in **DETAIL** Small Structures

in **DETAIL**

Small Structures

Compact dwellings
Temporary structures
Room modules

Christian Schittich (Ed.)

Edition DETAIL – Institut für internationale
Architektur-Dokumentation GmbH & Co. KG
München

Birkhäuser
Basel

Editor: Christian Schittich
Editorial services: Cornelia Hellstern, Cosima Strobl, Melanie Weber
Editorial assistants: Carola Jacob-Ritz, Diane Hutchinson,
Michaela Linder, Daniela Steffgen

Translation German/English: EUROCAT Translations, Sulzbach

Drawings: Ralph Donhauser, Michael Folkmer,
Daniel Hajduk, Martin Hämmel, Nicola Kollmann,
Elisabeth Krammer, Dejanira Ornelas

DTP: Roswitha Siegler

A specialist publication from Redaktion DETAIL
This book is a cooperation between
DETAIL – Review of Architecture and
Birkhäuser GmbH

Bibliographic information published by the German National Library
The German National Library lists this publication in the Deutsche
Nationalbibliografie; detailed bibliographic data is available on the Internet at
<http://dnb.d-nb.de>.

This book is also available in a German language edition
(ISBN: 978-3-920034-36-2).

© 2010 Institut für internationale Architektur-Dokumentation GmbH & Co. KG,
P. O. Box 20 10 54, D-80010 Munich, Germany and
Birkhäuser GmbH, P. O. Box 133, CH-4010 Basel,
Switzerland
www.birkhauser-architecture.com

Printed on acid-free paper produced from chlorine-free pulp (TCF ∞)

Printed in Germany
Reproduction:
ludwig:media, Zell am See
Printing and binding:
Kösel GmbH & Co. KG, Altusried-Krugzell

ISBN: 978-0346-0283-9

9 8 7 6 5 4 3 2 1

Contents

The fascination of small structures

Christian Schittich

Temporary pavilions made of bamboo touring through China for a cultural project, a tiny oasis in the woods devoted to the art of contemplation, a cube stripped down to its bare essentials lending a new meaning to the term "home extension" or a viewing platform projecting spectacularly over a rocky precipice: small-scale architecture is an area which is challenging and fascinating in equal measure for planners and designers. When space is a rare commodity, every detail and every function requires particularly careful consideration, making use of every last inch. On the other hand, small-scale construction projects generally mean that the architect is able to control the entire planning and building process right from the outset, exerting a direct influence right down to the most minute details, which is not always possible with larger projects. At the same time, this field of architecture also places particular emphasis on the intended usage, and above all the prospective users. This results in correspondingly direct feedback, with any faults and weaknesses generally becoming immediately apparent. Due to their manageable scale, microarchitecture projects are typically assigned to young architects at the beginning of their careers, as well as students.
They are often developed for temporary usages. For this reason and on account of the limited costs involved, such projects lend themselves to experimentation, as a means of trying out unconventional room scenarios, testing new structures and materials and showcasing visual effects.

At the same time, many examples of microarchitecture are sophisticated high-tech structures which are sometimes developed for extreme environments such as forests, deserts or high mountain areas. Microarchitecture blends seamlessly into product design here. The structures are versatile and flexible in the cause of efficiency. "This type of microarchitecture" notes Richard Horden, "is inspired by mobility, bionics and microelectronics. It follows the call for light and a lightness of touch, for new experiences and a better and closer relationship with nature. One aim here is to minimise the use of materials and energy and to combine transportation and accommodation." (see DETAIL 12/2004, p. 1422)
This publication considers microarchitecture in a broader context. The term is interpreted here as referring to anything which is small in scale, from a rough tree house to a high-tech tent, from architectural furniture through kiosks and bus shelters to small-scale homes, whereby the size of a "mini-house" may well vary between Munich and Tokyo.

Microarchitecture – experiments in space optimisation

Lydia Haack, John Höpfner

Our society is currently in the midst of a paradigm shift in which environmental and economic criteria are being reappraised. Issues such as climate protection and conservation of resources have resulted in a change in the image of architecture, which now seeks long-term sustainability and addresses the availability of raw materials and resources. We are faced with the challenge of devising solutions and concepts for our built environment that can be reconciled with these demands and limitations without any sacrifices in the quality of our buildings with the ultimate aim of creating a modern conception of architecture that takes account not only of technical design but also of conceptual methods.

An important contribution in this regard could be made by microarchitecture,[1] since it is by definition a self-restricting form of architecture that seeks to achieve as much as is required with as little as possible. If this self-imposed minimalism – for example the reduction in the living area – is not to be associated with a deterioration in convenience or a reduction in utility, we must inevitably arrive at a new conception of and approach to space. Spatial concepts for this microarchitecture cannot be formulated in the traditional way as a function of free-flowing space alone but must be developed in the form of precisely fitting sculptures. To ensure that the "tailor-made spatial suit" does not degenerate into a straitjacket, the minimisation of space should not be regarded in terms of its encapsulation but should achieve spatial quality through a varied and diversified sequence. If this happens, the self-restrictive efforts will offer potential for reorientation and enrichment and space-optimised modelling will become the driving force behind innovation.

Micro

Micro is the Greek word for "small". Micro-Architecture could thus be understood as the miniaturisation of architecture, the downscaling of structures, while retaining function and possibly form as well. Just as small-scale paintings are called miniatures, miniaturised architecture is called microarchitecture. Is microarchitecture then the reduction in size of architecture based on changes of scale and reduction in the structural volume? Or is it more like a bonsai, which whilst appearing at first glance to be merely a miniature tree is in fact a metaphor. The reduction in the size of the object is associated with an increase in its sensory quality and symbolises art and harmony between man and nature. Microarchitecture has the same potential to be more than just scaled-down conventional architecture.

Microarchitecture

Because of its unusual and sometimes spectacular appearance, microarchitecture is sometimes misunderstood as a superficial gimmick or fashion when in fact it has its own inherent rules of behaviour, much like the bonsai tree. A structure that appears eccentric is in fact an unusual way of stating a spatial relationship in a natural context while also expressing independence. As the link between outer and inner worlds, often with a particular relationship to the natural environment, space must be defined initially in terms of its limits but at the same time it also needs to extend beyond these limits. When the volume is compressed, there is less room for the normal buffer zones. Architects must develop limiting and delimiting strategies for the transition from inside to outside that are clearly visualised not only as constructed filters but also as separations and links. This multidimensional complex perception of space is one of the central focuses of space optimisation.

This microarchitecture is in no way a miniature version of architecture, a building designed haphazardly or on the basis of rationalising ideas, "shrivelled and starved deficient structures", but spatially compressed innovations that address different issues and that seek design harmony not through individual elements, but in the interaction and attractive force of all of the components involved. Space optimisation follows Mies van der Rohe's principle of "less is more", not through a reduction to less but a reduction to the essentials.[2]

Spatial boundaries

At the interface, the perimeter of the building, space is divided into two worlds and defined as such in architectural terms. Whereas the outside is subject to natural forces and the fluctuations caused by sun, wind and weather, the inside should be as comfortable as possible. Miniaturisation increases the demands on both the shell and the interior organisation. The planning of the various physical conditions in a confined space in order to ensure a high degree of comfort is a huge task that involves not only the building shell but also, because of the reduced space, the interior.

Aspects of spatial planning

Three-dimensionality

Because the optimum utilisation of all available space is of such vital importance in microarchitecture, the entire structural volume has to be taken into account at the planning stage.

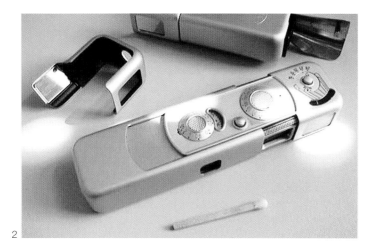

2

If the space were to be divided in the conventional manner into horizontal levels and furnished on this basis, we would have to make considerable concessions in terms of quality. The flexibility of the spatial concept becomes a central theme with a shift from two- to three-dimensional space division. The task to be confronted is not one of reduction but of reinterpreting and compressing the spatial sequence.

Compression
The compression of space calls for an exact understanding of human activity in space with a view to reorganising the interspatial functions.

In technology, miniaturisation is a common way of seeking improved efficiency. Developments leading to ergonomic improvements, reductions in weight and energy consumption and increased efficiency are all based on this consideration. Walter Zapp, for example, investigated the limits of technical feasibility and developed a camera, the Minox, in 1938 which in spite of its conventional mechanics was claimed by the manufacturer to be smaller than a cigar and weigh less than a lighter (fig. 2). Because of its smaller size and the new handling, the camera revolutionised photography and led to the development of today's miniature cameras. It also paved the way for the use of computer chips and nanotechnology instead of miniaturised mechanical parts.

The era of multifunctional appliances demonstrates how compactness not only influences user behaviour but also has a specific impact on the structural environment. If minimisation is seen as an opportunity for multifunctional design, it eliminates the physical distances and changes the spatial context and space requirements. Whereas architects used to require a drawing table of 2×1 m (2 m²), a 30-inch monitor on a 1.2×0.80 m (0.96 m²) table, if not a laptop without a table is sufficient today. The space requirement has thus been reduced by at least 50 per cent, not to mention the other changes. It is not therefore surprising that the most successful products of our time are often innovative miniature versions, such as the Apple iPhone or Daimler smart, because the change in utilisation also creates a new lifestyle. Smallness and multifunctionality have become the new status symbol. Functional compactness results in new user habits and perceptions, including the compression of space.

Ergonomics within reach and in action
"It would seem that perfection is attained not when no more can be added, but when no more can be removed."[3] It is not surprising that this quote, which describes one of the main features of compression, comes from Antoine de Saint-Exupéry. As a trained pilot, he knew that reduction is a complex process that is meaningful only with knowledge of all technical aspects and their interaction and with account taken of user-specific properties such as ergonomic considerations.

For thousands of years the human body has been the term of reference for length, width and height and for determining what is big and what is small. The static ideal in Leonardo da Vinci's Vitruvian Man is a person who touches a square or circle with his fingertips and the soles of his feet. Le Corbusier's Modulor sits, supports himself and is represented in a series of movements. Both of these criteria – the spatial volume within reach and the mobile use in action – are important for living in confined spaces. User behaviour influences action to the extent that space continuously changes. Thus the rigid spatial divisions in a micro-house give way to a division on the basis of utilisation. The greater the compression and the room for transition from one zone to another, the more carefully these spatial zones have to be planned. Each optimised user area is designed flexibly as a concept-dependent spatial sequence or as a collection of sub-areas. The conventional conception of space is replaced by a dynamic three-dimensional version in which physical nearness and user behaviour interact intensively.

Considerations regarding the interior

The utility of space depends on the interaction between the user and the spatial structure and, with increasing technological progress, on their relative demands. Historical models or examples from other disciplines serve as references for the relatively recent field of microarchitecture.

Optimised functionality

The compact kitchen designed in 1926 by Margarete Schütte-Lihotzky, known as the "Frankfurt kitchen", the forerunner of fitted kitchens as we know them today, was the result of efficient planning and led to a new and different utilisation (fig. 3). The functions in the small, fully-fitted working kitchen were optimised so effectively that it could be described as a command centre. There was room for only one person, the housewife. The rationalisation took the form of the "business-like" organisation of the household on the lines of Taylorism, the system of scientific management devised by Frederick Winslow Taylor, which involved both architectural and social restructuring.[4] The compact organisation of a standardised functional kitchen was meant to improve the efficiency and satisfaction of the housewife and to reduce the amount of non-creative housework so as to give her more time for creative activities. Through the visible organisation of work in the "command centre" the role of the housewife was revalued and the quality of work and leisure time enhanced.[5]

Superimposed functionality

As women became more emancipated, the spatial concept changed from a control centre to a workshop kitchen in which the husband was also allowed to cook.[6] One way of optimising space to this end was to create a functional overlap between the living space and the kitchen. The fixed distinctions between the roles within the household have become blurred and rigid planning for a particular user type is no longer meaningful, since the possible lifestyles diverge so greatly, from a one-person household to a patchwork family.

Compressed functionality

The minimised onboard kitchen in aircraft is a model for a development by which planning, be it for a kitchen-cum-living room or a minimised one-person kitchen, has to take account of "simplexity", i.e. on the basis of the simple utilisation of a complex technology enclosed in a spatial organisation (fig. 4). Objects are stored, refrigerated, prepared and

1 micro compact home, Munich, 2005; Horden Cherry Lee Architects and Haack + Höpfner . Architekten
2 Minox B 8x11 spy camera
3 "Frankfurt kitchen", 1926; Margarete Schütte-Lihotzky
4 Aeroplane on-board kitchen

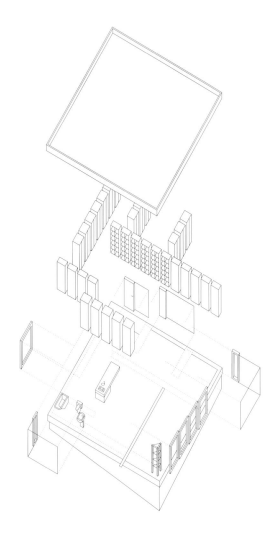

5

served in a small space planned down to the last millimetre. At the same time, the on-board kitchen is positioned so as to optimise the service in the confined space.

Multifunctionality
The Furniture House by Shigeru Ban, built in 1995 at Yamanakako also features function compression. Cabinet units inside and outside delimit and divide the room and also form part of the roof (fig. 5 and 6). The functions of the supporting elements and perimeter are combined with storage. The prefabricated cabinet units are assembled as modules to form the spatial structure. The cabinet/wall thus becomes a central and multifunctional structural component.

This multifunctionality can be seen even more clearly in the "Walden" project by Nils Holger Moormann. The free-standing wall fitted with all kinds of garden utensils is also a protective shell at the same time (fig. 7). The idea of creating a simple life outdoors was the inspiration for this superimposition of function and utility. A seating group, a retractable brazier and a shelter on the upper floor turn this habitable wall into an almost autonomous outdoor living and working area.

Dynamic functionality
The type of movable components described below help to enhance the efficient use of space. Space can be defined dynamically and temporarily by folding and shifting. Efficient storage space, for example can be enlarged with movable elements to form a spatial zone. The "temporary space congestion" becomes a design tool in spatial planning, using mobility to compensate for the confined space.
In 1924 Gerrit Rietveld applied the principle of free room division to his Rietveld-Schröder-House. Sliding walls enable the upper storey to be converted from open plan into separate rooms. The open layout can be varied and adapted to requirements.

Recent examples of variable room division range from simple elements such as the Softwall movable fabric wall by Stephanie Forsythe and Todd MacAllen, which can be extended from 5 cm to 5 m, to furniture with flaps and doors or retractable elements as room dividers.

The pink cabinet in 2Raumwohnung by Behles & Jochimsen has a kitchenette, machines, washbasin, storage space, lighting and serving elements that make for optimised compact utilisation instead of a conventionally furnished space (fig. 8). The furniture can be placed in an empty apartment and through folding down its components the layout can be defined and varied. The door-high element also has various built-in components behind flaps and pull-out units, turning this compact element into a multifunctional room divider.[7]

The Suitcase House by the EDGE Design Institute achieves the same effect with a sequence of boxes that remain hidden in the floor until their concealed functions are required (fig. 9). Seats or bathroom units appear when part of the floor is lifted up. The vertical floor element also acts as a room divider and encloses a newly defined space. With the use of mobile floor elements the neutral room can be turned into an individual space.

6

The micro compact home by Horden Cherry Lee Architects und Haack + Höpfner Architekten (fig. 1, 10, 11 and 21–23), inspired by Japanese teahouse architecture, uses many of the principles described here to superimpose function and utility.[8] Each occupant can make optimum use of the room by changing the room scenario as a function of the time of day or occupation; all areas can also be used without any modification. The interior is divided into four function areas – wet area, rest area, living area and cooking area – with a flowing transition between them. The rest area has a fold-down bed and is separated spatially and visually from the living area so as to provide an active differentiation between the two. By sliding or folding the fitted elements various user-specific forms of practical living can be achieved. Mobile fitted elements provide storage space. This variability (workplace, seating group, guest bed or sofa), the multiple use of space in the hall (kitchen, seating group, bed and dining table area) and the entrance (vestibule, WC, shower) and the exploitation of all available space through the use of drawers and pull-out elements for storage make for extremely efficient space utilisation. The arrangement of the functional elements nearby (refrigerator, microwave, storage area underneath the kitchenette next to the seats) is also highly ergonomic. The measures together provide mobility and a high degree of user convenience; and the compactness and rectangular form help save energy in manufacture and use.[9]

The different planning methods illustrate that not only does a well thought-out arrangement save space but also that the skilful positioning of compactly organised zones also creates multifunctional space. Using mobile elements a neutral space can be converted into a versatile spatial sequence. With individual multifunctional elements the space utilisation can be further improved. Compressed planning results in spatial concentration away from enclosed and dedicated rooms towards specific and multifunctional spatial zones. This change with variable zones creates a new type of utilisation in which the occupants are actively involved in the daily design and determine the optimum utilisation through their interaction with the space they live in.

Considerations regarding the shell

Because of the variability of the interior in microarchitecture, the shell also has to perform functions other than providing thermal comfort. Openings must be adapted to the variable space utilisation and capable of responding to an increased range of functions. A variable layout in a confined space as a function of daylight can result in different utilisations from living to sleeping but for that purpose the shell must be adjustable as well to allow both public and private use. The physical proximity to the perimeter demands not only mechanical control (opening, closing) but also a far more subtle approach and spatial differentiation in order to achieve both physical comfort and a visual sense of distance through an opening to the outside world.

5 Axonometric of Furniture House, Yamanakako, 1995; Shigeru Ban Architects
6 Furniture House, Yamanakako, 1995; Shigeru Ban Architects
7 Walden, 2006; Nils Holger Moormann
8 2Raumwohung, Berlin, 2006; Behles & Jochimsen
9 Suitcase House, Beijing, 2002; EDGE Design Institute

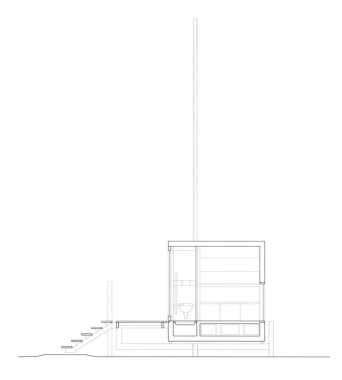

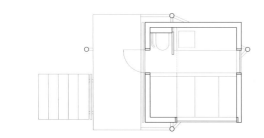

10

11

Dialogue between interior and exterior

Interesting historical models for flexible room division can be found in Japanese culture. The formation of interior space and the transitions between the interior and the exterior are formed through the subsequent filling of a skeleton framework. Like a structural grammar, which creates a fabric of relationships between the building components, the openings in the skeleton framework and the transitions between spaces are in the form of structure-filling elements, permitting a gradual and controllable transition from fully open to fully closed.[10] The wood and bamboo woven panels help to regulate the temperature naturally and form mobile buffer zones offering the ventilation required for the warm but humid climate in Japan. The flexible division and building structure are coordinated with the climatic conditions and permit gradual opening beyond the perimeter to the outside, as can be seen in the imperial Villa Katsura in Kyoto (fig. 12).

The flexible spatial transitions are a useful model for microarchitecture as they permit variation inside but also enable the living space to be expanded visually and actively with the aid of the mobile elements. The building structure, selected to comply with the local conditions, allows almost infinite control of the spatial perimeter. To this end, increased attention is paid to the design of the shell and its seamless controllability.

The position of the openings in the micro compact home is determined by a number of factors including view, lighting and use. The windows can be transformed to serve as solar protection, for privacy or to darken the room. A view outdoors is provided from practically any position in the room through the two openings (fig. 11), creating an impression of cosiness but with a reference to the outside world. The light coming through the low windows illuminates the work areas, focuses the gaze downwards to neutralise the disadvantage of the low ceiling and contributes in this way to a subjectively pleasant feeling of spatial comfort.
Other possibilities for taking account of the compression inside are provided by the ongoing developments in material-integrated technology and the transfer of new technologies to the building sector.

The microarchitectural skin

It is possible today to develop free forms at the interface of digital production and professional craftsmanship to produce new effects. The Mercury House by Arturo Vittori and Andreas Vogler investigates a new technology for working marble using a computer-controlled cutter to reduce double-curved thin-layer sheets to a thickness of just 4 mm. The idea is not only to optimise the form but also to investigate the relationship between material and design.
The innovative potential of material-integrated design will make it possible in future to investigate complex spatial relations and then to coordinate them with the material and design. It is thus conceivable that transitions will be able to take account not only of comfort but also of privacy while still being open to the outside as they have energy-conducting, climate-regulating and form-shaping properties.

Reaction to the environment

Architecture always relates to a context, which in turn is influenced by it. Small buildings are inevitably in direct contact with their environment because of the spatial proportions.

Microarchitecture creates a closer connection between man and nature. In many cases nature itself is used as a reference and as a direct or indirect model for different structures. Approaches include minimum use of material, the search for efficient supporting structures and surfaces and continuously optimised and refined structures adapted to the local conditions.

In dialogue with nature
Inspired by minimised shelters in remote locations, the design spectrum in the natural environment is influenced by experimental research stations with tent-like structures or adventure-oriented recreational buildings reminiscent of sporting equipment. Two opposing attitudes to this opening to the outside world can be observed.

Body/retreat "closed"
One of the first minimalist dwellings was the retreat in Pill Creek, Cornwall, by Team 4 (Richard Rogers, Susan Brumwell, Norman Foster and Wendy Cheeseman) in 1963, which may be regarded as a reference object for the development of microarchitecture. In the search for an intact and remote natural retreat, the architects designed a sunken shelter over a vizor-like projecting glass pulpit projecting over a cockpit-like interior. The space itself was enclosed and created a defined interior with various superimposed functions. The separation of the interior from the exterior highlights the concept of protection and cosiness, while the openings – which in fact break up the protective shell – provide generous communication between inside and outside and neutralise the perceived separation between them. Nature and shelter merge through the combination of closeness to the ground and absence of material since two thirds of the building is underground.

Structure/experience "open"
Another type of early microarchitecture sought a bond between the object and its natural surroundings in a different way. The free-standing objects established a relationship with nature not by way of a closed concept but through the transparency of its structure. Like a modular building, the framework structure enables the room to be opened or closed with all transitional phases between these two states. The spatial structures can then be filled with different levels, as in the case of the Beach Point mobile viewing platform.[11] Designed by Jürgen Schubert, Thorsten Schwabe, Peter Zimmer and Markus Kottmaier in the Department of Building Theory and Product Development at the Technical University of Munich, it features a combination of structural components such as frames and floors, in contrast to panelled protective accommodation like the flexible Ikos research station by the French architect Gilles Ebersolt (fig. 13). Through the development of a set of connected structural components that can be assembled without special tools and of designs that do not require a foundation, such structures can be adapted without difficulty to their surroundings. For example, the supporting framework on the research station, which is made of knock-

10 Section and plan of micro compact home, Munich, 2005;
   Horden Cherry Lee Architects and Haack + Höpfner . Architekten
11 micro compact home, Munich, 2005; Horden Cherry Lee Architects and
   Haack + Höpfner . Architekten
12 Old Shoin in Villa Katsura in Kyoto, view into the room with fireplace (irori)

12

13

down regular polygons, can be filled as required with solar protection membranes or waterproof coverings. The adaptability of such microarchitecture, which can be incorporated in a tree or suspended in a gorge, endows it with a naturalness that also ensures that the natural context is retained.

Reaction to extremes

Whether it is the utopian dreams that stimulate or inventive spirit or the extreme conditions to which we expose ourselves, it is clear that without curiosity or boldness we could not overstep borders and investigate new territory. Extremes help us to understand and have produced innovations in the past that have become routine features of our life today. The observations of the earth and weather during the first voyages around the world provided information about the global context. Pioneering space travel brought us innovations in telecommunications, navigation and new lightweight and extremely stable materials.

Technology transfer

The lightness required for space travel led to the optimisation and investigation of possibilities for combining material and design. A research project by Zoran Novacki in the Department of Structural Design at the Technical University of Munich is investigating transformable support structures whose behaviour in space is simulated by means of an animation entitled "Bridging Mars" (fig. 14). A combination of spatial shear mechanisms and telescopic elements enables the support structure to unfold automatically with a high pack factor and geometric flexibility. With the aid of cable systems the structure can be stiffened to become a usable support. This unfolding support structure uses a minimum of material and has a flexible structure that makes it highly versatile. Designs of this sort are ideal for temporary accommodation or mobile pedestrian bridges (fig. 15) but also conceivably as models for flexible and enlargeable spatial structures. The criteria required for space travel such as lightness, mobility and flexibility not only provide inspiration for new ideas but also make it possible to investigate the feasibility of concepts with material-efficient, space-saving and adaptable structures.

Human-centred design

Living in hostile and weightless conditions for long periods is a cause of extreme mental stress. Research in this area, e.g. micro-gravity projects[12], a cooperation between the space technology and architecture departments of the Technical University of Munich and the NASA Johnson Space Center in Houston shows the importance of distinguishing between working space and the private sphere particularly when existing for long periods in confined spaces. Every spatial design must be optimised as far as possible with account taken in particular of utility and personal wellbeing. Design features such as tactility and colour that contribute to improving environmental harmony are just as important as the simple handling of technical equipment. Safety can be ensured only if the occupants can orient themselves in a three-dimensional weightless environment (fig. 16 and 17). This human-centred design should be a basic prerequisite for all space-optimised planning. Just as the success of a mission depends on the mental state of a crew in a space station, wellbeing in a confined space is

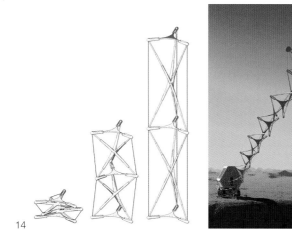

14

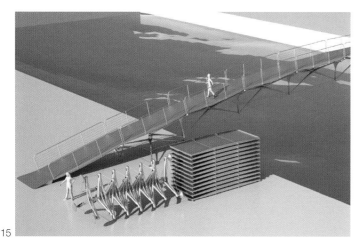

15

the prerequisite for the acceptance of a new building form such as microarchitecture.

In our dealings with space, research into weightlessness has also taught us how to organise extremely complex situations and to combine different disciplines. Three-dimensionality can be experienced literally. All space limiters are of equal value. The conventional top and bottom demarcation through walls, floors and ceilings no longer applies. This produces a completely new way of perceiving such limits, as in turnOn by the architects AllesWirdGut, which shows in an interesting and challenging way how we can make more active use of these surfaces, and in projects like the micro compact home, whose compressed form calls for multifunctional use of all available surfaces.

Human factor engineering

While we have set up comfortable homes for ourselves here on earth and design buildings primarily for our own conveni-ence, the structures in space and other extreme situations such as polar or desert regions or high mountains also have a life-preserving function. The material and energy flow must be recycled to run autonomously for long periods. In a high Alpine research station like Peak_Lab, designed by the Department of Building Theory and Product Development at the Technical University of Munich in cooperation with the Department of Architecture at the University of Applied Sci-ences and Arts Luzern, there are no conventional supply or disposal systems.[13] The research station is autonomous with a self-contained power-generating skin. Five separately transportable cells are suspended on a dismantlable light-weight structure and connected vertically to form the build-ing. The geometry and arrangement take account of the aerodynamics of the high Alpine site. Inside, the building is organised as a research station and adapted to the user-space interaction described earlier. The form is thus not only a question of design intelligence but also technical logic focusing on the aerodynamics and climate conditions on site. This may be described as human factor engineering, a basic prerequisite for sustainable and efficient spatial planning in microarchitecture.

The extreme conditions and the consideration of complex interrelations provide great potential for new ideas. These developments can also be applied to urban architecture. Experiments in microarchitecture are particularly suitable for the development in practice of the technical innovations pro-duced by progress in technology and the extreme require-ments on the building sites.

Multiplication and urban planning

The vision of creating entire urban structures with small building units has a long tradition, with projects featuring a collection of housing units such as Habitat 67 by Moshe Safdie in Montreal in 1967 or Nakagin Capsule Tower by Kisho Kurokawa in 1972. They are based on the concep-

16

17

13 Ikos flexible research station, 2004; Gilles Ebersolt
14 Bridging Mars, 2009; Zoran Novacki, drawing and animation of the transformable support structure
15 Utilisation as a mobile pedestrian bridge
16 Workspace for an astronaut, 2000; design: Björn Bertheau, Claudia Hert-erich, Arne Laub; tutors: Lydia Haack, Richard Horden, Andreas Vogler
17 Microgravity project, interior model ISS, since 1998; Department of Building Theory and Product Development at the Technical University of Munich

tual idea of the Metabolists – particularly Yona Friedman and Eckhard Schulze-Fielitz – of creating urban structures with prefabricated cells. Small room units are also important in the graphic work of Archigram. The autonomous state-of-the-art capsules could be adapted and readapted in accordance with the occupants' requirements. They soon became an ideal element for creating mega-structures as a means of reacting flexibility to unforeseeable urban growth. Today mobile structures are used to create low-priced temporary housing to cover short-term demands. A culture of container architecture has developed that meets the need for transportable and temporary housing but is not suitable as an alternative for urban planning because of its inflexibility and structural quality. The introverted boxes are at best stackable items that can be used in emergencies.

Microarchitecture is developed in context. As transformable and adaptable structures they can do more than overcome quantitative logistical problems. They are therefore particularly suitable as flexible components of dense urban development. As additional, repairing or stand-alone modules the small units can be adapted intelligently to their environment. Concepts include dockable or additional rooms, systems that can be enlarged on the matchbox principle, and even units that can be combined to form entire estates or colonies. The quality of the individual projects is notable in particular for the involvement in the structural surroundings and the adaptability to the different conditions. A project like the micro compact home calls for minimal interference with the structural surroundings thanks to the lightweight aluminium frame which can be adapted to different topographies and which raises the mini-house from the ground and at the same time emphasises the volume. The cube can thus be experienced as a free-standing object in its particular context. As a unifying urban element joining the housing units to one another, as well as a multifunctional spatial compression, access, forecourt zone, terrace and seating platform simultaneously, the frame logically extends the systemic optimisation of space from the interior to the exterior.

Through multiplication and combination, microarchitecture in an urban setting can develop a village or micro-urban character, as in the House before House in Utsunomiya by Sou Fujimoto Architects (fig. 18, 19). Here the house and garden – interior and exterior – form a harmonious structure that gradually takes on a natural form. Ten cubes were distributed seemingly haphazardly on a site, and the space playfully divided, creating open areas that offer varying characteristics for spending time.[14] Spatial enhancement achieved through the interplay of individual housing units can also be discerned in the Moriyama Housing Complex designed by Ryue Nishizawa (fig. 20). It is the combination of five compact stacked rental apartments with scattered detached structures that lend this complex its urban character. The staggered arrangement of the individual small white cubes and their openings has been precisely planned, as has the relationship between the open areas and paths. As a result, the network of paths traversing the area creates an "urban labyrinth" – a continuation of the spatial optimisation in an urban dimension.

Space optimisation and mobility
Product orientation
The advantage of small structures lies in their ease of transport. If a small building is built using a lightweight construc-

18

19

tion, moving it is relatively inexpensive. Switching from conventional construction methods to lightweight construction makes industrial production possible. Structures that had been unique are transformed into serially produced products that cost considerably less in comparison. In addition, product-oriented planning creates improved working conditions, as buildings produced in series, such as the micro compact home, can be prefabricated under better conditions in the factory. The resulting buildings can then be erected at the destination relatively quickly. Delays resulting from the weather, not to mention the defects and dangers that are an unavoidable part of a construction site, are minimised as a result.

Just as factory production has a positive effect on the quality of workmanship, planning processes that have been coordinated in advance, often including the development of a prototype, result in the optimisation of components and improved product quality. The coordination of the design and production processes can also lead to considerable reductions in the materials used. With the micro compact homes, initial efforts alone made it possible to reduce the waste for some building materials from 25% to only 5%. The opportunities presented by this planning method are clear. The further we go with product-optimised planning, the more efficient and higher quality our buildings can become. In the end it may even be possible to create structures that are entirely dismantlable, and thus fully reusable.

Although it has been more than 60 years since Richard Buckminster Fuller called for the elimination of the barriers between architecture and product design and introduced key components of product-oriented planning such as multiple production, location independence, lightweight construction and industrial production, even now this planning method is only beginning to establish itself, being found primarily in the prefabrication of individual components. His project, the Dymaxion Unit[15], which can be produced industrially and weighs only about three tonnes including furnishings, owes its inspiration to the aerospace industry. As Buckminster Fuller put it "maximum performance per pound of material invested"[16]: an optimised product at the interface between performance and materials utilised. The Wichita House, whose technology and structure had been developed even further, can be transported in a cylinder, giving visible expression to the concept of mobility, raised above the ground. This places it at the beginning of a development in which the objective was to minimise the use of materials through the harmonisation of design, technical and functional aspects, all to create architecture that is autonomous and transportable.

Product-related mobility

Although mobile living has deep roots in other cultures, as well as a permanent place in architectural discourse, a dislike of temporary housing resulting in part from history has continued to the present day.

The fact that the term "mobile" became laden with negative associations, such as makeshift, nomadic, even vagabond, is a result of two separate waves of production of temporary structures. Simplified structures suitable for self-assembly that were designed for colonisation in the 19th century and emergency shelters that were meant to provide fast, afford-

20

18 Floor plan of House before House, Utsunomiya, 2009; Sou Fujimotot Architects
19 House before House, Utsunomiya, 2009; Sou Fujimotot Architects
20 Moriyama Housing Complex, Tokyo, 2005; Ryue Nishizawa

able accommodation after both world wars came to define the image of replacement structures. Plans from both epochs, especially after World War II, on the other hand, resulted in some striking innovations. Former armaments factories began utilising their technical know-how to develop housing instead of weapons. Examples include the Dornier-Wohnzeug (somewhat similar to a caravan) from 1947 and the MAN-Stahlhaus (a steel house) from 1948. Yet neither efficient spatial planning nor technical innovations such as prefabricated room cells and novel new multipurpose furniture resulted in greater acceptance of mobile structures. Although the "quality of manufactured houses" was seen as being higher than those built using conventional methods, this still did not create a secure foundation for this type of construction, for it continued to be tainted by its association with its emergency origins.[17]

Micro-mobility

Global markets, short-term employment contracts, 'significant others' and temporary living arrangements have come to define the modern way of life. The spontaneity we demand has changed our point of view, making it clear that we will be caught up in a never-ending cycle of tearing down, building and renovating unless we begin working with structures that are flexible, adaptable or even mobile. A quote from the physicist Georg Christoph Lichtenberg sums up our current situation nicely: "I honestly cannot say whether things will become better by becoming different, but I can say this much: things must change if they are to become good."[18] Mobile architecture has two components: first and foremost a reduction of the structure itself, and, as a consequence, minimisation of the impact on its architectural surroundings. Yet this characteristic often causes a grave problem, a building that is adrift from its surroundings. If no links are established between a building and its environment, mobility will be viewed solely as transportable, movable, portable, yet not as versatile, adaptable or even dynamic, or in a positive sense as vibrant and attractive. In this case, the experiment involving the use of microarchitecture to achieve a contemporary optimisation of space would fail. Although the compact, lightweight and spatial-functional efficiency of microarchitecture means that it is usually transportable and thus closely associated with mobility, when designing its form there should be an interplay between the object and its surroundings, so that it always appears in context.

21

From prototype to serial production
Prototype development
Thanks to their reasonable size, examples of microarchitecture are particularly suitable for explorations of complex themes in structural form. Be it using simple models or fully developed prototypes, architectural dependencies can not only be tested in stages, but visualised at the same time. Model approaches range from individual components for new material applications to innovative new lightweight structures. The use of mock-ups makes it possible to conduct preliminary simulations of relative sizes and interior configurations, while proof-of-concept prototypes allow form and material applications to be examined. Even though these methods make studying a particular concept relatively affordable, and represent a vivid medium for communication between laypersons and professionals, they cannot replace the production of a prototype, which is necessary to test suitability for actual use.

Using prototypes such as the Desert House from Architecture and Vision (see page 130) and the micro compact home, spatial visions are tested under real conditions, whereby the interplay of all factors that are decisive for the acceptance of a project – from suitability for use to touch and feel – are tested simultaneously. The capital-intensive production of prototypes can be worthwhile financially if a project may be suitable for subsequent series production, and may also serve as a means via which the resulting optimisations can result in architecture that is successful and sustainable for the long term.

Serial production
On the basis of a mock-up which allowed the interior relationships to be examined, continuous adaptation and optimisation processes resulted in the first prototype of the micro compact home, which, in accordance with the principle of product-oriented planning, was able to combine technical, aesthetic and economic objectives by making the leap to small-scale series production.

The precision prefabrication of individual components and integration of all free spaces for the building's technical and electrical installations resulted in a multitude of multifunctional elements. The complex process of organising the compression of the building's technical, structural and design elements into an edge length of 2.60 metres, combined with the reduction of the weight from nearly 3 tonnes to 2.30 tonnes, was the basis for the simple transportability of the object using a car in compliance with road traffic regulations (fig. 21). It was only this measure that made it possible to achieve resource-saving versatility, delivering the maximum energy independence in line with the concept. Efficient functional organisation with a changeable interior is thus reinforced by the flexibility of the module, which results from its tremendous versatility (reuse, recycling).

While the first prototype was produced largely by hand, series production has resulted in improvements to the interior, as well as to the building's shell. The insulation of the outer shell was optimised using vacuum panels; as a result, heating energy requirements were gradually reduced to 91.5 % of those for the first object built, a figure which has since been reduced to only 62.1 % of the original value.

Concluding thoughts
Micro architecture represents an alternative to conventional structures not only because its smallness results in the con-

servation of resources, making it an economical and ecological alternative to conventional structures, but also because it demonstrates that a reduction in volume does not have to translate into a reduction in the quality of the space created. Although not all spatial optimisation approaches represent surprising new strategies, using modern technologies to build on the experiences of earlier generations, can still give rise to independent and innovative spatial solutions. In addition, the new interdisciplinary approaches detailed here, drawing for example on the automotive and aerospace industries, show that a unity of design, technical and functional optimisation can lead to improved, reduced, and structurally sturdier components, a result that is far removed from fears of standardised or even inferior products. Unlike its predecessors, the creation of microarchitecture today is characterised by the urgency of finding construction methods that are more frugal and use fewer resources, and its sometimes temporary character has a more positive resonance as a result of the increasing mobility of modern society.

Microarchitectural experimentation with spatial optimisation is taking place at the same time as a trend towards the development of new technical products whose smallness, multifunctionality and mobility have done more than bring them wider social acceptance. As a result, microarchitecture is not seen as an expression of doing without, but rather as added life experience, as innovation. The core concept – focussing on the essentials – is gaining increasing acceptance in an over-satiated society. Microarchitecture represents a contribution to the world of architecture that is both necessary and appropriate for our time. Like the Vitruvian ideal – functional, constructive and creative – it offers an alternative solution for architecture that is sustainable and suitable for real life.

22

21   micro compact home being transported, Munich, 2005; Horden
      Cherry Lee Architects and Haack + Höpfner . Architekten
22, 23 micro compact home, Munich, 2005; Horden, Cherry, Lee Architects
      and Haack + Höpfner . Architekten

References:
 1 Blaser, Werner (ed.): Light tech. Basel/Berlin/Boston 1995, p. 19
 2 Blaser, Werner: Mies van der Rohe – less is more. Zürich 1986, p. 12
 3 Original quote: "Il semble que la perfection soit atteinte non quand il n'y
    a plus rien à ajouter, mais quand il n'y a plus rien à retrancher." Antoine
    de Saint-Exupéry, Terre des Hommes. Paris 1939, p. 60
 4 Meyer, Erna: Der neue Haushalt. Ein Wegweiser zur wirtschaftlichen
    Hausführung. Stuttgart 1929
 5 Hoff, Claudia Simone: Designline Küche, Online magazine for Product-
    and Interiordesign, 7 November 2007
 6 Aicher, Otl: Die Küche zum Kochen: Werkstatt einer neuen Lebenskultur.
    Munich 1982
 7 see DETAIL 11/2007, p. 1278ff.
 8 see DETAIL 12/2004, p. 1470ff.
 9 Nerdinger, Winfried (ed.): Wendepunkt(e) im Bauen. Von der seriellen
    zur digitalen Architektur. Munich 2010, p. 168
10 Deplazes, Andrea (ed.): Architektur Konstruieren. Vom Rohmaterial zum
    Bauwerk. Ein Handbuch. Basel/Berlin/Boston 2005, p. 112
11 see DETAIL 5/1998, p. 782ff.
12 Lehrstuhl für Gebäudelehre und Produktentwicklung Technische Univer-
    sität München (ed.): Richard Horden Architecture and Teaching. Basel/
    Berlin/Boston 1999, p. 110–113
13 see DETAIL 12/2004, p. 1459ff.
14 see DETAIL 12/2009, p. 1356ff.
15 Neologismus aus Dynamik und Maximum
16 McHale, John: R. Buckminster Fuller. Make of contemporary Architec-
    ture, London 1962, p. 15
17 Ludwig, Matthias: Mobile Architektur: Geschichte und Entwicklung trans-
    portabler und modularer Bauten. Stuttgart 1998, p. 71
18 Lichtenberg, Georg Christoph: Sudelbücher. Berlin 1984

23

Pavilions – temporary prototypes

Peter Cachola Schmal, Philipp Sturm

Having already designed several flagship stores for the fashion label Prada over the last few years, Rem Koolhaas' Office for Metropolitan Architecture (OMA) was commissioned by Miuccia Prada to design and build a temporary pavilion on the space next to the historic Gyeonghui Palace in Seoul. So, in spring 2009, a 20-metre high white colossus, 180 tonnes in weight, with a curious tetrahedron shape and the promising name Prada Transformer, appeared right in the historic centre of the South Korean capital (fig. 2). The supporting framework of the oddly shaped contraption was made from steel tubes, which were wrapped in a white translucent membrane. Clever manoeuvring with a heavy crane allowed the Transformer to be turned onto any of its four sides. Each side had its own individual geometry: hexagon, rectangle, cross and circle, each shape corresponding to a specific use. The hexagon was used for fashion shows, the cross for art exhibitions, the circle for special events and the rectangle served as a cinema. Uses and functionalities shifted together with the architecture, and gave visitors a sense of being inside a futuristic drawing by Maurits Cornelis Escher. Six months after opening, the multifunctional cultural centre disappeared again.

That same summer, Sverre Fehn's Nordic Pavilion from 1962 served as an exhibition space for the Danish-Norwegian artists duo Michael Elmgreen and Ingar Dragset with their project The Collectors at the 53rd Venice Biennale. The two curators transformed the Nordic Pavilion, together with the adjoining Danish Pavilion, into a rambling, eccentrically furnished residence (fig. 1). Below Fehn's open concrete-fin roof, Elmgreen and Dragset showed pieces by their artist colleagues and examined the life and work of a fictitious inhabitant; an extravagant art collector whose body, meanwhile, was floating in the swimming pool. Yesterday's classic Modernist pavilion thus offered a space for today's contemporary art.

In 2010, in commemoration of the 400-year-old connection between the Netherlands and the city of New York, and with financial support from the Dutch government, the New Amsterdam Plein & Pavilion was erected in Lower Manhattan (fig. 9 and 10). The square – plein in Dutch – is situated at the eastern edge of Battery Park, where Henry Hudson is said to have first set foot in Manhattan 400 years ago. The brilliant-white, biomorphic pavilion serves as an information centre and restaurant, while also acting as an arts, media and light installation in its own right. The structure, its sculptural shape spreading out in four directions, builds on the concept of The Changing Room, UNStudio's intertwining prototype at the Venice Architecture Biennale 2008 (fig. 11).

Definition

Transient fashion collections, installations to celebrate the overheated art market and commemoration of historic events are just three examples of the different uses pavilions can accommodate, and illustrate the definition and function of contemporary pavilion architecture. These, typically small, buildings now tend to be set in a cultural context, as exhibition or event spaces, sometimes erected specifically for a particular event, such as Ludwig Mies van der Rohe's German pavilion, which was built for use by the Spanish King Alfonso XIII at the opening ceremony of the 1929 Barcelona World's Fair. A key characteristic of this type of building is its often temporary nature, which opens up many interesting possibilities from an architectural point of view. The term pavilion is derived from the Latin word "papilio" – meaning tent, or, more literally, butterfly – hinting at its flexibility in terms of space, time and function, as well as its military origins. No other type of building allows such profound statements on so small a footprint, whilst also often being short-lived – a great advantage as far as design and construction are concerned. Contemporary pavilion architecture frequently does not require a long shelf life, making it ideal for experimental architecture.

The pavilion is still a popular theme in 21st century architecture, as is impressively evident in numerous designs and structures from recent years, such as the Serpentine Gallery

2

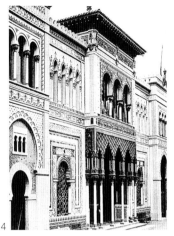

3   4

Pavilions or the summer pavilions designed by students at the Architectural Association in London. Other examples are the Burnham Pavilions in Chicago, designed by UNStudio and Zaha Hadid, or the inflatable Air Forest in Denver, created by Mass Studies in 2009. Not yet built are Coop Himmelb(l)au's planned 21 Mini Opera Space in Munich and the pavilion for the German Architecture Museum in Frankfurt by Barkow Leibinger Architekten. All of these are examples of pavilions within an arts and culture context and therefore generally subject to tight budget constraints. At the same time they allow – or demand – scope and opportunity for experimental and speculative work.

At what is probably the biggest world expo in history to date, in Shanghai in summer 2010, tight budgets are not an issue, or at least they are no obstacle for clients and architects. On either side of the Huangpu River, themed and national pavilions are being built with 7-digit budget figures, as if the economic crisis had never happened. An economically and financially powerful China is inviting the world to represent itself. Seen in a historical context, there is a slight retro feel about size-XXL country pavilions lining up on an area of 47,000 square metres. The host nation's pavilion alone is 63 metres high and towers above all other buildings. In Shanghai as at previous World Expos, the pavilion theme is used by some of the architects involved as an opportunity to experiment and to reflect on established architectural concepts. For example, Thomas Heatherwick's British pavilion presents an interpretation of the building envelope that is as unusual as it is spectacular. Gently swaying in the breeze are 60,000 transparent fibre-optic rods, used to draw daylight into the building, giving it the appearance of a giant hedgehog. Cho Minsuk of Mass Studies with his Korean pavilion, meanwhile, experiments with form and space by creating a three-storey multi-coloured building using twenty letters from the Korean alphabet.

From pleasure gardens to world fairs
The pavilion is not a phenomenon that only emerged during the great world fairs of the last 160 years. As far back as antiquity, in the Alexander Romance about the life of Alexander the Great (356–323 BC), there is mention of a mobile stone pavilion, in which the Candace, the Ethiopian queen, travelled to the battlefields of her armies. In Europe too, the existence of this type of building has been known for centu-

5   6

ries. But interest in pavilions only took off in the 17th century, during the era of world exploration and colonialism, when Europeans were discovering these ephemeral structures in new territories in the Middle East, India, Siam, China and Japan. As a place for festivities or religious rituals, the pavilion found its way into the parks and landscape gardens of European nobility. In his essay Upon the Gardens of Epicurus, written in 1685, the English diplomat and author Sir William Temple gives a detailed description of Chinese gardens.[1] Over the following years, inspired and guided by Temple's description, landscape gardens sprang up all over England, with winding paths, woodland glades, gazebos, statues and pavilions at their centre. Chinese design principles and philosophies thus began to influence European garden and park design and, following the Asian example, these new types of building became places of contemplation, meditation and stillness. In 1757, William Chambers, architect to the English king, who had travelled to India and China with the Swedish East-India Company, published a book of engravings entitled Designs of Chinese Buildings, Furniture, Dresses, Machines, and Utensils, depicting authentic drawings of Chinese architecture.[2] Chambers also created the first Anglo-Chinese garden, in London's Kew Gardens. Between 1757 and 1762 he erected a number of structures within the park, among them a mosque, a menagerie and a bridge. Still standing today are his Orangery, the ten-storey-high Pagoda, the Temple of Bellona and the Temple of Aeolus. Chamber's aim was to create an illusionist paradise in which every part of the world would be represented by a characteristic building. Until well into the 18th century, these parks and pavilions were used by the European gentry primarily as a pleasure garden and a refuge from society's constraints and conventions.[3] Examples, alongside Kew Gardens in London and numerous summer residences, are the Amalienburg in the grounds of Schloss Nymphenburg in Munich and the Petit Trianon in Versaille. Whereas, initially, European Rococo pavilions were mainly built as temporary shelters and open structures, their design and function soon moved towards closed buildings and miniature palaces. The era of the great explorers later inspired a number of fanciful exotic and nationalist designs. An example of this transition period is John Nash's Royal Pavilion in Brighton with its orientalising rows of domes and minarets, built between 1813 and 1823 for the Prince of Wales, George IV. In their totality, these Japanese and Chinese inspired buildings, the Ottoman tents and Moorish miniature palaces, can be seen as the predecessors of national pavilions at 19th century world fairs.

With the colonialisation of Africa and Asia, and in parallel with the industrialisation in Europe, world fairs as international showcases of crafts and technology became established around the middle of the 19th century. At the first World's Fair, the Great Exhibition in London's Hyde Park in 1851, the world's nations were still restricted to individual exhibition stands within Joseph Paxton's Crystal Palace (fig. 3). The next show, in Paris in 1867, could no longer offer sufficient space to accommodate all participating nations. The countries represented therefore began erecting temporary buildings outside the central exhibition hall, using their own designs. On the Champs de Mars in Paris, visitors to the fair were able to view all products of a nation or of a particular industry in one visit. National identity was no longer expressed just through crafts or industrial products, but also in the architecture and construction of the exhibition stand itself. Initially still arranged freely on the green field, at the Paris World's Fair of 1878 the pavilions were built for the first time along a streetscape (fig. 4). The "Rue des Nations" recreated the urban structures of the European city as defined by Georges-Eugène Baron Haussmann. Many of the countries represented no longer displayed just their national style, but also offered leading artists and architects of the time a space to show their work. The Paris-based artist Alfred Vaudoyer designed country pavilions in the respective national styles for Luxemburg, Uruguay, Peru and others. In addition to demonstrating national identity, world fair architecture at the beginning of the 20th century was also preoccupied with the convergence of arts and sciences. With his experimental theatre pavilion for the American dancer Loïe Fuller at the 1900 Paris World's Fair, the young architect Henri Sauvage gave a performance that was almost as spec-

1 Nordic Pavilion at the Venice Biennale in 1962; Sverre Fehn
Installation The Collectors by Michael Elmgreen and Ingar Dragset at the 2009 Venice Biennale
2 Prada Transformer, Seoul, 2009; OMA
3 Crystal Palace in London, 1851; Joseph Paxton
Exhibition building for the first ever World's Fair. Photograph from around 1900
4 "Rue des Nations", Paris World's Fair, 1878
5 "Pavillon de l'esprit nouveau" at the "Exposition Internationale des Arts Décoratifs et Industriels Modernes" in Paris, 1925; Le Corbusier and Pierre Jeanneret
6 Soviet Pavilion at the "Exposition Internationale des Arts Décoratifs et Industriels Modernes" in Paris, 1925; Konstantin Melnikow
7 Japanese Pavilion at the Hanover EXPO, 2000; Shigeru Ban Architects
8 German-Chinese Pavilion at the Shanghai EXPO, 2010; Markus Heinsdorff; the Russian Pavilion can be seen in the background

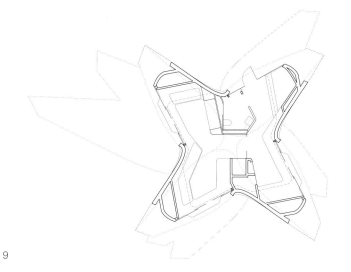

9

10

11

tacular as that of the dancer. The art of the moving image, still in its infancy, combined with Fuller's dance, inspired Sauvage to a design that seemed to have a movement of its own, its facade evoking images of Fuller's flowing dresses or of curtains at a theatre.[4]

A generation later, Konstantin Melnikov turned the utopian visions of the Russian avant-garde into exhibition architecture. His Soviet pavilion, a modern, open and transparent design in the spirit of El Lissitzky's "transformable spaces", graced the 1925 "Exposition Internationale des Arts Décoratifs et Industriels Modernes" in Paris, demonstrating the achievements of the Russian revolution, before Stalin replaced Constructivist experimental architecture with monumental designs a few years later (fig. 6). Also in Paris, Le Corbusier with his "Pavillon de l'esprit nouveau" showed a two-storey maisonette unit, which became the prototype for his later "machines for living". In the adjacent exhibition space, he also introduced his urban design vision for Paris with his "Plan Voisin" (fig. 5). Melnikov's Constructivist utopian vision, as well as Le Corbusier's two-storey steel-and-concrete villa, gave exhibition visitors a glimpse of avant-garde modern architecture at a show that was otherwise entirely devoted to Art Deco.[5]

The most important pavilion of the 20th century, and an icon of modern architecture, was Ludwig Mies van der Rohe's German pavilion at the 1929 World's Fair, better known as the Barcelona Pavilion. This paradigmatic masterpiece allowed Mies not only to play with a whole host of extravagant materials – travertine plinths, partition walls of black marble, green onyx and glass, red velvet curtains, polished steel and chrome supports – but also with the horizontal and vertical reflections of the Mediterranean skies, and of the exhibition visitors, in the two water basins and the dark glass walls. The Barcelona Pavilion has become a landmark of a new architecture of abstraction, where construction framework and space are allowed to develop independently of each other. Walls, floors and the "floating" roof slab are no longer defining boundaries, but form a continuous space, blurring the inside and the outside. Decades after the pavilion was dismantled its profound impact on architectural history had become evident, prompting the city of Barcelona in the 1980s to reconstruct this iconic symbol of freedom (from the Franco dictatorship).

Temporary pavilions for world fairs still belong to the most important experimental designs and buildings in 20th century architecture. In addition to those already mentioned, there is Alvar Aalto's Finnish pavilion for the 1939 World's Fair in New York, Sep Ruf and Egon Eiermann's German pavilion and Le Corbusier's Philips Pavilion for the 1958 World's Fair in Brussels, Buckminster Fuller's US pavilion and Frei Otto's German pavilion at the 1967 Expo in Montreal, as well as Kenzo Tange and Kisho Kurokawa's Metabolist fantasies for the 1970 Expo in Osaka. Also groundbreaking were MVRDV's Dutch pavilion, Peter Zumthor's Swiss pavilion and Shigeru Ban's Japanese pavilion for the Expo 2000 in Hanover (fig. 7).

Architectural prototypes and new spatial concepts
Its temporary character is one of the key advantages of the pavilion. It offers a quick and easy way to try out contemporary ideas and new spatial theories in architectural practice.

The buildings are not purely utilitarian, but offer a spatial experience. Their small size makes it possible to play with their proportions in relation to the human body; to experiment and explore spatial and physical characteristics. An example of this is the Philips Pavilion for the 1958 World's Fair in Brussels. Le Corbusier and Iannis Xenakis created a multimedia universal artwork of music and architecture. A cluster of nine hyperbolic paraboloids supports a suspended roof of pre-stressed concrete. Inside, no objects were on display, but instead visitors were able to experience a psychedelic sound installation of Edgard Varèse's "Poème électronique", played through hundreds of loudspeakers. The sounds were accompanied by images and film clips ranging from Le Corbusier's designs to clips of the Hiroshima bomb. The Pavilion, one of the first ever multimedia installations, created a new spatial experience and, at the same time, explored visitor reactions, not only to the multimedia environment but also to the building's floorplan: to what extent can the spatial experience determine human movement?

12

Today, architects such as UNStudio and Barkow Leibinger are using pavilions as an opportunity to experiment with form. Ben van Berkel sees pavilions as a launchpad, a kind of "generator" for ideas and solutions, which can then be developed further in more complex buildings.[6] New architectural elements and concepts can be tried out in these temporary buildings, for later use in more lasting architectural works. For example, UNStudio used its Changing Room pavilion to develop spatial concepts they had been unable to implement a year earlier in their American residential building project VilLA NM. Ben van Berkel, just like Le Corbusier, explores human proportions and spatial relationships. The neutral-white loops of the "Changing Room" object swirl like a giant double bow around the historic columns of a former shipyard. Lines turn into surfaces and then become space. The floor gradually merges into the wall and then the ceiling. On the inside, images projected onto the flowing surfaces create an additional contemplative space within the physical space. Berkel thus aims to convey to the visitor that quantities can be expanded or compressed (fig. 11). What in 2008 still only worked as a temporary installation in an exhibition hall, sheltered from wind and rain, now stands in its next, more permanent, incarnation, exposed to the elements as the New Amsterdam Plein & Pavilion on the New York harbour (fig. 10).[7]

Other architects, too, have used pavilions as prototypes to research new materials and construction methods. For example, Santiago Calatrava's daring roof constructions, first explored in his Kuwait pavilion at the 1992 Seville Expo, are later found on his high-speed train stations in Lyon and Liège. Bruno Taut's glass pavilion and Ludwig Mies van der Rohe's Barcelona Pavilion represent milestones in the use of glass as a construction material. Equally, Bernard Tschumi's Glass Video Gallery in Groningen is one of these prototypes of architectural design – and a case study for the glass

9, 10 New Amsterdam Plein & Pavillon, New York, 2010; UNStudio floor plan and photo during construction
11 The Changing Room at the Venice Biennale, 2008; UNStudio
12 Serpentine Gallery Pavilion, London, 2002; Toyo Ito & Associates with Arup
13 Tod's Omotesando Building, Tokyo, 2004; Toyo Ito & Associates with Arup

13

industry. The transparent pavilion is the first completely self-supporting glass building. All supports consist of glass panes held together with brackets.

For a few weeks every summer, London adds a further destination to its many sights and attractions. Architects who have not yet built anything in Britain are invited by the Serpentine Gallery to design the Serpentine Gallery Pavilion. Thanks to its temporary nature, the pavilion is exempt from most of the usual building regulations, and the architects can realise their visions with the only constraints being finance and timescale. The programme has been running continuously since 2000 with one short break in 2004. Some of these buildings, which receive much public attention, have subsequently been developed further, such as Toyo Ito's construction, which presented, for the first time, a new, non-orthogonal geometry based on a steel structure with the lines of force extending beyond the building's edges – a geometry that was to be copied over and over again (fig. 12). Ito himself re-used the principle three years later on the Tod's Building and the Mikimoto Building. Both of these buildings are on the popular fashion mile Ometesando Street in Tokyo and stand out as a result of their unusual geometry created by a network of lines and surfaces (fig. 13).

Most recently, a pioneering student project has raised eyebrows in the world of pavilion design. As their entry to the European Student Competition on Sustainable Architecture, Andreas Claus Schnetzer and Gregor Pils, both students at Vienna University of Technology, designed the Palette House. Made from 800 used Euro-palettes, the building won first prize in the competition and was subsequently shown at the Architecture Biennale 2008, directly on the Venetian Lagoon. The simple construction takes on today's ecological and economical challenges and can be built virtually anywhere. The cost-effective recycled product is used as the primary construction element for facade, ceiling and walls. Insulation and services are fitted between the palette layers. The flexibility of these relatively small modules gives the construction an enormous adaptability. The box-shaped building can be added to, made smaller or, if necessary, moved to another location. The palette house can be used as a weekend cottage, a low-cost home, for example in developing countries, or as temporary shelter in disaster zones. The easy handling and wide availability of the wooden palettes are a particular benefit, and this, combined with low energy and material requirements, make the concept economically viable. The Vienna students' Palette House was well received by visitors at the Biennale in Venice, as well as in Vienna and in the townships in Johannesburg (fig. 14).

The DAM Pavilion
To celebrate its 25th anniversary in summer 2009, the German Architecture Museum (Deutsches Architektur Museum, or DAM) in Frankfurt was planning to erect a temporary pavilion in the park of the nearby Museum for Applied Art – where it would be joining Richard Meier's newly renovated cubes and Kengo Kuma's inflatable tea house (see p. 122ff.). The space was to be designed to accommodate cultural events, with an auditorium for about 100 people, and to be used as a café with outdoor seating during the day (fig. 18). The Berlin-based architect Barkow Leibinger, working with the Stuttgart engineering studio Werner Sobek,

14 Palette House, Venice, 2009;
Design: Andreas Claus Schnetzler, Gregor Pils
Tutors: Karin Stieldorf, Pekka Janhunen, TU Vienna
15 Swoosh summer pavilion in London
Design: Valeria Garcia Abarca, AA London (concept)
Tutors: Charles Walker, Martin Self
16–18 Design for the DAM Pavilion in Frankfurt/Main, 2009;
Barkow Leibinger, Architekten

14

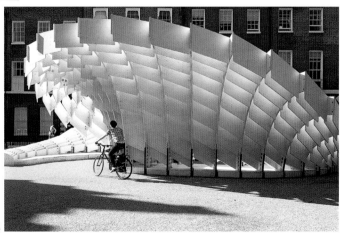
15

envisaged a light structure, made from curved steel tubes and covered by a translucent skin, arranged around a small tree at its centre. Using the economic model of the Serpentine Gallery Pavilion in London, the DAM Pavilion was to be financed entirely through sponsorship. Due to the financial crisis in autumn 2008, the project had to be aborted, but was documented in an exhibition in summer 2009.

"A pavilion is neither building nor pure experiment. It oscillates between the speculative and the pragmatic. We see it as an interesting vehicle (a prototype or model) for gauging the boundaries and possibilities of speculative work. It adds perspective to themes that exist, incomplete, somewhere below the surface. The pavilion, for us, is a measure and a filter to help legitimise and understand the value of our research."[8] This is how the architects Frank Barkow and Regine Leibinger understand pavilion architecture. Designing and constructing pavilions, however, does not just offer vast opportunities. It is also a tremendous challenge in sustainable architecture. The requirement to minimise material use and to enable complete disassembly and recyclability of the materials used was a key condition in the design and construction of the DAM Pavilion.

The café and auditorium are accommodated within a ring of several crescents encircling a small courtyard with a tree (fig. 16 and 17). Digital technology makes it possible to shape the standardised steel tubes individually into multiple radii thereby creating a bespoke shape from a system of tailor-made steel tubes. This framework is then covered with polycarbonate tiles, which are mounted onto Velcro loops. To screen out the sunlight and avoid overheating of the internal spaces, solar panels are fitted onto suitable roof areas and some of the tiles are printed opaque. Generously sized air vents ensure good ventilation.
At the DAM exhibition, a several-metre-long section of the tile-covered steel tubes was shown at full size to give visitors a sense of the spatial experience. This 1:1 mock-up clearly gave everyone a taste for more.

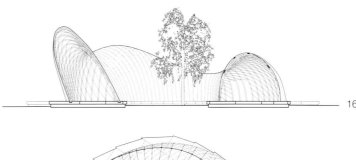

16

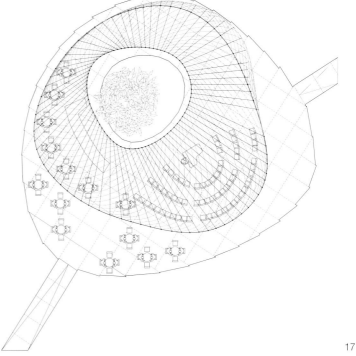

17

References:
1 Sieveking, Albert Forbes: Sir William Temple Upon the Gardens of Epicurus: With other seventeenth century garden essays. Newcastle upon Tyne 2008
2 Chambers, William: Designs of Chinese Buildings, Furniture, Dresses, machines and Utensils. New York 1980
3 Bußmann, Kerstin: The Pavilion. A History of Enduring Transience. In: The Pavilion. Pleasure and Polemics in Architecture. Frankfurt am Main 2009, p. 36
4 Bergdoll, Barry: The Pavilion and the Expanded Possibilities of Architecture. In: The Pavilion [3], p. 17ff.
5 Ibid., p. 23
6 van Berkel, Ben: Pavilions. An Interview by Karen Murphy. In: The Pavilion [3], p. 81f.
7 Ibid.
8 Barkow, Frank; Leibinger, Regine: Between the Speculative and the Pragmatic. In: The Pavilion [3], p. 171

18

Tree house – dream house

Andreas Wenning

Tree houses have a long tradition and were built by our fore-fathers many thousands of years ago. They were high off the ground and concealed between the branches and leaves to provide protection from dangerous animals and enemies. Life in and with trees was therefore a question of survival. For some peoples it is still so today (fig. 1). Later on, people began to use tree houses for enjoyment and leisure. The treetop house developed from a vital necessity to a synonym for adventure, romance and freedom. It became a place for adults and children to experiment with their building skills and to play.

The destruction of natural habitats and our environment today also makes tree houses into places of protest. Environmental activists use them to demonstrate in favour of the preservation of forests and individual trees. In art, literature and film, they have also provided a setting for imaginative and futuristic scenarios.

There are different interpretations of what actually constitutes a tree house. For some people it must be built completely in the tree without any supports connecting with the ground. This is a very restricted definition. Obviously, tree houses must be connected in some way with trees and built off the ground. The house could enclose some of the tree or interact with its natural growth. Supports can be used to strengthen the structure and shore up the tree itself. The desire to be in the trees, to enjoy the view and to experience nature is the decisive factor.

The tree house as building task

Although tree houses are buildings, they tend to be constructed in a confined space and rarely on the basis of specific architectural plans. This could have something to do with the simplicity of the planning and hence the modest fees that can be demanded. The fact of planning with a living foundation is an unusual one for an architect to confront. Tree houses are thought of as playgrounds that are difficult to reconcile with the problems and planning procedures that normally occupy architects. The small demand for professionally planned tree houses in the past could also be explained by the generally accepted idea that they belong to the do-it-yourself sphere.

Tree houses are generally associated with a traditional formal language with a pitched roof and transom windows, but there is nevertheless something innovative in the way they can be designed using modern resources. They have increasingly become an object of study and are occasionally planned and executed professionally, opening up a new area of application for architecture in this way.
The special feature in the planning and erecting of a tree house is the interaction with the tree. There is also a need to take account of the natural habit and the very private wishes of the person for whom the house is built. The finished product will be a place to feel comfortable and private but also somehow exciting and in touch with nature. It can – perhaps should be – very small so as to create a haven of retreat for the user. The design of this micro-space in the tree can vary considerably. It can be simple or luxurious, adapted to or contrasting with its surroundings.
The interaction between the structure and the living environment is particularly important. Trees must not be overloaded and require sufficient freedom to move in the wind and continue to grow without restriction.

The first stage – planning permission

Professionally constructed or large tree houses are regarded legally as structures and could be subject to planning permission. The type of planning permission will depend on the local legislation and judgement of the building authorities. Small children's tree houses do not normally require explicit planning permission. In some German state authorities the cut-off point is specified as 30 m³ gross volume. This limit can quickly be exceeded because the volume underneath

1 Korowai tree house in New Guinea

the tree house and the terrace are also included in the calculation. The distance from neighbouring properties might also have to be taken into account.

Selecting the tree

The tree in which the tree house is to be built must be vital and stable. A healthy tree will not be as quickly overloaded and can also accommodate the tree house for a longer period.

The tree must therefore be examined. A tree that looks vital is not always necessarily safe and a tree that is not well supplied can be stable enough for a tree house. The main growth phase should be completed. In structural terms the main growth period may be regarded as having been terminated when the tree has reached two thirds of its possible height. Oak and beech trees can grow to a height of 25 to 30 metres, for example, and can thus be regarded as being sufficiently stable for a tree house when they have reached 15 to 18 metres.

Even a layperson should be in a position to distinguish an intact tree from one that is damaged, and this is generally sufficient for an initial appraisal. If a tree crown has sparse foliage or dead branches, for example, it could well be suffering from fungal infestation that can interrupt the connection between the roots and the crown.

Professional tree experts should then be consulted to confirm whether the tree is suitable or not.

Structure and materials

Wood is the commonest and most ideal material for a tree house. European larch, Douglas fir and oak are particularly weather-resistant and suitably coloured as basic materials. Because of their strength, tropical woods are often superior to indigenous varieties, but their environmental compatibility must also be taken into account.

Metals, fabrics and plastics can also be considered because of their structural properties and weight. They offer the possibility of making lightweight structures, which could be of great advantage. The cost, natural appearance, harmonisation with the tree and ageing properties are further arguments in favour of wood, however.

The facade can be in the form of a single layer or multiple layers with insulation.

2　　Load-bearing strap
3　　Steel cable to secure a tree house substructure
4, 5　"Zwischen Eiche und Erle" (between oak and alder), Osnabrück, 2006

2

3

4

Because of the height, assembling a tree house presents greater difficulties than a building on the ground. It is therefore advisable to preassemble as many components as possible on the ground or in a workshop and then to raise them into position with a rope winch or crane. Beams or terraces can be attached to the tree if necessary before the facades and roof elements or even the entire tree house are hoisted into place. Tree climbers can often get to inaccessible higher reaches safely without scaffolding or ladders.

Securing the tree house

The tree must be able to move freely even in a storm and its natural growth should not be impeded. The securing of the structure to the tree is thus of vital importance. The material used should not grow into or damage the wood cambium. In this regard, flexible suspension is a good alternative, the tree house being secured to the tree by means of adjustable fittings, steel cables or looped straps (figs. 2 and 3) that are also used for securing the tree crowns. If there are no forks in the trunk or branches to attach straps, it might be necessary to fix anchor bolts or screws in the tree. This method should be used only with coniferous trees, whose resin is thick enough to ensure bonding that will prevent the development or spread of rot in the trunk.

Description of projects

The area around a horse riding centre 30 km to the south of Bremen offered the ideal conditions for building a tree house. There was a well equipped workshop, a vast panorama and, most importantly, a healthy stock of tall trees. The enclosed section of the tree house and the terrace were preassembled as a single element and suspended between two beech trees (fig. 6). The narrow, boat-like triangular 5.6 m² room was hoisted by means of a truck-mounted crane onto a previously installed substructure made of untreated larch. The trapdoor entrance is reached by climbing 9 m on a system of vertical and diagonal ladders. Narrow bottom-hung windows on the walls, a skylight and the horizontally glazed top of the tree house structure provide plenty of daylight and an almost unimpeded all-round view. The initial project was the first on the "baumraum" label, and further projects in Germany and other countries were to follow, some of which are described here.

6 Tree house at Plendelhof, Bassum, 2003
7 Cliff Treehouse, New York State, 2007

6

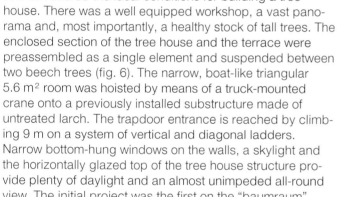

5

7

The semi-circular tree house structure "Zwischen Eiche und Erle" (between oak and alder) with large south-west-facing glazing and windows was built next to a small stream on a property in Lower Saxony (fig. 4). Two V-shaped trunks support two long oak terraces at different heights integrated into the living structure and incorporating the branches. Stainless steel components and straps passing over the tree crown support the terrace and part of the 10 m² cabin. Two conical stabilisers prop up the back of the tree house. The interior made of untreated oak and light grey wool felt consists of a large bed area, a bench, several large drawers and a shallow sideboard (fig. 5).

The Cliff Treehouse, an enclosed cabin on a steep cliff next to a tree, was built on a private property north of New York City (fig. 7). The load is distributed between two short steel supports at the top and two V-shaped struts underneath the protruding part of the house. Access is via the cliff and then on a narrow and gently inclined ramp to a terrace built around a maple tree. A walkway then leads to the cabin. The outer formwork is in the form of sawn silver-painted larch planks, giving the structure a dynamic metal-like effect. The tree house was prefabricated in Germany and the components shipped to the USA, where it was assembled in cooperation with an American building company.

Private individuals are not the only ones to build tree houses. Weberhaus has included one as an attraction in its World of Living residential and theme park. The elliptical structure stands next to an oak tree and rests on seven conical supports made of Siberian larch standing at different angles to one another and hinge-mounted to the tree house and concrete foundation. The precise positioning was simulated on models and then optimised using a structural program. The terrace and stairway are supported by guys attached to the tree after the stability of the oak had been verified by means of tensile tests and computer simulations. The crown of the load-bearing oak can be studied from the domed interior by means of a patchwork of photographs and texts in German, English and French explaining the diverse nature of the tree as a living entity (fig. 8).

On the outskirts of the town of Melle is a tree house named "Zwischen Magnolie und Tanne" (between magnolia and spruce) on a private property embedded in dense brush (fig. 9). It was designed as a retreat and guest room but also as a play area for the owners' grandchildren. It can be used in addition for business meetings and small receptions. The layout is in the form of two right-angled surfaces at different heights. Because there was no available tree with sufficient load-bearing capacity, the terrace and enclosed cube rest on a carefully made brushed stainless steel support. The two sections are jointed by steps. The wood facade is made of weather-resistant tatajuba, while the walls and fitted furniture in the 14 m² cabin are in red-stained oak (fig. 10).

The special feature of the "Backstelze" in Eberschwang is its long and narrow terrace and separate sculptured tree house (figs. 11 and 12). The terrace is suspended from two oak trees and a birch while the tree house itself is supported by asymmetrically positioned oak poles. The outer skin is covered by a back-ventilated weatherproof steel facade. The red-varnished terrace and supports match the rust-coloured

13

metal surface. Oblique windows provide a view in all directions and are in harmony with the overall form. There is also a horizontal glazed surface looking down onto the small stream underneath the tree house.

Outlook for tree houses

The idea of creating a space in a tree for private leisure or commercial purposes has immense potential. A tree house could be designed for seminars, meditation and relaxation and even as a restaurant (see "Tree house restaurant near Auckland", p. 102ff.). The tourist industry has also now discovered the attraction of tree houses. The trend towards nature and the environment has brought about an increase in the demand for such exotic accommodation, ranging from simple hostels to luxuriously fitted tree houses that can now be booked in many places around the world. There are some accommodations in Asia designed indirectly to protect the rain forests by drawing the attention of aware tourists to the importance of forest preservation. They also offer the local population a viable alternative to predatory exploitation of the primeval forests.

Tree house utopias

Exceptional and spectacular settings such as those found in the northern Californian forests provide an ideal location for unusual tree houses. Computerised visualisations and new lightweight materials make it possible to develop and build free forms. The stairway of the Winding Snake, for example, coils up around a mighty sequoia to a metal cabin (fig. 13). In the Loop utopia (fig. 14), the stair ramp defines the floor, sides and ceiling of the tree house. Inspired by the South Seas, the spherical cocoon and organically shaped terrace of Palm Fiction hang between palm trees next to the sea. This tree house could be mass-produced using boat-building principles (fig. 15).

Tree houses are a form of microarchitecture and could conceivably be constructed in many places. They could also be adapted for water, desert or ice or even built on the roof of a high-rise building in the city.

8 World of Living, Rheinau-Linx, 2008
9, 10 "Zwischen Magnolie und Tanne" (between magnolia and spruce), Melle, 2007
11, 12 "Bachstelze", Eberschwang, 2008
13 Winding Snake rendering
14 Loop rendering
15 Palm Fiction rendering

14

15

Mobile architecture

Gerhard Kalhöfer

Mobility and experimentation

Mobile architecture refers in the first instance to the territorial mobility of objects and their transport to another location. By extension, it can also refer to immovable architecture that can be transformed for different utilisations. In both cases architecture moves and is sent on a journey, at the end of which another situation or condition awaits it.

Travel in general requires a concentrated focus on the things that are taken on the journey: they become smaller and lighter. When travelling, utility and convenience are all that matters. Travel should not be cumbersome. The same is true of architecture: if it becomes mobile, its scale inevitably changes and it becomes microarchitecture.
Size often matters to architects, however. The larger a project, the more important it becomes, and quantity also enhances reputation.
What then is the attraction of microarchitecture?
One factor is certainly the continuity, from planning to execution, which is only possible with small projects. All aspects are planned, checked and implemented down to the last detail directly by the architect. Large projects, by contrast, require a team for their completion. This means that many tasks and steps are outside the planner's control. For beginners, microarchitecture is thus a perfect introduction to the working world and at the same time permits all of the skills learnt while studying to be tested in practice. Seemingly small tasks are more controllable, thereby reducing the risk of failure. The smallness means that complex operations are more concentrated and at the same time more manageable.
As with research projects, architects can use small models to establish basic principles for larger projects. The experimental character is used by many young offices to address specific topics discussed in the world of architecture and to develop innovative solutions. Micro-projects are particularly suitable in this regard, because their size makes the underlying structural concept more readable and permits spectacular spatial effects to be achieved without major construction work. In this way many extreme and experimental projects have been completed by new entrants to the profession with considerable practical and in some cases financial input of their own. For many young architects, such as AllesWirdGut in Vienna, for example, they are the launching pad for a career, in their case through the drawings and full-scale models for TurnOn, their experimental housing project (fig. 1).

Zero distance

Microarchitecture follows similar rules to product design. The users and the objects are approximately the same size and can thus confront one another at eye level. This has consequences: greater attention has to be paid to the user's movement and his relationship to the object when using it. Mobile projects in particular demand that the planner imagines situations and factors in possible and anticipated actions. He is called upon to consider the function of the space over time and to describe scenes and processes. At stake is the spatial behaviour and the social interaction. This should also be reflected in the drawing, which is the architect's working tool and instrument for communication. It must include people not just as staff but to illustrate the particular function, since the size and direct proximity to the user can reveal weaknesses and errors. If the mobile elements have a before and an after, this must be reproduced in the drawing. A plan shows how feasible the transformation option is and whether it is based on a human scale.

Unlike architecture, microarchitecture can focus intensively on specific situations and users. For all the standardisation of design, tailor-made projects are possible, as is the case in product design, where buyers can personalise even mass-produced items. Many mobile projects by Kalhöfer-Korschildgen are based initially on the user's specific demands. In the Social_Indicator designed in 2010 the multi-purpose corpus corresponds to the user's lifestyle by incorporating stairs, kitchen and a retractable 6 m dining table that reacts to the changing space requirements. It is the central hub of social activity and can accommodate up to twenty-three people. When completely extended, it projects onto the terrace, thereby removing the separation between indoors and outdoors (fig. 2).
The possibility of directly experiencing a building through its human scale increases the likelihood that its complexity will be perceived and understood. This creates a much closer attachment by the user than with large buildings, an attachment that is frequently reinforced by interactive elements. A person who can change his environment through his interaction with the building or can set it in motion loses the traditional respect for perfectly designed architecture, and a direct relationship is more easily formed.
As the quality in microarchitecture is not defined by size, thereby excluding all possibility of monumentality, it can only express itself through more sensitive means such as complexity and distinctiveness. The absence of monumentality

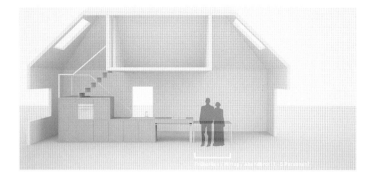

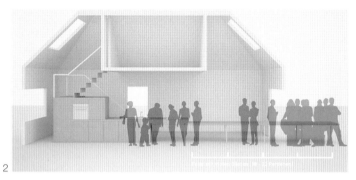

also permits a new type of irreverent architecture that can also contain self-referencing irony or humour. The unusual feature of a building, its ability to question itself through its mobility, produces a reaction of amazement. The occupants of the building do not perceive its mobility or part-mobility solely in conceptual terms. The building is not only an object but, through its mobility, a living communication partner with equal rights and one to be treated with humour. The essential significance of mobile architecture is not necessarily its practical versatility; it can also be expressed in terms of zero distance, laughter and amazement by the building-owner at meetings, by workers on the site and by visitors at parties when they experience this mobility (fig. 3).

Temporary space instead of form

Through its movement, mobile architecture gives space a temporary character. It is interested in the user's action rather than the effect of its outer appearance. The spatial design is also important, of course, but it takes a back seat when the space is also a setting for action. The distinction by Louis Kahn between rooms that are useful and rooms that are used presupposes the importance of interaction. Mobile structures thus not only define the space they occupy but also offer utility-serving elements. Lars Lerup compares architecture with theatres offering props with which users can design their own play. As the users bring individual experiences and ideas, they are not "responding organisms", but active individuals who define the building by appropriating it.[1]

In this conception, mobile architecture becomes a process rather than a form. Our experience of space is transformative and without form, a sequence and a progression.[2]

Appropriation is one of the key terms for understanding mobile buildings. It is fundamentally an active process but has both static and dynamic aspects. When understanding and categorising space, intellectually entering a place through the senses, appropriation is static; it is only when it is personalised, modified and adapted by the occupant that it becomes dynamic. It is a question of occupying the space physically, conceptually and emotionally. The appropriated space is a stable framework and point of departure for action and discovery. Associations with the structural environment are created in the interaction between assimilation and transformation by means of an architecture that not only prescribes but also stimulates. The opposite, expropriation, takes place in dominating or anonymous buildings that do not permit active confrontation and interaction.[3]

Mobile projects achieve their aim only with the cooperation of the user. If he is offered a series of reasonable possibilities, the architecture will be certain to move. The logic of the different options before and after the movement and their advantages also facilitates implementation with the workers on site. The strategic and conceptual approach as opposed to a formal one makes the projects so robust that they can withstand a limited amount of "adaptation" and formal modification by the executing companies, as it is not the form but the different spatial arrangements that count. Who-does-what arguments and classic role scenarios no longer apply. Discussion can focus not only on form and its precise execution according to the drawings but also on a process and its technical implementation (fig. 4).

Self-determination rather than outside influence

Small buildings are usually designed interactively, since their smallness often means that they need to expand in space in order to be used for diverse purposes. Mobility is frequently achieved only through extension to the surrounding area and access to and use of it.

Lack of interest by users was one of the criticisms of mobile architecture in the 1960s. As there is no indication that the interest by planners in transformable mobile buildings has decreased – the many publications and projects on the subject would appear to show the opposite – the conditions must have changed since then. Although contemporary mobile architecture uses the same mechanisms as in the 1960s, it now encounters emancipated users who can move confidently in a product world of endless choice. Liberalisation of society is no longer an issue. People are used to reflective living in which socialisation takes place against a background of continuous change and transformation of the familiar world. For this generation, choice and mobility are no longer an obstacle. Technology is adapted to the consumer and can be discovered with ease. The scenic quality that results corresponds perfectly to the lifestyle of today's leisure society and its hedonistic consumer behaviour. Apple products are the best example of this successful association of emotion and product. For this reason, mobile interactive projects are appreciated differently today.

Added to this is the blurring of the boundaries between the public and private realms and the infiltration of public life into the private sphere. Both ask questions of the built-up space and result in a functional dissociation from fixed loci. An incredible variety of architectural choices and furnishing options and the resultant demands and contradictory wishes of users call additionally for spatial and practical flexibility. It is no longer a question of compensation strategies seeking solutions. The attempt to react to complex demands with simple images is retrograde and today's social reality calls for understanding and incorporating the qualities and opportunities presented by the new-found freedom. In contrast to the 1960s, mobile architecture today has come of age.

Concentration of functions

This social development is leading to greater specialisation in all areas, including architecture. We are undergoing a process of categorisation and duplication that breaks down familiar associations and defines them more precisely. Mobility now permits functions that were separated by the process of specialisation to be reintegrated without losing their inherent characteristics. The spatial merging takes place through change of location. Hybrid or transformable architecture overcomes functional distinctions. Mobility allows the creation of something new while the different functions continue to co-exist. Today's mobile architecture shows indications of a concentration of functions.

4

1 TurnOn in movement, 2001; AllesWirdGut
2 Social_Indicator, conversion of a 1970s house, Waldesch, 2010; Kalhöfer-Korschildgen
3 "Fahrt ins Grüne" in movement, mobile extension of a half-timbered house, Remscheid, 1997; Kalhöfer-Korschildgen
4 Workers next to the "Zimmer mit Aussicht", mobile roof terrace, Cologne, 2008; Kalhöfer-Korschildgen

5

The movement of buildings is a sensory moment and would therefore be sufficient on its own as a design motivation. Mobility only makes sense, however, if it links functions effectively. Experimental projects can convince even critical and conservative users if the functional advantage of a solution removes their scepticism with regard to conceptual poetry or the very mobility that is a prerequisite for the different functions to be taken advantage of.

Alienation of function

How are functions integrated in mobile architecture? Sometimes, related functions can be called up sequentially by means of a transformable object. In other projects several functions have been linked unconventionally with one another. This hybrid combination is often disconcerting, as conflicting or non-matched functions are often juxtaposed. In many cases, the meaning of the initially alienating and subjective combination becomes apparent only through use. The artist and architect Allan Wexler uses this combined function concept in many projects. He offers the user of his objects a complex view of everyday items and rituals. In his Dining Building with Window Chairs, windows and chairs have been combined. Access to the room is possible only by setting the architecture in motion and retracting the window chair. If the user sits down, no light can enter the room because his back blocks the opening. The overhead light is the only remaining source and focuses attention on the centre of the room – the table and the socialising space. The absurdity of this combination of functions increases the user's perception of the process and enhances the sensory significance of the utilisation (fig. 5).

Type

With territorial change, the movement of mobile architecture can be active or passive. A building can move itself – with the aid of its own technology, motor and wheels – or it can be moved.

In both cases the size, volume and weight have to be reduced, since under normal circumstances only regular means of transport are available. Heavy loads for oversized objects are subject to special authorisation procedures and are not an option for conventional projects. The only other possibility is cost-intensive air transport by airship or helicopter. The reference dimension is the road and the maximum size of lorries. In Europe the maximum height of a standard European semi-articulated heavy goods vehicle is 4.00 m and the maximum width 2.55 m. The length can vary: 18.75 m for an articulated train and 16.50 m for an articulated lorry. A longer version of the same width but up to 25.25 m vehicle length and 60 t total weight has only been approved to date on an experimental basis.

All mobile architecture must comply with the EU measurements for heavy goods vehicles. If it exceeds 2.55 m in width, the object needs to be assembled on site.

While the transportable height of 2.60 m is the same as the minimum height in architecture for habitable rooms, the maximum width restricts the design freedom. The only possibility as a result is function-driven rooms in which the technical solutions have high priority. The freely available and non-defined space is thus small and viable only through tight coordination of a compressed technological configuration. The addition of several transportable modules can solve this dilemma. The problem here is often in the dominance of the

6

7

uniform and banal-looking structural form that is produced. In spite of these deficits, a modular and transportable construction method can also have a high architectural and sensory quality. This can be seen typically in the mobile architecture of Oskar Leo Kaufmann and Albert Rüf, which makes use extensively of wood materials. Their project System 3 was shown at the Micro Compact Home exhibition at the MoMA in New York. The system is based on the distinction between "serving space" and "naked space". The element containing the entire building engineering has a prefabricated serving unit and is enlarged through the fitting of additional wall, floor and roof elements to become a freely usable space. The unusual width and large freely available surface area eliminate the possibility of a container-like atmosphere being created. The innovation consists of the combination of unit-based and element-based systems (fig. 6 and 7).

The container is the classic example of standardised passive territorial mobility. Because it is standardised it can be transported in various ways by road, rail or ship. The means of transport chosen will depend on the space requirements and cost-effectiveness. The size is determined by the storage and transport dimensions. The American truck width of 2.44 m is taken as the basis for the width of containers. There are two types: 20-foot containers (6.058 × 2.438 × 2.591 m) and 40-foot containers (12.192 × 2.438 × 2.591 m). Special versions such as air freight containers, which slope on one side, are adapted to the vehicle transporting them, but the underlying principle and construction are the same as with standard containers. Two thirds of international freight traffic is carried out in containers. They are robust and cost-effective; their interchangeable side elements make for increased flexibility and they have an average service life of twelve years. These advantages have made containers into an architectural symbol of globalisation and a favourite in student designs at college. Emotionally speaking there are two aspects: a functional banality and the poetry of transboundary mobility. The architectural approach to containers is also paradoxical: architects are enthusiastic about the possibility of standardisation but nevertheless show through their personalisation of these standard products that they question it after all.

However, mobility also means that the building itself is transformable and adaptable. Transformable projects are planned mostly for housing. One of the classic themes is the dissolution of the spatial separation and the creation of a relationship between indoors and outdoors. The disappearing windows in Mies van der Rohe's Villa Tugendhat are a classic example. Shigeru Ban developed this idea of dissolving spatial separation in a most radical manner with his Case Study projects. Living Room by Formalhaut is one of the most lyrical projects in this regard. The 2005 residential building in Gelnhausen uses different media to create an interaction between indoors and outdoors, occupants and the city. The participation of many different artists creates not only an architectural but also a welcome interdisciplinary effect; the result is highly complex spaces of high formal and artistic quality. Venturing outdoors with the shifting balcony not only enlarges the room but also creates an interaction between indoors and out-

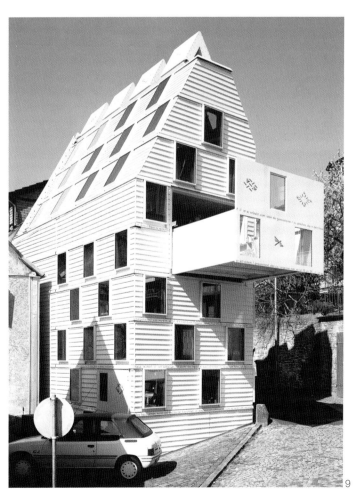

5   Dining Building with Window Chairs, 1983; Allan Wexler
6, 7 System 3, New York, 2008; Oskar Leo Kaufmann / Albert Rüf
8, 9 Living Room, Gelnhausen, 2005; Formalhaut, seifert + stoeckmann

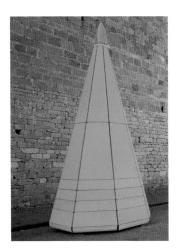

10

doors. The motorised balcony is like a classic filing cabinet drawer mounted on two rails with rollers and three-way bearings. It takes just three minutes to slide it into the desired end position (figs. 8 and 9).

Uses of mobile buildings

A distinction should be made at the outset between projects for the public sphere and those for the private sphere. In public buildings, approval procedures and safety aspects are the decisive and often exclusive criteria for mobile architecture. Applications for private users are just as work-intensive but have fewer liability risks for the architect.

Mobile urban architecture usually means consumer buildings, e.g. kiosks extending into the public space. Their disappearing outer shell has a signal effect and can also be used as a flexible storage space for the goods to be sold (fig. 10). Market stalls that can be erected and dismantled quickly are another example. The market stall by the Norwegian office Rintala Eggertsson can be folded to the size of a rectangular box that will fit in a small transporter and contains the aluminium structure necessary for its erection. To transport it from the car park to the erection site it can be fitted with two wheels and two feet – much like a wheelbarrow – before being transformed into its final state as a market stall (2 × 2 m) with roof, sales areas and shelves. Through this metamorphosis the object is capable of reacting precisely but without difficulty to the relevant situation (fig. 11 and 12). Another application for quickly erected mobile buildings is as temporary buildings. Kept permanently available for emergencies following wars or natural disasters, they can be transported rapidly by road or air to the site of the emergency. The large amount of accommodation that is generally required calls for small items that can be transported in large numbers and in a short time for assembly as emergency shelters for entire families. In this case the logistical and technical considerations are of prime importance (see fig. 8, p. 54).

Other mobile buildings serve cultural or social purposes. The Rheinpegel_Raumlabor installation by Kalhöfer-Korschildgen featured an art exhibition by the Montag Foundation that referenced the Rhine. An additional elastically mounted interactive floor level that tilted when walked on was installed in a room in a historical villa. The soft, flowing and instable nature of the river was symbolised by the fluctuating "level" of the floor. If the visitor stepped on the floor at its edges, the floor tilted to one side revealing a blue base with a quotation by Schiller inscribed on it: "Strongly it bears us along in swelling and limitless billows"[4] (fig. 13). The New York Voter Registration Center by Allan Wexler was designed to encourage college students to register for the 2008 presidential election. The foldable pegboard structure could be transported in a small vehicle and erected in a few minutes. To reduce the weight, the areas of material that were not structurally relevant were cut out. An American flag is incorporated in the sandwich construction and can be seen through the cut-outs. In addition to its symbolic character, it also performs a structural role as the hinge linking the individual panels, making it easy to fold the walls and roof into position (figs. 14 and 15).

A large proportion of mobile architecture is devoted to housing. The user is offered a space for assembly that can be

11

12

44

adapted to his particular requirements. The main considerations are saving space and flexible applications. The Bed/Sitting Rooms, also by Allan Wexler, for an artist's home for the Mattress Factory Art Museum illustrate this concept. Different items of furniture can be slotted into cut-outs in a partition and used on either side as a sofa or bed, depending on how far they are pulled out. The lighting is rotatable and can also be used on both sides of the partition. The wheels on the furniture items are designed with deliberate simplicity and lack of sophistication. The layout can be changed at will several times a day. The project is not about engineering but the option of changing a room layout in a dwelling. A variety of configurations are available for one or two people: a single person could have a single bed on one side and seating on the other; a couple would want a double bed on one side and a sofa on the other; two people on either side of the partition would have a single bed for one and a sofa for the other; a single person could also have a bedroom on one side and an empty living space on the other (figs. 16 and 17).

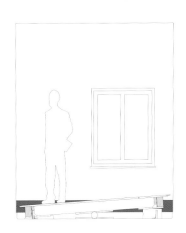

Furniture and mobility

The mechanical methods of transformation have been developed and refined over the centuries on furniture. The basic principles have remained practically unchanged, however. Sigfried Giedion describes this development in detail in his book Mechanization Takes Command, pointing to the etymological connection between 'mobility' and 'meuble' (French for furniture). In fact, French distinguishes between movable items – 'meuble' or 'mobilier' – and immovable ones – 'immeuble' – which is also the word for building. Movable items are called 'meubles' because they accompany their owners when they travel. In the Middle Ages the mobility of furniture was connected with moving from place to place. The trunk was the medieval container. Its size and weight made it mobile. Household goods were always packed and their owners were ready to move at any time. It was not the lack of space, as was the case in the early modern era. Giedion emphasises that medieval mobility was that of a nomadic being with deep insecurity and fear of loss. The noble's castle was practically empty when he was away because he could not know what the situation would be like on his return.[5]

As society became increasingly stable in the sixteenth century, household goods no longer needed to be constantly on the move. The principle of mobility was used not to change locations but for flexible use. The result was functional hybrids: trunks that served as tables or, with hinges, as benches. In the late Gothic era furniture was made mobile by using rotating axles (dowel pins and hinges) so that they could be employed, for example as desks for reading, writing or painting.[6] The reversible benches described by Giedion are also unusual: the backrest is mobile so that users can sit either facing or with their backs to the fire.[7] The principle was further developed in the nineteenth century in railway carriages. Even today there is a single-track tramway in Porto, Portugal, that operates in this way: at the terminus, the tram

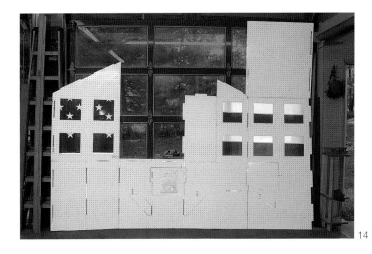

10 Stalls, Pisa, 1997; Leonardo srl, Salvatore Re Architetto
11, 12 Square market stall, 2008; Rintala Eggertsson
13 "Rheinpegel_Raumlabor", room installation for the exhibition "Blick zurück nach vorn" by Montag Stiftung Bildende Kunst, Villa Ingehohl, Bonn, 2008, Kalhöfer-Korschildgen
14, 15 The New York Voter Registration Center, 2008; Allan Wexler

cannot turn around so the passengers simply move the back-rest so that they can once again sit facing the direction of travel (fig. 18).

Rococo refined these mechanisms and created lightweight and complicated furniture whose mobility combined practicality with concealment: the furniture was opened up to show what it could do.[8] The designs at this time featured sophisticated technical innovations, e.g. spring-loaded hidden drawers. Mobility at this time always had something playful about it.

After the Middle Ages, when the mobility in furniture was designed for moving from one place to another, came practicality and convenience, and then in the nineteenth century America the concept of transformability. This was due to the lack of space: there was not enough room for dedicated single-function furniture, and at the same time multifunctionality saved money. The American Shakers tried to live independently through their own industry and inventiveness and developed many pieces of combined furniture notable for their excellent workmanship and elegant appearance. There were many patents for mechanical devices for converting a folding chair into a lounger or a table into a bed. A typical American invention is the fold-away bed, an extension of the principle used in railway sleeping compartments that in many American households did away for the need for a separate bedroom.

Mechanisms

The classic modern style took the American principle of austerity one step further. In effect, the purpose was to achieve efficiency by allowing rooms to be used for two different functions. In the 1920s, systems based on folding mechanisms were the primary starting point for mobile projects. Executed on a larger scale as building components, the principle of transformation meant that walls themselves could be rendered unnecessary. Individual room components could be rearranged as desired and their functions redefined. Examples include the Maison de Verre by Pierre Chareau and Haus Schroeder by Gerrit Rietveld, which were designed as oversized items of furniture. While working with Richard Neutra in Berlin, Erich Mendelsohn created an apartment whose central component could be rotated, similar to a stage. This can be positioned to create various room combinations, reducing the floor area that has to be devoted to access.

In the 1960s, groups such as Archigram and Haus-Rucker-Co moved from simple mechanical systems that had been in use for centuries to computer-controlled processes; the results of their efforts were more of a glimpse of future developments than representative of the state of the art, however. Their relatively theoretical projects assumed the development of new materials and focused on such things as the use of surfaces as information media and extreme variations of space, from the body-sized shell to larger spaces for social activities. Even so, folding has remained the key mechanism for versatile objects right to the present day. A good compendium of the mechanical principles of mobility has already been provided in the book "Collapsibles" by Per Mollerup. The folding mechanism controls the adaptation, allowing the object to be made larger or smaller. The sequence of use and non-use or changed use is usually expressed through an adaptation of the size. The closed, passive state represents a reduction in

16

17

18

volume, making it possible to save space or to transport the object. If the object is active, it is opened and expands into the room.[9]

The hinge serves primarily as a sturdy connection. Depending on the material and utilisation, however, the mechanism can change. Textiles make use of folding or folds for transformation. Scissor arms are familiar from everyday items such as awnings and disappearing stairs. Telescopic arms are utilised in the lifting apparatuses of lifts and working platforms. Fan-shaped structures are vulnerable to technical problems and are seldom used – they can most often be found on objects or pieces of furniture. Inflatable pneumatic systems play a special role, as they can facilitate the elastic expansion of rooms or the creation of temporary urban structures. They offer the best possibilities for creating versatile spaces in contemporary architecture (fig. 24). While an expansion of space is what first comes to mind, pneumatic structures can also be used to create interactive floors and walls. On the occasion of the "Wie wohnen – heute?" exhibition marking the 75th anniversary of the Weissenhofgalerie in Stuttgart, Kalhöfer-Korschildgen took Mies van der Rohe's vision of the wall, which permitted a fluid conception of space and entirely new ground plans, and updated it using the technologies and materials available today. In conjunction with mobile objects, pneumatically controlled walls mean that almost any ground plan can be realised. While the technical infrastructures are housed in the hard wall shells, extendable pneumatic walls can function as information media and be used as furniture (fig. 21).

Soft tech instead of high tech

The acceptance of interactive mobile architecture increases if the transformability is comprehensible and different functions or possibilities are easily recognisable. As technology is required for transformation processes to take place, its role always has to be considered: is an automatic high-tech solution to be used or is a soft-tech tool preferable with which the user starts and controls the process?[10]

Simple solutions are to be preferred to complicated ones as they are easier to plan, execute, manufacture, operate and service. Soft-tech solutions are also less expensive and more attractive for the user. It is frequently the users themselves who insist on understandable mechanical components, not only because of the rapid and uncomplicated operation but also for their solidity. Service life and durability are the main criteria. In most cases operation is therefore manual, even if a servo control could be used (fig. 22). A project can be more easily accepted if the user is involved in the transformation process. By taking part in the operation, by triggering and controlling the technology involved the user has an emotional attachment that personalises the project.

The use of established technology is also to be preferred. Dedicated technical solutions are often complicated to plan and prone to failure in operation. Standard technical components from other disciplines can often be incorporated in a new design situation.

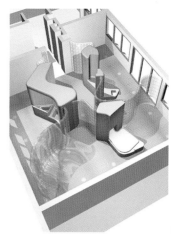

21

22

16, 17 Bed/Sitting Rooms for an Artist in Residence, Mattress Factory Art
        Museum, Pittsburgh 1988; Allan Wexler
18 Tramway in Porto with foldable backrest
21 Mies_Update, Weissenhofgalerie exhibition, Stuttgart, 2002,
        Kalhöfer-Korschildgen
22 Sliding "Fahrt ins Grüne" (see fig. 3)

Thus in "Zimmer mit Aussicht", a conventional free-standing sliding door is used for the vertical side movement. It rotated 90 degree for fitting and can be operated easily with a pulley and counterweight (see p. 136ff.).

In the Bonn pavilion "Raum auf Zeit – Zeit im Raum" for the Montag Foundation the inside-outside link is created by reversing the principle used for opening and closing a garage door (see p. 118ff.). Instead of opening inwards, the garage door opens outwards. Everyday components are misappropriated in this way for new situations, deliberately disconcerting the user. This avoids established actions and utilisation rituals. By mixing rational and irrational moments the application is given an additional tension and ludic element. This is completely in line with a society that needs consumption not only to satisfy its needs but also for emotionality.

Options, decisions and control

The self-evident use of mobile architecture calls for a conception of what the result might look like. Spatial transformations are not always immediately evident. It is important for users to be able to imagine the different statuses. They must be offered a holistic image, much like a Cubist painting. Only if the different alternatives are comprehended can the actor make use of the various options available. Elegance in use is ultimately a question of simple decisions and the ability to control them. It is certainly not a question of the quantity, where the user is offered many apparent alternatives that are ultimately devoid of meaning.[11]

As mobile architecture changes, the process and associated questions are of decisive importance. When should the change take place and how long should it last? The time factor also plays an important role in the acceptance of mobility.

Transformable objects must be capable of rapid and simple movement. The time taken for a function to be set up is decisive. The time at which the object is used is also of relevance. The aim is to improvise with architecture and to offer alternatives for the user. These alternatives need to be clearly structured so as to reduce the number of options available and support the user. Changes should not be haphazard or continuous in the manner of our neurotic fast-paced society. The options and transformability of a design can be structured clearly and sensibly by means of a defined rhythm – seasons (as in the case of "Fahrt ins Grüne", fig. 3), changes in temperature, day-night alternance or medium-term cycles for changes in location, atmosphere or function. Rhythm is also a familiar space-time concept for the user. Because the transformation intervals remain comprehensible, rhythm offers a feeling of continuity even while the change is taking place. In a sense it may be described as a restructuring of time in a deconstructed space. The cycle provides a scale on which the user can recognise order and free flow.[12]

Most of the works of George Bernard Shaw were written in a small and modern garden house designed by the writer himself. The wood-boarded house is mounted above and below on steel pillars and can be rotated by hand. In this way the 6 m² room, writing desk and bookshelf can follow the sun. This is something that the user can understand immediately. Time and motion are interrelated and their speed and duration predefined (fig. 23).

23

References:
1 Lerup, Lars: Das Unfertige bauen. Architektur und menschliches
   Handeln. Braunschweig 1986, p. 139
2 Guiheux, Alain: Architecture Action – Une Architecture Post-Théorique.
   Paris 2002, p. 10
3 Kruse, Lenelis; Graumann, Carl-Friedrich; Lantermann, Ernst-Dieter:
   Ökologische Psychologie. Weinheim 1996, p. 127 and 223
4 Schiller, Friedrich: Der epische Hexameter. In: Musen-Almanach für das
   Jahr 1797. Tübingen 1796, p. 67
5 Giedion, Sigfried: Mechanization Takes Command. 1948, p. 306
6 Ibid., p. 316
7 Ibid., p. 316 and 324
8 Ibid., p. 361 and 364
9 Mollerup, Per: Collapsibles. Munich 2001
10 Gili Galfetti, Gustau; Piloto, Pisos: Model Apartments. Barcelona 1997,
   p. 12
11 ebd. [3], p. 112
11 Geißler, Karlheinz A.: Die Orientierung am Rhythmus. In: Zeit, Zeit-
   verständnis in Wissenschaft und Lebenswelt. Bern 1997

Further reading:
Bellanger, François: Habitat(s): Questions et hypothèses sur l´évolution de
   l´habitat. La Tour d'Aigues 2000
Cook, Peter: Archigram, Basel 1991
Dell, Christopher: Prinzip Improvisation. Cologne 2002
Edition Nautilus: Der Beginn einer Epoche. Texte der Situationisten.
   Hamburg 1995
Gideon, Sigfried: Raum, Zeit, Architektur. Zurich / Munich 1998
Gleich, Michael: Mobilität. Hamburg 1998
Harloff, Hans Joachim: Zur Grundlegung der Wohnpsychologie, Report
   Psychologie 5,1989

23 Writing shed of the writer George Bernard Shaw, Ayot St Lawrence,
    1902
24 "Küchenmonument" (Kitchen Monument), with The Art for Places project,
    South Sefton, Liverpool, 2008; raumlaborberlin

24

Big and small – the convergence of architecture and design

Oliver Herwig

Waste, or rather the appeal to collect waste, shines gold. Since 1996 gold-painted prefabricated concrete units have been standing on the outskirts of Landshut with italic lettering, as if Hild und K Architekten had wanted to pay homage to Robert Venturi and the old casinos in Las Vegas (fig. 2). A wall for recycling containers runs between two new transformer stations and bus stops. The Munich architects took Landshut's motto "Year of Gold" literally to give a touch of class to the banal recycling depot. Seldom has enjoyment of small things been presented so ironically and with such a wink. The wall became an appeal to discover the waste depot as a place of added value. An almost Nietzschean revaluation and a successful marketing idea at the same time.

In Japan, Germany and the United Kingdom, many designers are showing an interest in small structures that otherwise disappear in the mass of commonplace mass-produced and cheap goods, seemingly in protest against the seriousness of big business. Microarchitecture is perhaps the last area of experimentation of the modernists, who are generally more focused on large, lofty and long-lasting items. In 1994 Oswald Mathias Ungers described the essence of architecture in numbers, size and proportions: "The ideal structure, the perfect form is the focus of interest."[1] Ungers ends his essay "Mass, Zahl, Proportion" with a quote by Wittgenstein that illustrates much of the thinking of the modernists, namely that architecture is coercive and ennobles and cannot therefore exist where there is nothing to ennoble.[2] Microarchitecture attempts bravely to prove the opposite. Nobility and banality appear both to be progressing in step. In 1964 Susan Sontag published her famous "Notes on Camp", creating the basis for a systematic discussion of kitsch as the ambivalent driving force behind our mass culture. A decade later Venturi, Scott Brown and Izenour came out with "Learning from Las Vegas", an anthropological and architectural investigation of the heart of banality and commercialism, which shows that buildings function with great vitality beyond the sphere of planning and controlled aesthetics, if only as cheap accommodation, rainproof shelters with applied symbols.[3]

Mass society and its symbols are apparently a source of constant irritation and misunderstanding. The prevailing opinion even today is that architecture is the real thing and that design is just fashion, packaging and application. On one side are the architectural theorists focusing on structures and problem solutions, durable or even eternal answers. On the other side are packaging artists, designers and stylists who are more interested in the wrapping than the content.

The intensity of the process and the time taken cannot serve as criteria for distinguishing architecture and design. It is more the contrast between one-off and mass-produced items that have set the two disciplines apart since the Industrial Revolution. In 1910, fifty million of Thonet's chair no. 14 had been manufactured. For all its lack of comfort, it had become a modernist symbol for a chair, combining the functional logic of preformatted square timber and mechanical assembly. Chair no. 14 was mass produced between 1859 and 1930 in a practically unchanged form. No building or architectural design can make a claim of that sort.
Until recently industrial manufacture was the typical feature of design, and architecture was characterised by a mixture of craftsmanship and industrial building technology. Computers have changed the rules of the game, however, and the distinctions between disciplines have become blurred as a result. Digital design, rapid prototyping and computer-controlled manufacture are undermining the traditional distinction between one-off and serial production. In contrast to what Adolf Loos claimed, one-off items can be created with the same effort as mass-produced ones. Has design suddenly become a question of scale?

Our world is dominated less by megalomaniac buildings than by intelligent interventions, anonymous kiosks, ticket machines, bus stops, toilets, advertising pillars, snack bars and tourist information counters. Microarchitecture in the form

2

of mobile and autonomous structures slot into the infrastructure like mobile phones in the telecommunications network: invisible, unremarkable and yet highly efficient. They use it and give it meaning. Although part of the hardware they give an insight into the software needed to animate complex structures like a city. Microarchitecture and mobile buildings demonstrate the flowing transition between architecture and design – objects filling space or using it.

The entire building world on the table

Where does design end and where does architecture begin? Alessi is not the kind of company to provide incisive answers to this question. Since 1979 the Italians have preferred to commission post-modern heroes to create their Tea & Coffee Piazza collection: Michael Graves, Hans Hollein, Charles Jencks, Richard Meier, Alessandro Mendini, Paolo Portoghesi, Aldo Rossi, Stanley Tigerman, Oscar Tusquets, Robert Venturi and Kazumasa Yamashita designed the silver tea and coffee services with milk jugs, sugar bowl and tray in limited ninety-nine piece series. The project was masterminded by Alessandro Mendini, who sought to make a fundamental statement.

Mendini was not interested in household items alone: he wanted a portable architecture manifesto that creates images rather than ideology. To do this he attempted to re-emotionalise buildings and squares that in his view had been reduced for decades to pure functionality. Miniaturisation and domestic microarchitecture provided the manufacturer Alessi, who was emerging as a manufacture of post-modernist rhetorical figures, with the ideal vehicle. The Tea & Coffee Towers col-

lection curated by him illustrates the problem of using product design as a laboratory for architectural ideas and concepts. It represents a generation of architects[4] that was visibly less constrained by contrasts like theory and practice, large and small, illusion and reality (figs. 3, 4). Their collectors' items show how many architects have managed to blend architecture and design. It is difficult to decide whether Ben van Berkel's Tea & Coffee Towers, computer-generated free forms for the dining table, are not in fact a form of mini-architecture. The design method determines the product. CAD programs for free-form surfaces were used in the various projects by UNStudio, particularly in the much acclaimed Mercedes Benz Museum, which Hanno Rauterberg in DIE ZEIT described as a symbol of digital modernism.[5] Are art museums and coffee pots spiritually related? In spite of the shared basis, architects and designers use very different CAD programs to generate objects. Yet digital modernism has opened up a new vista, distinguishing not between one-off and serial production but only between good and bad design.

The furniture designed by Zaha Hadid also clearly owes a lot to computers. Both the name and the form are geomorphological. The "Glacier" and "Moraine" sofas for Sawaya & Moroni, for example, three-dimensional vector graphs or designer art for the home, resemble collisions, designed accidents in the living room. Hadid's large-scale programmatic dissolution of form and function has no convincing small-scale counterpart, nor does it represent the reinvention of living in the digital era. UNStudio's Circle modular sofa landscape by Ben van Berkel, a flexible seating group made up of six elements that can be reformed into new concave and convex forms, is much more pragmatic (figs. 5, 6).

Long live levity

In the late twentieth century, the Italian author Italo Calvino formulated six demands for the future: lightness, quickness, exactitude, visibility, multiplicity and constancy. The much quoted Six Memos for the Next Millennium[6] is much more than a literary inventory. Calvino provided a blueprint for our lives that was quickly reflected in theoretical design ideas. He demanded a "lightness of reflection"[7] and a "weightless seriousness",[8] even before terms like sustainability dominated discussion.

Lightness is precisely what Richard Horden aims for as he turns his back on the massive constructions of the past and looks to flexible forms that do not impose themselves on anyone, least of all the natural environment. "Touch the earth lightly" is the motto of Horden, who will be head of the Department of Building Theory at the Technical University of Munich until 2010. "In future," he prophesied, "we will have to learn to manufacture with considerably less effort."[9] How flexibly and at the same time sturdily can we build? And how much material is required by a meteorological station, a boathouse or a workshop? Not much, to go by the prototypes. The projects developed by Horden with his students are more like yachts about to drop anchor, or bold combinations of tent and surfboard.

Cliffhanger is the name of a platform made of plastic and metal. Like a swallow's nest on a cliff face looking down on Lake Garda, it is used by yachtsmen and climbers as a place

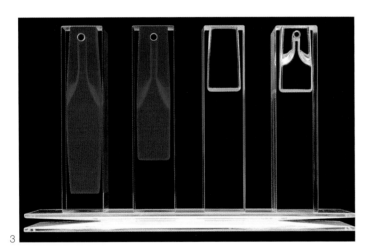

3

4

to rest, sunbathe and observe. For those who have had enough of spartan minimalist constructions, the Sky Motel might provide a better alternative. In the simulation, the aerodynamic aluminium snake is suspended directly underneath the Brenner motorway. At a height of over 70 m, it offers a breathtaking view of the Alps while the heavy goods vehicles above it labour their way over the pass. "It is always possible to use less material," says Horden. How often had he asked would-be architects: "How heavy is it?" in order to obtain a more elegant revised version.

The O_2 Village in the heart of the student village of Freimann shows how architecture of this sort can look in practice. The student housing authority commissioned a miniature estate consisting initially of seven housing cubes. The 6.50 m² micro compact home by Horden, Cherry, Lee Architects of London and Haack + Höpfner Architekten of Munich has flexible and retractable furniture that permits the inside to be transformed in moments. The mobile housing model offers a low-cost alternative for students in a city with little affordable housing.

Lightness resounds in the building world as a subversive appeal to use resources more intelligently. Ephemeral architecture created as it is needed and disappearing again like fair booths or tent cities could solve one of the central modernist dictums: less is more. Or, as Calvino put it: "We approach the new millennium riding on our tub without the hope of finding more than we bring ourselves, for example through lightness." [10]

What minimum? Microarchitecture for living

Shigeru Ban, who lives in Japan, where micro-structures occupying every niche are typical of the huge cities there, is known worldwide as the designer of the Japanese pavilion at Expo 2000 in Hannover. Together with Frei Otto he created an arching mesh of cardboard tubes up to 40 m long and 12 cm thick. They are slotted together and tied with polyester tapes. The roof is formed by a specially impregnated fabric of textile and paper. The building was a spectacular success, overshadowing the fact that the architect had already designed refugee housing on the same principle for the UN High Commissioner for Refugees in Rwanda (fig. 8). He tested fifty prototypes, all made of cardboard tubes that had to be resistant in particular to termites. Ban devised a construction made of prefabricated plastic connectors with canvas stretched over them to protect from wind and weather. He had already used a similar system in 1994 after the devastating earthquake in Kobe, creating emergency accommodation out of old beer crates filled with sand and vertical cardboard tubes, materials that were easy to dispose of and which cost barely 2,000 euros per unit.
Necessity – and by extension war – is the mother of invention. The Eureka RDS (Rapid Deployable System) military tent by Johnson Outdoors, which he claims is the fastest tent to erect in the world, is something of a design wonder (fig. 9). It is 10 m in length and can be erected by four or five people

1 Iris Dome, Hannover, Expo 2000; Hoberman Associates
2 Recycling depot, Landshut, 1996; Hild und K Architekten
3 Tea & Coffee Towers, 2000; Wiel Arets for Alessi
4 Tea & Coffee Towers, 2003; UNStudio for Alessi
5, 6 Four-piece Circle seating group, 2005; UNStudio for Walter Knoll
7 MYchair, 2008; UNStudio for Walter Knoll

5

6

7

8

in just fourteen minutes. This is possible thanks to a folding aluminium frame weighing just 315 kg developed by Chuck Hoberman. It joins scissor systems to three-dimensional support structures. This was also the basis for the kinetic toys that can be pushed, pulled and rotated to form three-dimensional objects.

There are few signs of this minimalist approach in central Europe. Building is a serious business, a question of norms and regulations, distances and established standards. It is thus hardly surprising that microarchitecture has reached a level of perfection here that goes far beyond the pragmatic or necessary.

When the Munich concept artist Stefan Eberstadt presented his Rucksack House in 2004, an amoeba-like two-ton cubic structure that docked onto an existing building and co opted its infrastructure, it attracted considerable interest (fig. 10). Even the tabloids jumped on to this exotic construction without realising its subversiveness. In principle Eberstadt had carried over the principles of his art – black holes and white surfaces – to the third dimension and created an art cube suspended high over the street looking more like perforated metal than a floating room. The Rucksack House was perceived variously as a work of art, habitable sculpture or the answer to the urban demand for change and trans-formation. It took almost five hours to dock it onto a pre-pared building front. A vehicle-mounted crane lifted up the box, a tubular steel cage with plywood and birch panels, where it was attached to prebored holes in the facade. That would not have been sufficient to hold it in place and two steel cables lashed the windowed parasite home to the building. Fortunately, the windows on the floor are made of 2.5 cm anti-crash acrylic glass. The unusual concept was shown at the Architecture Biennale in Venice as part of the Convertible City theme of the German pavilion in 2006 (see p. 133ff.).

Small is fashionable: Bibi and Eik Kammerl, Katrin Alden-hoven and Jörg Pottrick from Planungsbüro Kammerl und Kollegen, formerly Exilhäuser, have been able to fill files just with newspaper clippings about their "Zusatzraum" (Additional Space). The cube made of acrylic glass, an alu-minium frame and plywood, is designed as an extension for living rooms or studies and can be used as a workshop or summer house, for example. There was even a report about it in SPIEGEL SPEZIAL in an article about summer houses.[11] The publicity was to no avail: a favourable press appears to be insufficient. Enquiries were not followed up because it was impossible to find a manufacturer willing to mass-produce the object. In between architecture and design there appears to be an area that tends arbitrarily to shift one way or the other. Neither materials nor size offer an absolute framework but are merely points of reference for categorisation. Context and utility alone decide what will be perceived. In this regard, "Zusatzraum" may be seen as a designer summer house or microarchitecture, depending on the perspective.

Size does not provide an indication of content. Su-Si is 12.63 × 4.33 m in size and weighs twelve tons. Its use is unspecified and it can function as a workshop, office, exhibition pavilion or second home. Johannes and Oskar Leo

9

Kaufmann, who designed the wooden container, named the design after the first owners, Susanne and Siegfried, who wanted to live extravagantly in their own home, but did not even own a piece of land, which the architects also arranged for them.

Su-Si consists of a 43 m² room divided into three zones. The bedroom and bathroom are on the outside and the living room is in between. The advantages of this practical minimalist design can be found in the finishing, with spruce on the outside and silver fir on the inside. The interior furnishing can be chosen and provided by the customer. The only constraint on size is the vehicle transporting it. And because it was designed for transportation in one piece, the structure also needed additional reinforcement.

If Su-Si is a luxury trailer combining American pioneer spirit with European standards and sophistication, Cocobello opens up an entirely new category of mobility (figs. 11, 12). The steel house on wheels by Munich architect Peter Haimerl gave the same performance every day at the entrance to the Satellite exhibition at the Architecture Biennale in Rotterdam 2003. Cocobello consists of three nested components that can be extended horizontally and vertically. Thanks to its integrated lifting mechanism it can be loaded and unloaded without additional lifting tackle. The closed container can thus be transformed in an hour into a 42 m² unit. It is a form of mobile architecture that slots into the urban network, creates space of its own and also suggests other uses; a nomadic structure that borrows from vehicle and aircraft engineering and design. Its round corners and wide panoramic windows make it look more like an elaborate mobile home than a piece of mobile architecture.

Mobile homes are in any case a logical consequence of mobile architecture, as campers turn motorways into moving cities and Americans extend the principle of "my home is my castle" to every mobile foundation. Perhaps this is a result of the history of American settlers, with their endless wagon trains, or perhaps of the fact that today's enterprising pensioners are no longer content to be shunted off into old people's homes. They prefer to take their mobile homes and head for California or Texas where they can enjoy life in the company of like-minded fellow travellers. Mobile homes are a culture of their own, from the VW Bully with tent roof to transportable homes that can be shored up and secured with bricks. The idea of "here today gone tomorrow" is a romantic and pragmatic extension of nomad culture that exchanges the standardised suburban existence for a taste of freedom. The mobility of housing also encourages a willingness to accept a more flexible definition of architecture. In many places today there are pavilions and mobile structures that are erected for a period of time and then disappear again, temporary buildings with a built-in shelf life and illusions of nomadic and lightweight existence.

10

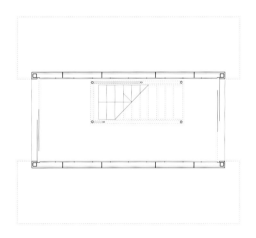
11

12

8 Shelters after the earthquake in Rwanda, 1998; Shigeru Ban Architects
9 Erection of Eureka RDS (Rapid Deployable System) tent, 2006; Chuck Hoberman for Johnson Outdoors Eureka Brand
10 Assembly and attachment of Rucksack House during an installation for plan05 in Cologne, 2005; Stefan Eberstadt
11, 12 Cocobello mobile workshop, Munich, 2001; Peter Haimerl

13

Infrastructure: architecture or works of art

The borders between architecture, art and design are shifting. In the best teahouse tradition, the annual show of pavilions at the Serpentine Gallery does not only show the latest architectural designs but also describes the aesthetic parameters of good taste. The experiments often have just one thing in common: they are not permanent, and this freedom gives the temporary pavilions a transparency in art and design that is otherwise difficult to find.

When the sociologist Lucius Burckhardt noted heretically in 1981 that design was invisible, he caused an uproar in the established world of design. The former lecturer at the College of Design in Ulm was attacking the heart of the system. He did not want to content himself with criticising the cosmos of well or badly designed objects, a world divided into things, but drew attention to the underlying structures. Instead of restricting himself to the design of a vehicle, for example, he targeted the phenomenon of mobility. Burckhardt believed that objects acquired their inherent structure through interactions in the design process.[12] Designers could be tempted to reveal the invisible aspects of a supply infrastructure when they build transformer stations, petrol stations, kiosks and pavilions, but in doing so they enter into conflict with industrial designers, who are devoted to the design of everyday objects.

Die-cast architecture, outsized design components that can be entered or lived in, are features of the Serpentine Gallery pavilion in London by Rem Koolhaas in 2006. His airy structure had a helium balloon for a roof, floating above the 5 m ground floor with its polycarbonate walls. The flexible interior altered with the weather. When the weather was cold and windy, the balloon collapsed and insulated the ground floor even further. The wall and balloon roof also served as a projection surface for light installations and films. The Dutch architect designed a mobile advertising column, an information balloon, which lived up to the standard not only of its predecessors but also of the pavilion by Olafur Eliasson and Kjetil Thorsen, who the following year constructed an illusory space made of steel and dark stained plywood whose dimensions were hidden from the viewer. Temporary, experimental and anything but solid, many of these pavilions stimulated the senses. And they are not alone: crossing boundaries is a feature of all of the individual disciplines.

Are these striking objects pumped-up design components, overblown works of art or simply compact buildings? Thomas Heatherwick links architecture, design and visual art to form a new whole. He sees himself as a three-dimensional designer. He is interested in how to create a better and stimulating environment for people. He demonstrated this with his spectacular series of wood and aluminium summer houses or "sitooteries" (from the Scottish "sit oot", i.e. to sit in the open air). "Sitoterie II" at Barnards Farm in Essex looks like an extraterrestrial artefact: 5,000 hollow spikes filled with orange acrylic glass serve as "windows" for the 2.40 × 2.40 m cube and also lift it off the ground (fig. 14). The light collected in the centre makes the work glow.

Heatherwick, who studied product design at the Royal College of Art in London, recently demonstrated his practical sense when the Kensington and Chelsea borough council in

14

London asked him to design new newspaper kiosks that would resist graffiti. The architects-artists-designers at Heatherwick Studio took the task very seriously and designed a functional kiosk: presented in 2009, it look like an oversized knight's helmet. The oval kiosks were transported in one piece to the site where they were to be set up. They are made of columns of flat-rolled steel with 2 mm steel sheets welded between them, panelled inside with plywood and outside with brass. In the morning the gleaming shell is slid to the side to open up the kiosk and in the evening it is closed like a visor, much to the displeasure of the graffiti scene (see p. 94ff.).

In twentieth century design theory, the question of content and form, technology and shell has frequently proved problematic. In his book Never Leave Well Enough Alone, Raymond Loewy, a gifted stylist who designed the Shell symbol and the Lucky Strike pack, describes his first major commission, to modernise the appearance of a Gestetner copier: "So I decided to limit my efforts to amputation (the four legs) and plastic surgery on the body." Loewy proposed a facelift: "I would simply encase all the gadgety organs of the machine within a neat, well-shaped, and easily removable shell. Then I would redesign the wheel, the crank, and the tray. The whole unit would then be placed over a set of four slender but sturdy legs, painted a pleasant colour, and sent back into the business world."[13] But what if the machinery is so large that its encapsulation produces a work of architecture? Deffner Voitländer Architekten from Dachau used the design of a municipal gas transfer station to carry out an interesting experiment on an encapsulation that both enclosed and revealed (fig. 13). The lemon-coloured shell made of glass fibre reinforced plastic and the waste gas pipes protruding from the roof present technology in a tangible form: pipes, bars, switches and valves adorn the outer shell like a technical drawing. The 'black box', the obscure inner workings of technology, is projected onto the outside. At night the station glows from the inside like an outsized lamp. Is this a disproportionately sized design? Or is it "just" architecture? Either way the shell is vital to a discussion of such borderline distinctions. It is self-reflecting and pragmatic and also inexpensive. Loewy was able to extract a pragmatic lesson from aesthetic decisions and to present a design logic that can even be applied to the gas transfer station: "The shell, concealing all the gadgets which were previously exposed, had other advantages. Being visible, they had to be finished carefully, nickel-plated and polished by hand. A very costly process."[14]

Was Loewy the master of redesign; the ingenious reworking of existing designs in order to improve them and to make them more striking and successful? Is the quoting of icons and predecessors now an accepted practice in the world of design? Designers rarely venture into the world of architecture, and even then only with the aid of architects. Frankfurt designer Bernd Hilpert from unit-design smiles as he considers the claim to universality of architects, who regard themselves as total artists, towering over everything. Together with

15

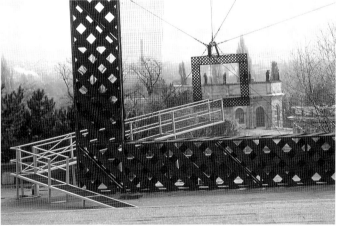

16

13 Gas transfer station, Dachau, 2004; Deffner Voitländer Architekten
14 Sitooterie II, Barnards Farm, Essex (UK), 2003; Heatherwick Studio
15 Viewing tower at Wetterpark Offenbach, 2006; bb22 architekten und stadtplaner together with unit-design
16 Frame Building at documenta 6 in Kassel, 1977; Haus-Rucker-Co

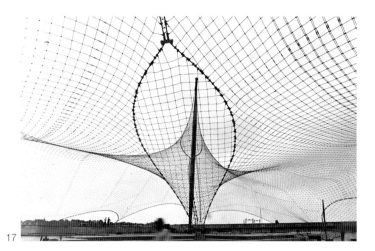

17

18

Jan Schulz from bb22 architekten und stadtplaner, unit-design drafted Wetterpark Offenbach in 2005 and 2006, a large landscaped park at the headquarters of the German Meteorological Service full of objects and crowned by a 10 m tower, whose panoramic frame quotes the Landschaft im Dia installation by Haus-Rucker-Co at documenta 6 in Kassel in 1977 (fig. 16). The designers were interested less in building than in structured communication. The tower is a visible object, a collaboration between designers and architects (fig. 15).

Large utopias with little material

At the former Stuttgart Institute for Lightweight Structures, the architect became a scientist as he investigated the surface tension of soapsuds. The modern architect, he demanded, must take the best and most suitable, regardless of where it comes from. He must invent, experiment, develop and investigate.[15] The search for minimalist architecture, be it mechanically pre-stressed membranes, octopus-like roofs at open-air events, cable net constructions that cover large surfaces with minimal effort, or pneumatic structures, is Frei Otto's vocation. He was responsible not only for large projects like the City in the Arctic project study in 1971 or the roof of the Olympic Stadium in Munich in 1972 but also for elegant miniature architectural projects like the ten umbrellas for the Pink Floyd concert tour in 1976, which are among the most subtle architectural designs of the 1970s: umbrellas like mushrooms growing upward on long stems and gradually unfurling.

"Don't fight forces, use them", was one of the basic principles of Frei Otto's American counterpart, the inventor and all-round scholar Richard Buckminster Fuller. Whether inventing the term "Spaceship Earth" or marketing the Dymaxion principle,[16] Buckminster Fuller included branding and marketing in his comprehensive design philosophy. "To do more with less"[17] became a catchphrase. Moreover, Buckminster Fuller put it into practice with the Dymaxion House, which was suspended like a sailing boat from a central mast.
"Mr. Fuller, fortunately, is not an architect," said Harvey W. Corbett, chairman of the Architectural League, introducing a discussion on the Dymaxion House on 9 July 1929. "Still more unfortunately, he is not an engineer. He isn't any of those objectionable things that we all know about."[18] Corbett was enthusiastic about Buckminster Fuller's approach.
"There is no reason, as I see it, why houses shouldn't be manufactured in mass production on just as large a scale as other commodities are made and used in that way," he continued.[19] Nothing came of it, but Buckminster Fuller continued to exert an influence – as a teacher.
He erected structures made of aluminium, wood, cardboard, paper or bamboo, Plexiglas panes made domes into lightweight light installations. At the 1967 Montreal Expo his geodesic domes and Frei Otto's membrane roofs showed how small the world had become (figs. 17, 18) as the Old and the New World competed for design supremacy. On the one side there was the massive geodesic dome by the Americans made of short rods connected at their intersections and growing into polyhedrons and covered by a plastic skin. On

19

17 German pavilion at Montreal Expo, 1967; Rolf Gutbrod, Frei Otto and
   Fritz Leonhardt
18 US pavilion at Montreal Expo, 1967; Richard Buckminster Fuller
19 Airquarium; Axel Thallemer

the other side there was an artificial landscape, a floating tent roof made of steel cables and translucent polycarbonate. Technology, architecture and engineering art came together to form fascinating new lightweight structures.

What has become of the blubbering utopias of the 1960s, like the 120 tons of water bubbling at the foot of Festo's Airquarium hall (fig. 19). The ring is filled to bursting to stabilise the dome. Its plastic fabric shimmers sky blue. No support, nothing but air keeps the 8 m hemisphere up. Visitors enter through an airlock. The membrane arches upwards so elegantly that it is difficult not to be fascinated by the elegant arch. Airquarium introduces water and air quite naturally into the building material canon alongside wood or stone. Even more, they become catalysts of pure form, in which structure and shell – the skin and bones of a building – come together. The inspiration for the pneumatic hall came from bubbles, which spread their load evenly over their entire surface. All that was needed was to fill it up and install the building engineering to make it into a mobile event and exhibition space: two steps that are more appropriate to the filling of a soda-making machine than a work of architecture. And that was the attraction of it.

Big and small

Size loses itself when miniaturised. As all-in-one designers, architects prefer comprehensible seemingly banal tasks. There are pragmatic reasons for the blurring of the borders between building and industrial design: both professions work with the same tools, CAD programs and CNC and rapid-prototyping production. The chasm between one-offs and mass production is disappearing, to be replaced by a race for ideas, regardless of where they come from. They come together in works like Design-Lexikon Deutschland: Peter Behrens and Dieter Rams, Walter Gropius and Luigi Colani, trained designers, artists and aerodynamic engineers, characterised by additional titles such as "architect and product designer" or "architect, furniture and product designer".

If microarchitecture is in fact located somewhere at the interface of design, art and building, where distinctions become a matter of opinion, another perspective presents itself to help distinguish between exhibition items, housing parasites and housing containers; namely their social relevance. Microarchitecture in central Europe offers temporary high-tech solutions to specific demands, but in less developed countries they become vital necessities, skilfully improvised solutions for all those who cannot afford a real house themselves. Where does architecture begin? This question is commonly applied to primitive huts but could well be asked of all minimalist housing structures. The minimalism that is praised as an aesthetic principle in affluent societies becomes a matter of survival in others. Between the extremes of high-priced minimalism and pure need some remarkable solutions have emerged, sophisticated microarchitecture for all contexts, regardless of the resources behind their development.

References:
1 Ungers, Oswald Mathias: Mass. Zahl. Proportion. In: O. M. Ungers – Architekt. Stuttgart 1994, p. 10
2 Ibid., p. 11
3 Venturi, Robert; Scott Brown, Denise; Izenour, Steven: Learning from Las Vegas. Boston 1972
4 Will Alsop, Wiel Arets, Gary Chang, David Chipperfield, Denton Corker Marshall, Dezsö Ekler, Massimilliano Fuksas, Future Systems, Zaha Hadid, Toyo Ito, Tom Kovac, Greg Lynn FORM, Alessandro Mendini, Morphosis, MVRDV, Juan Navarro Baldeweg, Jean Nouvel, Dominique Perrault, SANAA and UNStudio.
5 Rauterberg, Hanno: Barock aus dem Rechner. In: DIE ZEIT Nr. 45/2005
6 Calvino, Italo: Six Memos for the Next Millennium. Cambridge 1988
7 Ibid., p. 25
8 Ibid., p. 37
9 Herwig, Oliver: Muskelbepackte Luftnummern. Leichtbaukonzepte gewinnen in der Architektur immer mehr an Bedeutung. In: Frankfurter Rundschau 27 September 2003
10 ebd. [6], p. 48
11 Beyer, Susanne: Laube, Liebe, Hoffnung. In: SPIEGEL SPEZIAL Nr.4/2008
12 Burckhardt, Lucius: Design ist unsichtbar. In: Design ist unsichtbar. Helmut Gsöllpointer, Angela Hareiter und Laurits Ortner (eds.). Vienna 1981, p. 13–20
13 Loewy, Raymond: Never Leave Well Enough Alone. New York 2002
14 Ibid.
15 Bach, Klaus; Burkhardt, Berthold; Otto, Frei: Seifenblasen. Forming Bubbles (IL 18). Stuttgart 1987, p. 11
16 Neologism created from the words "dynamism" and "maximum"
17 See Joachim Krausse (trans.). Krausse, Joachim: Buckminster Fullers Vorschule der Synergetik. In: Buckminster Fuller, Richard: Bedienungsanleitung für das Raumschiff Erde und andere Schriften. Dresden 1998, p. 213–306
18 Joachim Krausse and Claude Lichtenstein (eds.): Your Private Sky: Richard Buckminster Fuller – Discourse. New York 2001
19 Ibid.

Summary of projects

Page	Project	Usage	Dimensions	Structure
	Urban and scenic spaces			
62	Observation tower on the Mur River terrain: loenhart&mayr architekten und landschaftsarchitekten with osd - office for structural design	Leisure facility	9.10 × 9.10 m	Steel
66	"Top of Tyrol" summit platform LAAC Architeken	Leisure facility	10 × 15 m	Weatherproof steel
69	Temporary bamboo pavilions Markus Heinsdorff	Pavilion	11.35 × 7.60 m (Navette)	Bamboo
74	Transport shelters in Darmstadt netzwerkarchitekten	Infrastructural	7.00 × 3.46 m 7.00 × 5.55 m	Steel
78	Market stalls in Augsburg Tilman Schalk Architekten	Sales	2.84 × 5.50 m (Uhl) 3.92 × 6.72 m (Müller) 3.60 × 6.72 m (Neubert)	Solid wood/steel structure
	Public spaces			
82	Theatre podium in Rotterdam Atelier Kempe Thill architects and planners	Cultural	40 × 5 m	Fair-faced concrete
86	Pavilion at Lake Geneva Bakker & Blanc Architectes	Bistro	2.80 × 10.14 m	Steel
90	Pavilion in Zurich phalt architekten	Workshop, office and storeroom	8 × 7 m (building) 16.00 × 12.50 m (roof)	Steel-skeleton
94	Newspaper kiosks in London Heatherwick Studio	Sales	4.43 × 3.03 m	Steel
97	Kiosk at lake "Staufensee" near Dornbirn Wellmann Ladinger	Sales	3.60 × 7.10 m	Fair-faced concrete
100	Temporary bar in Porto Diogo Aguiar and Teresa Otto	Restaurant	3 × 3 m	Steel frame, timber frame
102	Tree house Restaurant near Auckland Pacific Environments Architects	Restaurant	10 × 8 m	Wood
105	St. Benedikt Chapel in Kolbermoor kunze seeholzer architektur & stadtplanung	Religious building	3.08 × 5.54 m	Fair-faced concrete
	Mobile spaces			
108	Chapel in Lustenau Hugo Dworzak	Religious building	5.00 × 2.50 m	Timber post and beam
110	"Sehstation" in North Rhine-Westphalia Andy Brauneis	Town "look-out"	12.00 × 6.80 m	Timber frame
112	Mobile log house olgga architectes	Accommodation	2.50 × 6.00 m 2.50 × 3.00 m	Wood
114	Transformbox Bernhard Geiger with Armin Kathan	Survival	60 × 50 cm (Rucksackhouse)	Wood
118	Convertible pavilion Kalhöfer-Korschildgen	Pavilion	3.20 × 3.20 m	Steel
122	Tea house in Frankfurt am Main Kengo Kuma & Associates with formTL	Events	9.00 × 4.60 m	Self-supporting pneumatic membrane
126	Aero House Richard Horden, Wieland Schmidt, TU München, Helmut Richter, TU Wien, with students	Accommodation	2.70 × 1.30 m	Carbon fibre-reinforced plastic
130	"Desert Seal" tent Architecture and Vision	Survival, accommodation	2.35 × 1.25 m	Membrane, inflatable A-frame construction
133	Rucksack House Stefan Eberstadt	Accommodation	2.50 × 3.60 m	Steel
	Private spaces			
136	Mobile roof terrace in Cologne Kalhöfer-Korschildgen	Accommodation	4.40 × 3.00 m	Steel, plywood facing with sheet steel lining
139	Bedroom and playroom furniture h2o architectes	Accommodation	2.96 × 1.28 m	Wood
142	Summer houses in Berlin Hütten & Paläste	Leisure facility	5.00 × 3.17 m (MiLa)	Wooden post and beam
145	Beach houses in Domburg WTS Architecten	Accommodation	3.52 × 7.52 m	Steel frame, timber frame
148	Residential building in Tokyo Claus en Kaan Architecten with Souhei Imamura/Atelier IMAMU	Accommodation	11.00 m × 4.50 m	Steel frame
152	Residential building in Munich meck architekten	Accommodation	4.80 × 16.00 m	Reinforced concrete, timber frame
157	Renovation of students' apartments at the Olympic Village, Munich arge werner wirsing bogevischs buero	Accommodation	4.20 × 3.15 m	Precast reinforce concrete
162	Capsule hotel in Kyoto Fumie Shibata, Masaaki Hiromura, Takaaki Nakamura, Sigma Architectural Design	Accommodation	2.15 × 1.07 m (Capsule)	Capsule: glass-fibre-reinforced plastic

Observation tower on the Mur River

Architects: terrain: loenhart&mayr architekten und
landschaftsarchitekten, Munich/Graz
Structural planning: osd - office for structural design,
Frankfurt am Main

**The observation sculpture with its two winding
stairways continuously offers new views to those
making their way up and down its steps.**

The Mur River, which marks the border between Austria and
Slovenia, is located in the "European Green Belt" running
along the former Iron Curtain from the Arctic Ocean to the
Black Sea. The Mur River has been retuned to nature, and
this observation tower makes an architectural statement at
the mouth of the Saßbach, alongside the Mur hiking and
cycling trail running through the woods along the river.

The journey is the architectural reward
On their way to the observation point, the stairway takes visitors along a spiral course until they reach the highest point.
They must climb 168 steps in all to reach a small observation
platform which is 27 m high. From here, a separate stairway
takes them back to the ground, meaning the visitors on the
way to the platform do not encounter those on their way
down. This continuous movement through space is made
easier by a pleasant gradient ratio of 15.20/28.50 cm and the
decision not to incorporate intermediate platforms, as they
would have interrupted the flow of movement. The journey to
the tower's highest point is rewarding in itself, as the continuously changing vantage points reveal the varying ecological
height levels of the riverside forest. The form which the staircase sculpture took was the result of an integrated process
arising from the interplay of form, movement and load-bearing
structure. The architecture, which was designed in analogue
model studies, was developed and scaled up digitally in dialogue with the planning for the load-bearing structure.

Concept behind the load-bearing structure
The hybrid load-bearing structure that was used involves
rigid nodal connections in conjunction with tensioned cables
and compression struts. The primary load-bearing structure
comprised of tubular load-bearing and supporting elements
functions as a spatially coherent bar-type supporting structure, ensuring the tower's stability. While the vertical cables
control the vibration behaviour, the cables winding upwards
horizontally control the top displacement. This intelligent
cabling arrangement means that no additional vibration
damping is required. The double spiral's geometric crossing
points are also the points of intersection of the load-bearing
system. The load-bearing elements taper as they rise, in
keeping with the reduced structural requirements, in order to
reduce the materials needed.

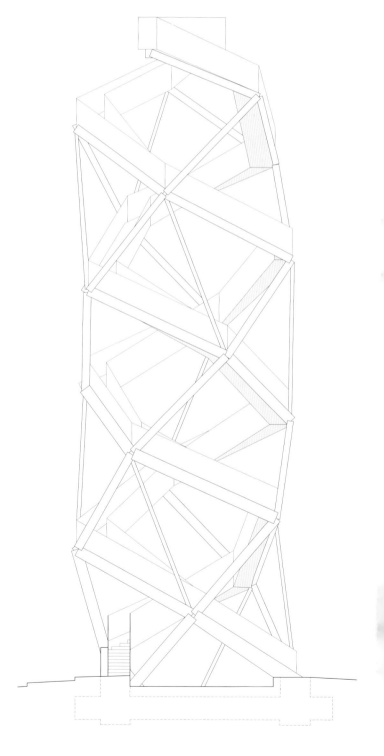

Elevation · Top view
Scale 1:150

Project data:

Usage:	Leisure facility
	Fixed
Structure:	Steel
Dimensions:	9.10 × 9.10 × 26.60 m
Construction costs:	€490,000
Year of construction:	2010
Construction period:	6 months

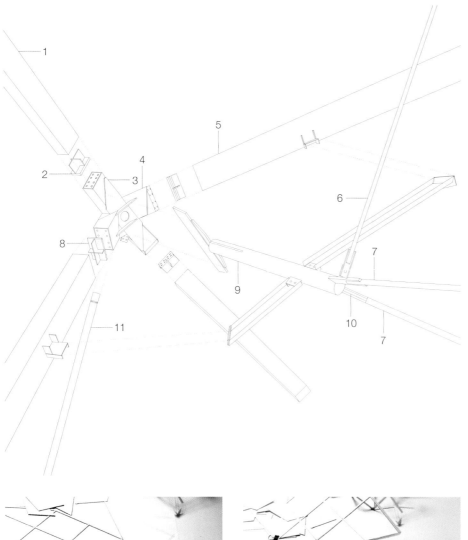

A

The complexity of the nodal connections made it necessary to conduct thorough 3D planning. A modular principle was developed for the primary details that could be transferred to all other nodes. In spite of variations in scale and material strength, this recurring node geometry principle made efficient production and high quality execution of the structure possible.

A Tubular supporting element
B Tubular load-bearing element
C Primary structure
D Secondary structure
E Entire structure

1 Tubular steel, 350/250/12.5 mm
2 Erection joint, tubular load-bearing element with bolt connection inside, high-tension plate 40 mm with 8 high-tension screws, diam. 27 mm
3 Rigid tubular supporting element transition, steel sheet box, 325/275/15 mm
4 Rigid tubular load-bearing element steel plate, 25 mm with steel fins, 20 mm
5 Tubular steel, 450/250/12.5 mm
6 Tensioned cable for longitudinal reinforcement, inside, hardened steel, diam. 24 mm
7 Tensioned cable for lateral reinforcement, hardened steel, diam. 32 mm
8 Erection joint with bolt connection inside, high-tension plate 50 mm with 8 high-tension screws, diam. 33 mm
9 Tubular steel collar, diam. 193.7/17.5 mm with rigid tubular load-bearing element, sheet steel strut, 20 mm
10 Connecting lug structure to the tensioned cable, steel lug, 35 and 47 mm
11 Compression struts for longitudinal reinforcement, outside, tubular steel, diam. 152.5/20 mm

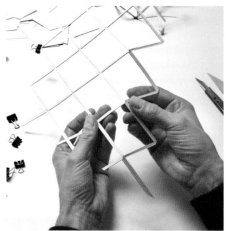

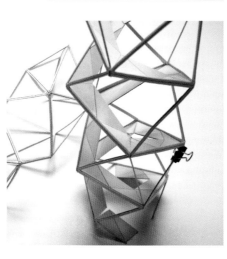

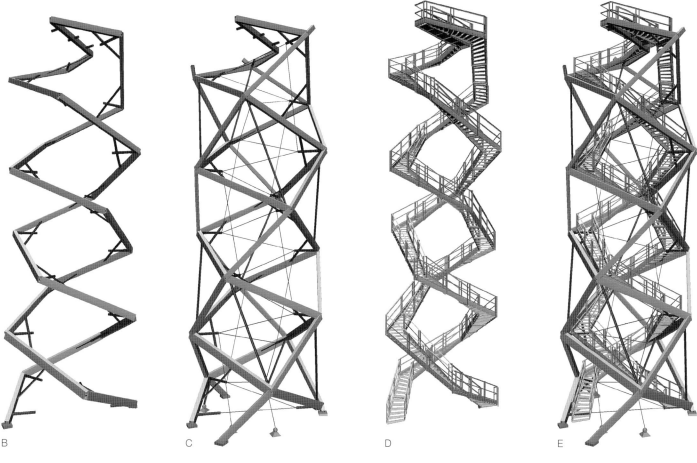

B   C   D   E

"Top of Tyrol" summit platform

Architects: LAAC Architekten, Innsbruck

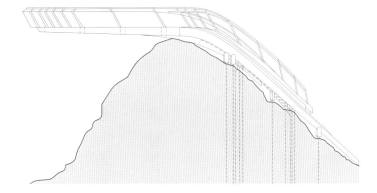

This summit platform on the ridge of the Great Isodor juts out far over the rock face to offer a fascinating panoramic view of the surrounding alpine landscape.

Barely an hour's drive away from Innsbruck, the Stubai glacier offers visitors a broad choice of recreational activities in summer and winter alike. The "Top of Tyrol" summit platform is a further attraction here, affording a fascinating panoramic view over the Tyrolean mountains from an altitude of over 3200 m. From the mountain station of the Schaufeljochbahn cable railway, a number of steps lead up to the ridge of the Great Isodor and on over open terrain to the platform protruding over the edge of a rock face. Sand-blasted steel struts support a grid floor. The flowing contours of the platform hug the rocky ridge and blend into the local topography. A monolithic rail with a larch wood hand bar follows the platforms contours, emphasizing its dynamic lines.

Similarly to the glacier landscape in which it stands, the platform also alters its appearance throughout the seasons. In the summer the weatherproof steel construction blends in with the red colour of the rock landscape which stems from the abundance of ironstone, while in the winter the bars disappear in the snow and only the struts protruding over the north face remain visible.

The planning and production process

The load-bearing structure is designed as a distorted grid construction. The curved plate steel struts protruding 9 m over the precipice take the form of box girders with a triangular cross-section. The upright steel plates which rest against

the mountain are stabilised with buckling-resistant bracing. The grid floor is fitted between the struts measuring around 50 cm in height. The supporting forces are discharged linearly via a foundation and pointwise via the rock anchors on the side of the mountain slope. As the platform is situated in a high alpine location subject to permafrost, the foundations had to be produced with 15 m long rock anchors in the tension zone and a reinforced concrete foundation in the area of the compression zone.

Due to the exposed location, the entire scope of installation work was carried out using a helicopter. A high degree of prefabrication, the simplest possible erection joints and perfect fits were essential for this purpose. A key challenge in optimising the design involved adapting the individual components to the helicopter's load-handling limits. Direct exposure to the local weather conditions required due consideration in planning the entire site facilities, concreting work and installation of all the components. The approx. 80 m² platform was installed within the space of just six weeks.

Project data:

Usage:	Leisure facility
	Fixed
Structure:	Weatherproof steel
Dimensions:	10 × 15 m
Construction costs:	€300,000 (gross)
Year of construction:	2009
Construction period:	3 months
Assembling period:	6 weeks

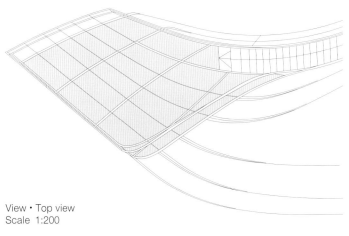

View · Top view
Scale 1:200

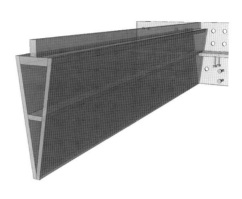

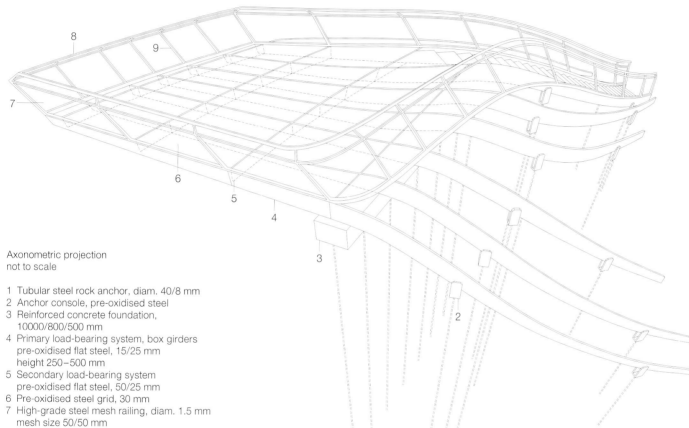

Axonometric projection
not to scale

1 Tubular steel rock anchor, diam. 40/8 mm
2 Anchor console, pre-oxidised steel
3 Reinforced concrete foundation,
  10000/800/500 mm
4 Primary load-bearing system, box girders
  pre-oxidised flat steel, 15/25 mm
  height 250–500 mm
5 Secondary load-bearing system
  pre-oxidised flat steel, 50/25 mm
6 Pre-oxidised steel grid, 30 mm
7 High-grade steel mesh railing, diam. 1.5 mm
  mesh size 50/50 mm
  fitted to 50/25 mm flat steel
8 Larch wood hand bar, 70/25 mm
9 Pre-oxidised steel railing support,
  25/25/80 mm, prefabricated and welded

Temporary bamboo pavilions

Architect: Markus Heinsdorff, Munich

"Navette pavilion" project data:

Usage:	Pavilion
	Temporary
Structure:	Bamboo
Clear room height:	3.60 m
Gross volume:	198 m³
Gross floor area:	55 m²
Dimensions:	11.35 × 7.60 × 4.20 m
Construction costs:	€29,975
Year of construction:	2007–2009
Construction period:	6 months

The traditional, sustainable building material bamboo has been joined with modern translucent mesh to turn the pavilion into a work of art.

Since autumn 2007, these temporary pavilions have been making their way to various Chinese cities as part of the "Germany Esplanade" exhibition, where they serve as municipal installations for a variety of objets d'art. All of the pavilion types have been designed as modern, multifunctional spaces, each of which has its own form and special features. The pavilions range in size from 36 to 142 m², are of modular design and can be connected into groups in various arrangements. The primary building material for the pavilions is bamboo tubes, as well as laminates which the architects developed especially to combine bamboo rods to create boards. As one of the oldest of all building materials, bamboo is gaining in importance on account of its sustainability. At 20 metres a month, it grows faster than any other plant, and its hollow tubes mean that it is not only light and elastic, but also a very

stable and long-lasting building material. The outside walls consist of vertical bamboo tubes and bamboo laminate bars running horizontally around the structure which are connected using brackets; the facade material can vary. Mesh made from metal or cloth is woven through the bars. The spaces this creates in between allow air exchange. An additional membrane is fitted in the interior to protect from rain. It is also possible to create a smooth single-leaf facade using acrylic glass. In both cases, the pavilion is translucent, and the interior light shines out at night. The doors, which are also covered with mesh, can be positioned anywhere within the facade grid.

As a result of the pavilions' round forms, the horizontal bamboo-tube roof girders come together radially. In some of the pavilions they are also placed on top of a central support, while other pavilions do without these supports. The translucent roof membrane is fitted almost like an umbrella, running from the ridge point to the edges, where it is secured to a steel frame running around the structure using cables around a steel railing.

Sections · Ground floor plans
Scale 1:250

A Dome pavilion,
  Gross floor area: 36 m²
B Diamant pavilion
  Gross floor area: 72 m²
C Navette pavilion
  Gross floor area: 55 m²
D Central pavilion
  Gross floor area: 69 m²
E Lotus pavilion
  Gross floor area: 142 m²
F Conference pavilion
  Gross floor area: 121 m²

aa

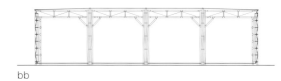
bb

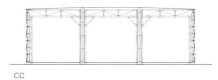
cc

a ──────── a

A

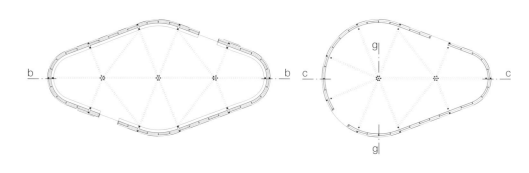

b ──────── b

B

c ──────── c

g
g

C

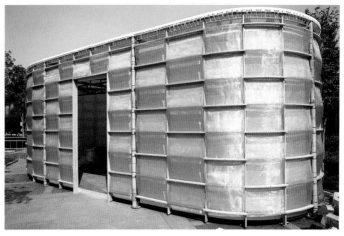

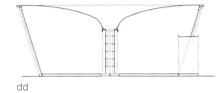

dd

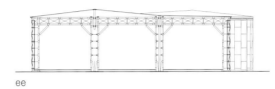

ee

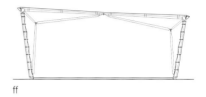

ff

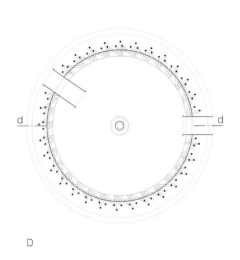

d — d

D

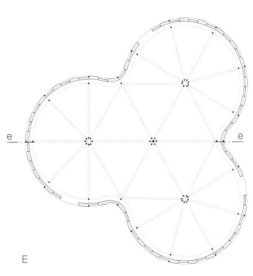

e — e

E

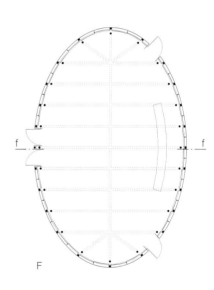

f — f

F

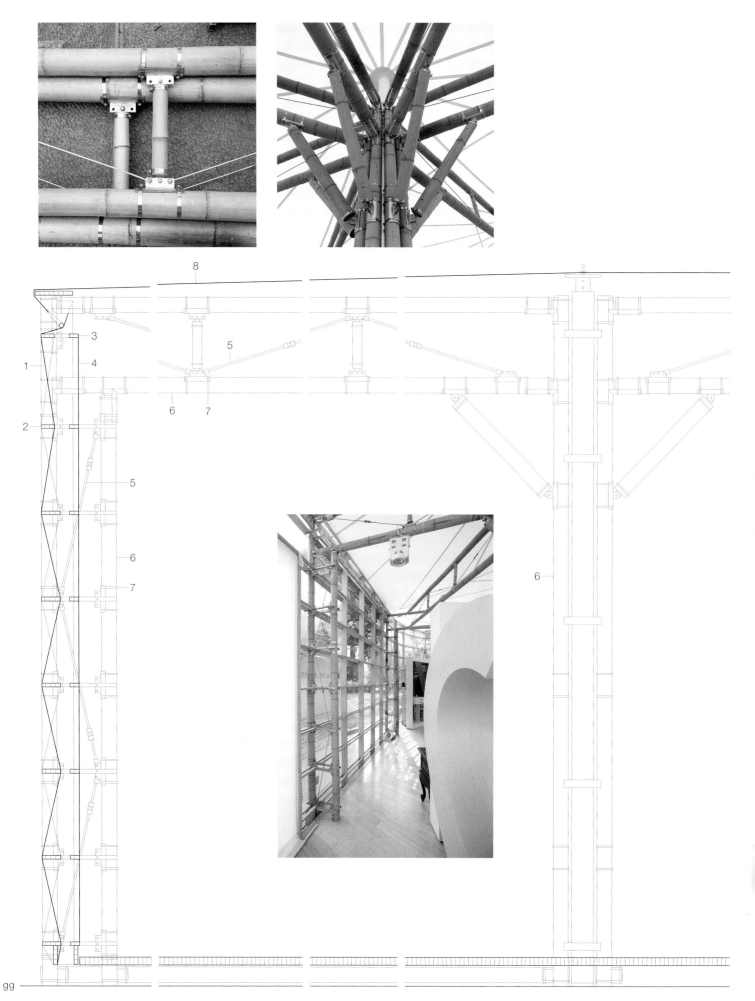

The form of the Navette pavilion is similar to a drop of water, the curves of which create a stable structure that is 3.60 metres high. The supports for the outside walls and the horizontal roof girders have been made using bamboo tubes that are connected like a ladder with a spacing of 35/40 cm. The load-bearing structure is given additional stability by tensioned steel cables. The facade's metal mesh has been woven through the horizontal bamboo laminate bars running around the structure. The additional height-adjustable central support is a rigid structure comprised of bamboo tubes that have been grouped together. Diagonal struts support the horizontal roof girders. All of the bamboo tubes are either equipped with cast brackets that can be bolted together, or are joined using shell-shaped steel brackets developed by the architects and steel clamps.

Vertical section   Scale 1:20

1 Stainless steel mesh woven between facade bars mesh size 1.12 mm, wire diam. 0.25 mm, weight 0.58 kg/m²
2 Facade bar running around the outside of the structure, bamboo laminate 100/20 mm
3 Facade bar running around the inside of structure, bamboo laminate 40/20 mm

4 Fabric inside wall
5 Tensioned steel cable, diam. 5 mm
6 Bamboo tube, diam. 80 mm
7 Galvanised steel half shell bracket joined using steel angles, length 100 mm
8 Roof membrane 1.2 mm with eyelet rivets approx. 100 mm apart, attached to the tubular steel railing, diam. 20 mm, using overlapping cables

Transport shelters in Darmstadt

Architects: netzwerkarchitekten, Darmstadt

Clear geometric sculptures in three colours rise up out of the ground in the railway station forecourt, providing information and shelter for waiting passengers.

The aim of this project was to provide rail travellers arriving in Darmstadt with a clearly laid out urban setting in which they can find their bearings and to offer them appropriate amenities in which to wait for public transport services. The previous tangle of roads, traffic islands and stops which travellers had to negotiate on their way to the main station entrance has given way to a spacious urban environment structured by the transport shelters' original architecture.

Arrangement of the modules
The new buildings unfold from the ground to form a family of geometrically abstract sculptures in blue, yellow and green. The right-angled Z-, L- and T-shaped modules, each tilted over at an angle of 90 degree, serve as information signs, shelters and ticket dispensers in one. Overhanging surfaces produce a columnless roofed-over area affording shelter from the weather. Four modules are arranged in an imaginary rectangle in front of the station building. The two T-modules serve as tram stops, while the two Z-modules are bus stops. To the south, on the other side of an additional T-module, is the regional bus services area incorporating four narrow L-modules. In the north the mobility centre serves as an information point and forms the front end of the square.

Functions
The steel construction is surrounded by frameless glazing on both sides. This glazing takes the form of laminated safety glass with coloured PVB films inserted between panes. The underside of the roof is provided with a grating. The modules incorporate ticket dispensers and displays presenting key information, including dynamically updated travel data on local and long-distance services, such as departure times. Lighting is also integrated. During daylight hours the sun lights up the translucent coloured glass sculptures, while at night they are transformed into glowing objects which incorporate the railway ensemble into an all-embracing lightscape and illuminate the waiting area.
A glass panel fitted in the middle of the rectangular bench offers additional protection from the weather. It also incorporates a display case for additional information.

Structural design
The primary supporting structure combines steel girders with a horizontal cross girder at the end of the overhang to form a rigid frame. The secondary supporting structure runs in transverse direction, consisting of two T-profiles which are joined pointwise by steel plates. The coloured glazing is fitted to supports which are attached to this secondary structure. Guttering on the outer edges drains water off the roof's horizontal glass surface. The vertical rain pipe is concealed within the construction. The interior glass panels can be opened by means of hinged fasteners for inspection purposes.

T-Module

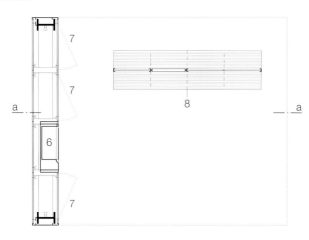

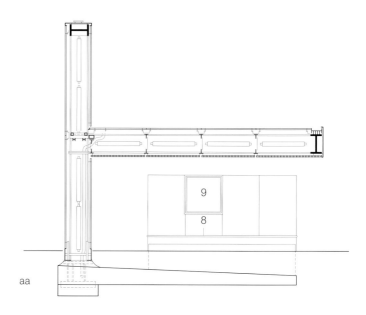

aa

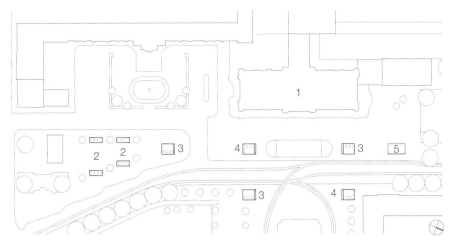

Site plan
Scale 1:2000
Floor plan · Sections
Scale 1:100

1 Main railway station
2 L-module for regional
  bus services
3 T-module for tram
  services
4 Z-module for municipal
  bus services
5 Mobility centre
6 Ticket dispenser
7 Maintenance flaps for
  lights
8 Bench
9 Display case for
  timetables

Section L-Module

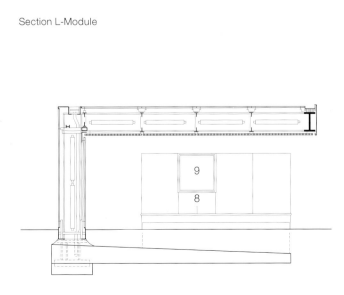

Section Z-Module

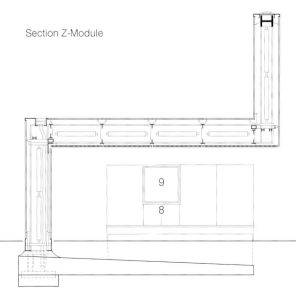

Project data:

Usage:	Infrastructural
	Fixed
Structure:	Steel
Clear room height:	2.60 m
Gross floor area:	110 m² (total)
Roof-over area:	272 m² (total)
Dimensions:	7.00 × 3.46 × 3.30 m
	(L-module)
	7.00 × 5.55 × 6.10 m
	(T/Z-module)
Construction costs:	€2 million
Year of construction:	2005
Construction period:	18 months

Vertical sections Z-module   Scale 1:20

1 Laminated safety glass, ESG-H 10 + 12 mm, with intermediate layer of coloured PVB films and etched-look matt finish
2 Steel girder, I-section 500 mm
3 Stainless steel countersunk-head point mount, screws, diam. 16 mm
4 Steel girder, I-section 500 mm
5 Reflector light, 1×54 W, dimmable, 1-10 V
6 Steel channel section, 80 mm
7 Canted sheet plate, 4 mm
8 Steel channel section, 140 mm
9 Internal gutter, gutter sheet on wooden substructure with 1 % lengthways slope
10 Continuous steel angle, 125/75/8 mm
11 Drainage pipe, diam. 70 mm

12 Steel profile T-shaped, 100/100 mm
13 Flat steel, 300/400/8 mm
14 Rectangular hollow steel profile, 120/80/5.6 mm
15 Grating, 30 mm, with welded in perforated plate, removable with socket-head screw
16 Steel I-section, 340 mm
17 Display case, opening on two sides
18 Laminated safety glass, 2× 10 mm
19 Bench:
   Seat surface of standard bankirai profiles, waterproofed and glued, 40/68 mm, outer edges rounded
   Substructure timber beams, 53/60 mm
   Steel profile Z-shaped, 65/140/65 mm 8 mm thick
20 Flat steel, 150/20 mm
21 Flat steel T-shaped, welded, 252/183/20 mm

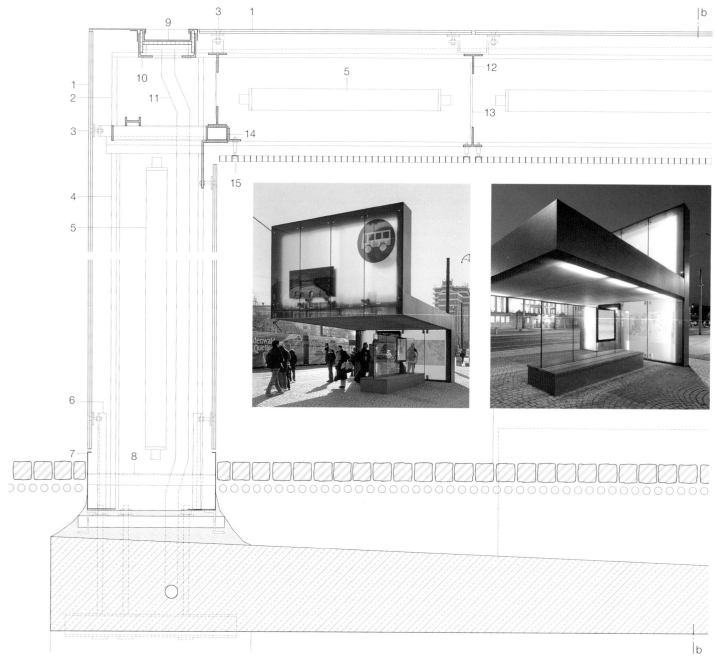

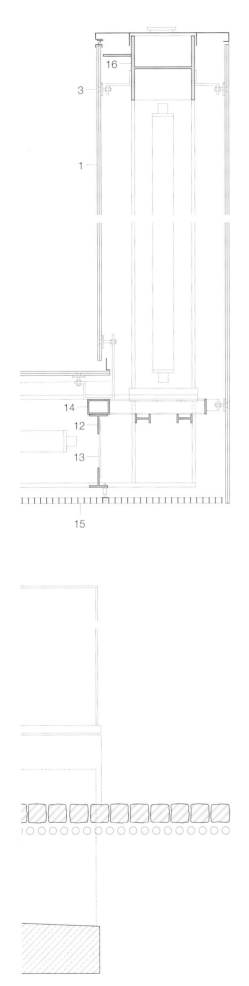

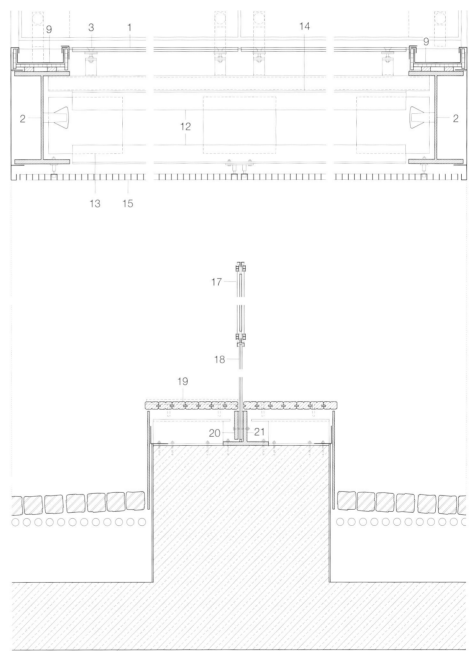

bb

Market stalls in Augsburg

Architect: Tilman Schalk Architekten, Stuttgart
Landscape architect: Helleckes Landschaftsarchitektur, Karlsruhe

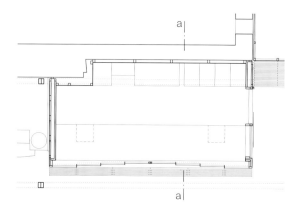

The newly designed Marktbrunnenplatz, or Market Fountain Square, has been given a coherent appearance, with homogenous paving and identical market stalls bordering the square.

With its central location between Fuggerstrasse and Annastrasse, the Stadtmarkt market lends Augsburg a touch of big city flair. Its alleyways, squares and market stalls make it like a city within a city, and its new structure has been designed to suit the products on offer. The open area has been divided into a vegetable alley, fruit alley, fish alley, baker's alley, flower alley and temporary farmer's market. The historic Fleischhalle, or Meat Hall, located near the centre is where butchers sell their wares, while the Viktualienhalle, or Victuals Hall, offers a wide range of international delicacies. In 2005, as a result of the widely varying appearances of the market stands, the low quality of the spaces and poor functionality of the access routes, the City of Augsburg held an architectural competition for restructuring the Stadtmarkt market. In order to keep the impairment of market activities to a minimum, the pavement and market stalls were to be renovated and renewed over the course of multiple phases.

Designing the square

The Marktbrunnenplatz to the east of the Fleischhalle serves as the interface between hectic pedestrian zones and a vibrant market. The goal of the new arrangement was to create an urban space that is an inviting location for spending time while also providing orientation. The dominant main facade of the Fleischhalle has been refined with a long canopy whose proportions are in keeping with neighbouring structures. The central square is bordered to the north and south by the new market stalls that have been placed perpendicularly to this. Light granite slabs highlight this new addition to the urban environment. In order to retain a uniform overall appearance, the area for vehicles adjacent to the square was paved using a stone matrix asphalt whose colour mixture was coordinated with that of the granite slabs. The space around the market fountain was cleared, making it the focal point of the square.

Architecture of the market stalls

The space-defining steel-glass roofs have been designed using a simple architectural style, and their translucent tensioned ceilings flood the sales areas with a pleasant light. Due to the fact that impact loads are to be expected, the steel structure must meet high static requirements. Shadow joints running vertically profile the welded supports, giving them an appearance of lightness. The sales booths arranged beneath the structure have been created using a prefabricated solid wood system, the most cost-effective method for this purpose. They are freestanding, and set off from the roof, the projection of which is sufficient to protect the area in front of each stall from the weather. The size and type of facade openings in the booths vary in accordance with the goods being offered, ensuring that each stall has a distinctive appearance. Sliding elements of the same height as the building provide generous openings in the facade. The fibre cement cladding of the closed areas has been painted an unobtrusive shade of green, providing a neutral backdrop for the products being offered.

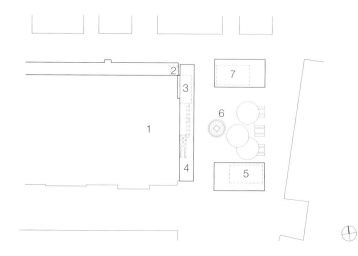

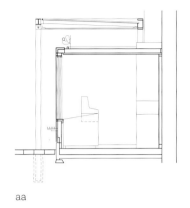

aa

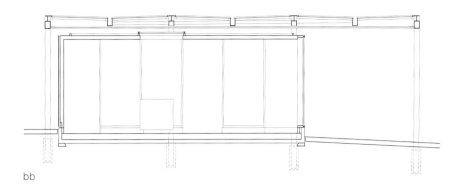

bb

Site plan
Scale 1:750

Floor plans · Sections
Uhl market stall and
Müller market stall
Scale 1:100

1 Fleischhalle
2 Storage area
3 Uhl market stall
4 Canopy
5 Neubert market stall
6 Market fountain
7 Müller market stall

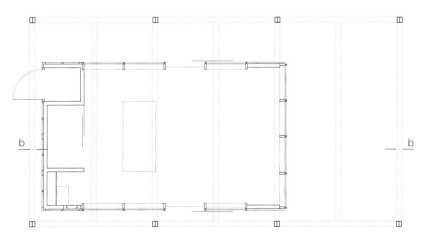

Neubert market stall
Floor plan
Scale 1:100

Vertical sections • Horizontal section
Scale 1:20

1 Fixed glazing laminated safety glass, 32 mm
2 Post and rail facade
  glued-laminated wood, 180/50 mm
3 Solid spruce elements, 98 mm
4 Fibre cement slab, 8 mm
  fixed on aluminium door system
5 Steel profile, 120 mm

6 Flat steel, 10 mm
7 Fixed glazing laminated safety glass, 16 mm
8 Light and acoustics mesh, polyester,
  translucent
9 Steel profile, 140 mm
10 Roof structure:
  Sealing: EPDM sheeting
  solid spruce ceiling elements, 95 mm
11 Aluminium profile worktop, 40/20/4 mm,
  bolted
12 Floor construction:
  In-situ concrete heated, 190 mm
  vapour barrier, thermal insulation, 100 mm
  frost blanket gravel

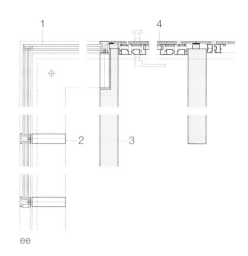

ee

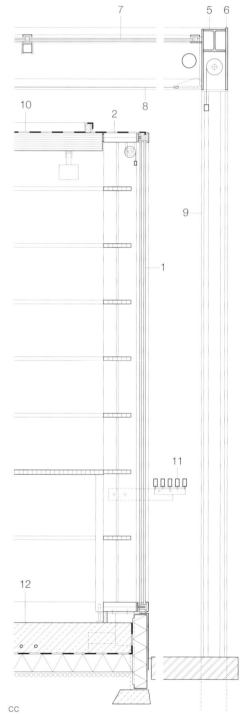

cc

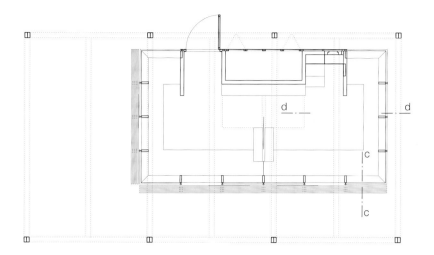

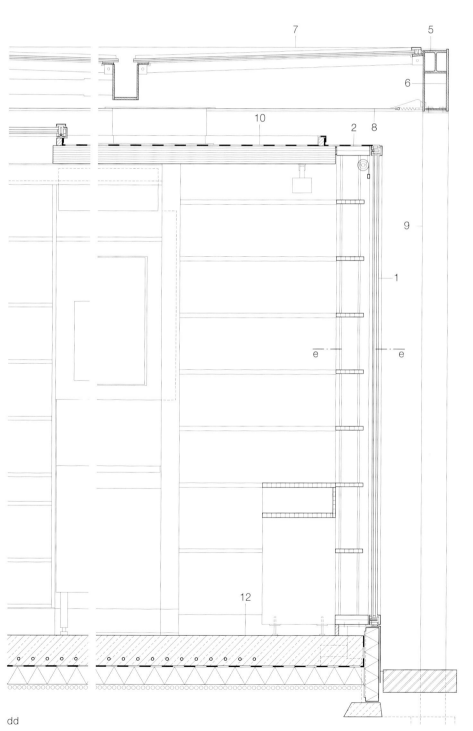

dd

Project data:

Usage:	Sales
	Fixed
Structure:	Solid wood/steel
Clear room height:	3 m (Roofing)
	2.50 m (Market stalls)
Gross volume:	240 m³ (Market stalls)
Gross floor area:	66 m² (Market stalls)
Dimensions:	2.84 × 5.50 m (Uhl)
	3.92 × 6.72 m (Müller)
	3.60 × 6.72 m (Neubert)
Construction costs:	€550,000 (gross, building structure alone)
Year of construction:	2008/2009
Construction period:	9 months

Theatre podium in Rotterdam

Architects: Atelier Kempe Thill architects and planners,
Rotterdam

The city podium on the bank of a canal in the middle of Rotterdam serves as a theatre stage while also providing a "roofed-over empty environment" for creative usage.

The reconstruction of Rotterdam after the devastation inflicted in the Second World War gave rise to Grotekerkplein square between a church and a canal. Despite its central location the square stands at a remove from city life due to the lack of any shopping streets linking it to the public areas. A competition to revitalise this area of the city envisaged a small theatre pavilion for performances and as a meeting place for the city's residents.

The resultant 40 m long podium closes off the western side of the square as a counterpart to Sint Laurenskerk church, creating a distinct boundary which separates the square from the Delftsevaart canal. The open and transparent nature of the structure ensures that visual links with the surrounding area are maintained and avoids any sense of confinement.

Spatial concept of the podium

The theatre podium is designed as an open stage for the city's inhabitants. The restrained building offers an empty space which has not been assigned any specific function. The aim is for the people of Rotterdam to discover this space on their own terms and put it to creative use. The monumental roof of the podium provides a befitting setting in which to stage meetings in an original manner.

The stage environment is created by two 5 m high service buildings in conjunction with a 50 cm thick base and the roof which spans the two volumes. The stage faces onto the square and water. Performers can face either side, or the stage itself can be used as a seated auditorium.

The southern service building accommodates the 70 m long textile stage curtain. Depending on the event, this curtain can be used to modify the size of the stage or serve as a backdrop. The movement of the curtain in the wind highlights the temporary nature of the events.

The northern service building houses the WC, changing room and prop room for the artists. A kitchenette here doubles as a small café.

Robust and fine materials

The podium is made of fair-faced concrete and stainless steel, to withstand the effects of everyday use, weather and vandalism. The concrete surface is additionally sealed with an anti-graffiti coating.

The roof consists of prestressed concrete, enabling an unusually slimline design with a thickness of just 50 cm at the edge and 75 cm in the middle. To provide the fair-faced concrete with the finest, lightest surface possible, titanium oxide aggregate was added as a whitener and large shuttering panels measuring 10.00 × 2.50 m were used. All technical installations such as electrical wiring and the curtain rail are integrated into the construction.

Fixed between the two concrete slabs, the service buildings are set apart by stainless steel mesh facing. The mesh panels are an unusually large 5 m in width, to produce a seamless finish. The buildings are each accessed by two room-high stainless steel doors produced specifically for this project. An LED light strip behind the stainless steel mesh illuminates the structure from within after dusk.

Project data:

Usage:	Cultural
	Fixed
Structure:	Fair-faced concrete
Clear room height:	5 m
Gross volume:	1200 m³
Gross floor area:	200 m²
Dimensions:	40,00 × 5,00 × 6,25 m (2× 5 m long service buildings, spanned by 30 m unsupported roof)
Construction costs:	€798,500 (net)
Year of construction:	2009
Construction period:	15 months

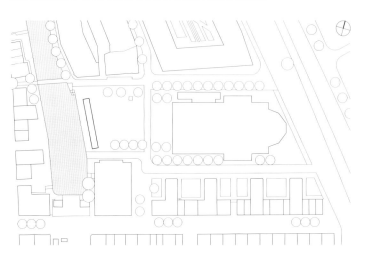

aa   bb

Site plan
Scale 1:3000

Sections
Floor plan
Scale 1:250

1 City podium
2 Service instal-
  lations/store
  for curtain
3 Kitchenette/
  changing
  room

83

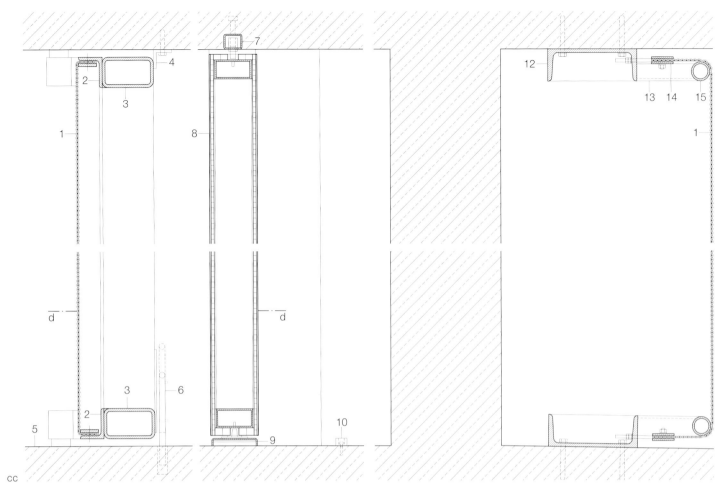

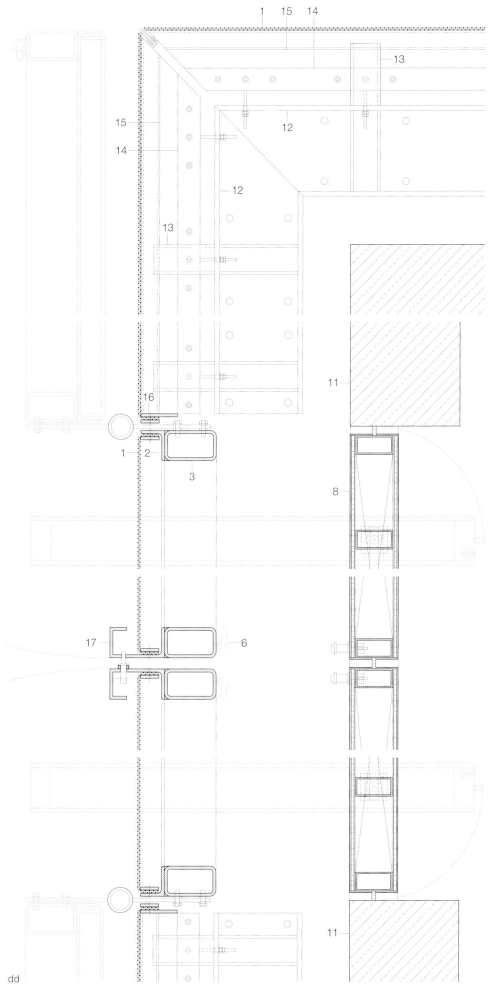

Detailed sections
Scale 1:10

1 Stainless steel mesh, approx. 7.5 mm,
  approx. 14.8 kg/m², consisting of warp
  cables and weft rods, each of 3 mm diam.,
  panel sizes, 1250 (5000)/5000 mm
2 Stainless steel profile, 65/80/8 mm,
  welded to door profile
3 Door frame, tubular stainless steel,
  140/80/8 mm
4 Door stopper, stainless steel profile,
  50/50/8 mm
5 Base slab, fair-faced concrete, power-trow-
  elled with 0.8% gradient, 300–320 mm
6 Fixing rod, diam. 16 mm, to clamp door in
  stainless steel sleeve in concrete floor
7 Tubular stainless steel embedded in
  concrete, 40/50/3 mm
8 Door leaf:
  Aluminium sheet, 2 mm, bonded to
  multiplex panel, waterproof, 8 mm, bonded to
  aluminium frame, 100/50/4 mm
9 Stainless steel profile, 125/20/3 mm
10 Stainless steel sleeve to clamp the door,
   diam. 30 mm, height 20 mm
11 Fair-faced concrete, 300 mm
12 Steel channel section, 240 mm, with drainage
   holes of 15 mm diam. for rain water
13 Steel channel section, 80 mm, welded to
   steel tube and steel channel section, 240 mm
14 Bolted sheet steel clamping profile,
   2× 60/5 mm
15 Tubular stainless steel, diam. 50/5 mm
16 Bolted stainless sheet steel clamping profile,
   100/8 mm and 50/8 mm
17 Door handle, composite profile in stainless
   sheet steel, 8 mm, welded to angle section

Pavilion at Lake Geneva

Architects: Bakker & Blanc Architectes, Lausanne

Pavilions in modular design accommodate various usages and can be extended according to requirements.

The promenade on the shore of Lake Geneva offers high recreational value. For those not content to stroll along and take in the scenery there is a yacht club, a landing stage for boats and fishing areas. Over the years, however, structural problems have arisen, such as the increasing road traffic around the lake and the heterogeneous character of the new buildings on the promenade. This prompted Geneva's municipal authorities to launch a competition aimed at providing the various service amenities on offer here with a cohesive identity. The winning project by Bakker & Blanc Architectes proposes a single type of building for all types of use, varying solely in terms of size and the design of the directly surrounding area.

Variety of different sizes

The vertical orientation of the planned pavilions directly at the lakeside – only a prototype has been installed to date – breaks with the structure of the development behind the waterfront and emphasizes the link between the Eaux Vives and Pâquis residential areas and the promenade. The gaps between the small structures are intended to provide views of the lake. Protected areas arise which are shielded from the traffic. The basic unit is a cubic structure stripped down to the bare essentials with a gently inclined gable roof, standing on a rectangular base without a projecting roof or canopy. The pavilion's modular design enables various types of building to be produced for the most diverse types of use. The smallest possible unit, with a modular dimension of 2.00 × 2.80 m, is a public toilet designed in accordance with the needs of disabled people. The kiosk incorporates a second unit. The existing prototype, which is in use as a catering stand with a restaurant and kiosk, represents the largest of the envisaged variants, measuring 10 m in length. Adjoining the cube is a textile sunroof providing a shaded environment for tables and chairs. When the hatches are closed in the evening, a plain cube remains which does not impose itself on the public space.

Design

The steel frame construction is designed with rigid corners. Hatches which can be opened by means of gas pressure-operated cylinders offer a glimpse of the individually designed interior. The patina on the outer shell of bronze sheeting conceals the marks left by daily use, transportation and the weather. The metal sheets have been mounted on sandwich panels and seamlessly welded together. The material cites the bronze sculptures which are prevalent throughout the town. Delivered and set up in the spring, the pavilions are loaded onto lorries and transported away again in the autumn, to make space for the boats which are hauled ashore for repair in the winter.

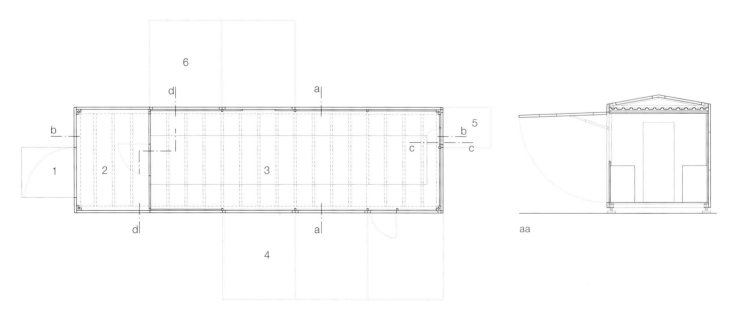

Floor plan · Sections
View of side facing road
Scale 1:100

1 Delivery point
2 Store
3 Kitchen/dispensing area
4 Restaurant
5 Kiosk
6 Ice cream sales

Axonometric projection
Building types

A Restaurant
B Ticket sales/
  Sailing school/Kiosk
C WC facility

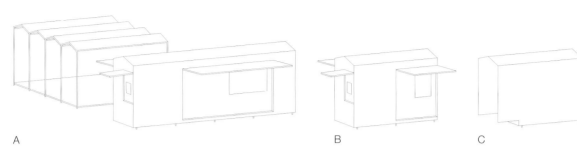

A   B   C

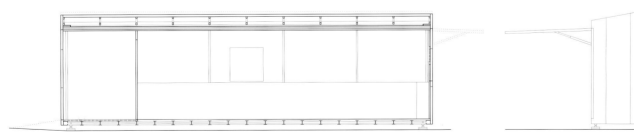
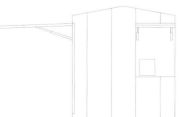

bb

Project data:

Usage:	Bistro
	Mobile
Structure:	Steel structure
Clear room height:	2.50 m
Gross volume:	73 m³
Gross floor area:	28 m²
Dimensions:	2.80 × 10.14 m
Prototype costs:	€258,393
Year of construction:	2006
Construction period:	1.5 months

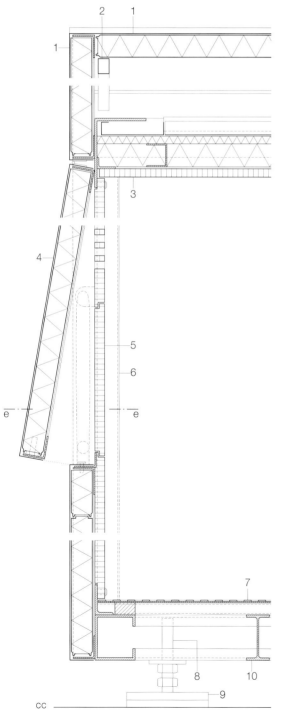

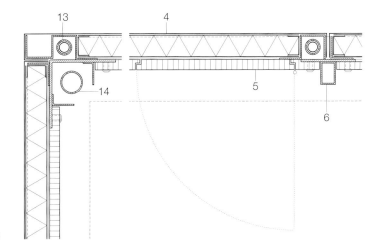

ee

Detailed sections
Scale 1:10

1 Bronze-brass sheeting
 pre-patinated, 1.2 mm
 fully bonded with
 60 mm aluminium-
 polyurethane panelling
2 Steel profile,
 40/30/2 mm
3 Three-layered panel,
 27 mm
 thermal insulation
 rock wool, 60 mm
 thermal insulation, 20 mm
 thermally insulated
 trapezoidal sheet metal,
 40 mm
4 Panel in steel frame,

60/60/5 mm
 some panels designed
 for opening
5 Opening wing three-
 layered panel, 27 mm
6 Tubular steel pillar,
 60/40/4 mm
7 Rubber tiling, 2 mm
8 Levelling thread,
 150 mm
9 Metal disk, 220/20 mm
 on rubber base,
 220/20 mm
10 Steel I-beam, 120 mm
11 Grating, 35 mm
12 Lifting eyebolts,
 accessible via flaps
13 Gas pressure cylinder
14 Rain pipe, diam. 60 mm

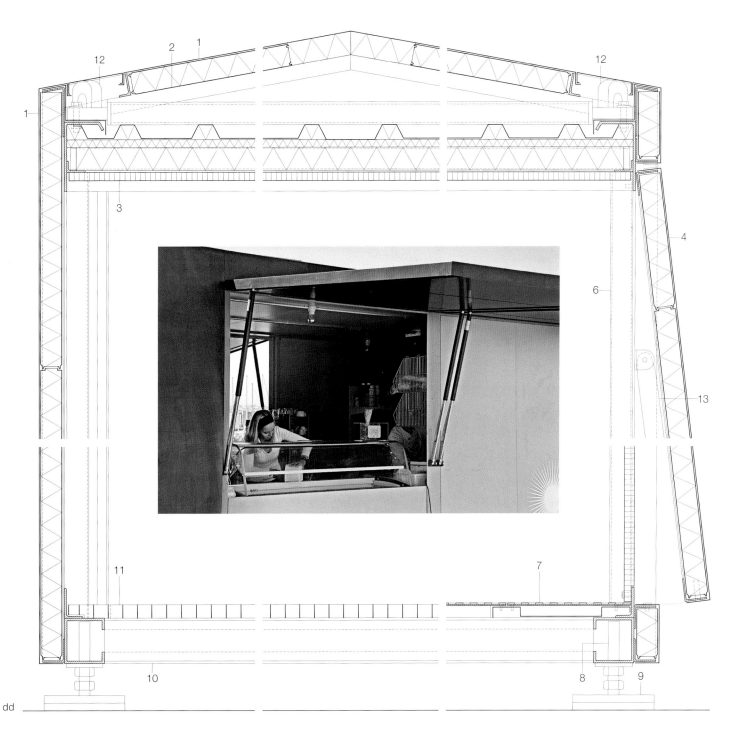

dd

Pavilion in Zurich

Architects: phalt architekten, Zurich

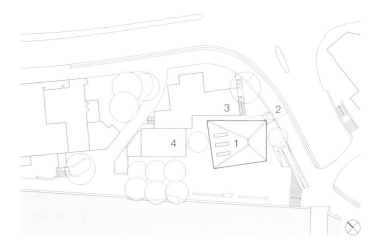

This little workshop tackles the theme of metal in structure and facades and offers various usage possibilities.

The centrally located Dynamo youth cultural centre has been offering young people a range of opportunities to work with design since it was established twenty years ago. The goal is to provide young people free spaces in which they can develop their own initiative, take responsibility and put their creative ideas into practice. Another creative locus has now been created between the banks of the Limmat River and a group of listed historical buildings housing the various parts of the cultural centre: the new metal workshop. As a result of extensive construction work, provisional storerooms had to be torn down and replaced with a new office and storeroom. The striking new mushroom-shaped pavilion lends structure to the formerly heterogeneous square, creating a new space. Its prominent projecting roof occupies the entire permissible building area, creating a roofed, support-free outdoor work area that can be used all year round. The facade can be opened on a large scale with simple folding doors, making it clear to the outside world when the workshop is in use.

Special "workroom"

The workshop's structure and facade are reflective of its function: A load-bearing steel skeleton structure rises above an insulated wooden office "box" and storage room. The entire building is enclosed by an industrially produced, perforated steel sheet which gives it a homogenous appearance. Its deep perforation ensures sufficient strength to withstand mechanical forces, while also fulfilling aesthetic requirements. The corrosion-resistant, hot dip galvanised shell offers a playful contrast to the red colouration of the new asphalt that resulted from the rusting iron shavings created during the steel working process. Depending on the lighting and the observer's vantage point, the building can appear transparent or closed; night can reveal glimpses of the illuminated interior, or its shiny metal shell can obscure it from view when the sun is shining. This interplay between transparency and opacity, between lightness and solidity, gives the pavilion its unique appeal. The perforation of the facade embellishment also makes it easy to hang hooks, signs and other items from it. The signage for the outdoor workshop has been created by using the perforation as a grid, with black rubber knobs serving as pixels.

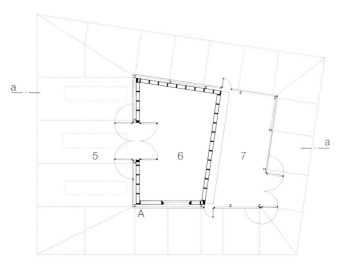

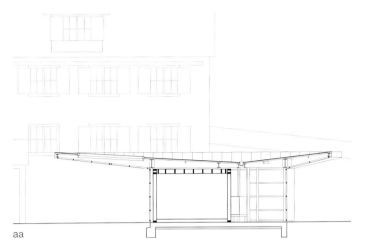

aa

Site plan
Scale 1:1000
Ground floor plan
Section
Scale 1:200

1 Metal workshop
2 WC/cloakroom
3 Jewellery workshop
4 Restaurant
5 Roofed work area
6 Office
7 Storeroom

Project data:

Usage:	Workshop, office and storeroom
	Fixed
Structure:	Steel skeleton structure
Clear room height:	2.40 m (office)
	2.83–3.42 m (outdoor work area)
Gross volume:	160 m³
Gross floor area:	49 m²
Dimensions:	8 × 7 m (building)
	16.00 × 12.50 m (roof)
Construction costs:	592,000 Swiss francs (gross)
Year of construction:	2008
Construction period:	4 months

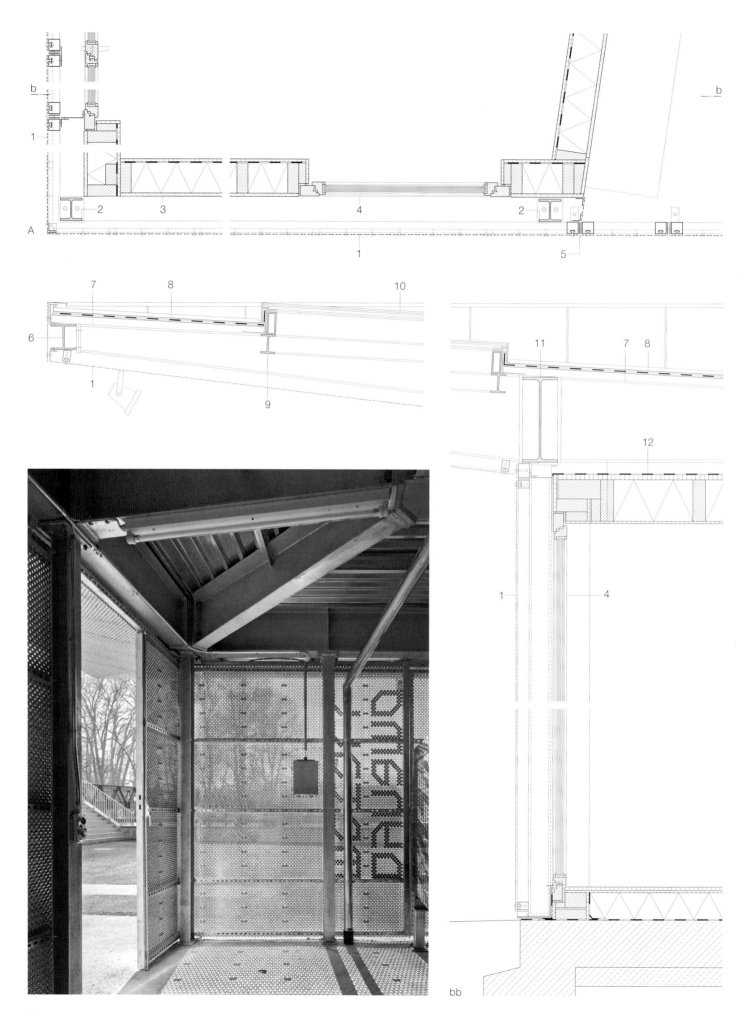

Detailed sections   Scale 1:20

1 Stamped steel sheet, punched, hot dip galvanised, 2 mm
   Substructure: steel profile, hot dip galvanised, bolted, 60/60 mm and 60/40 mm
2 Steel I-column, 120 mm
3 Wall structure: Particle board, cement-bound, 18 mm, thermal insulation cellulose, 160 mm, vapour barrier, oriented-strand board, 15 mm
4 Wooden windows with triple glazing
5 Flat steel profile, 100/20/5 mm as a mount for a padlock
6 Steel I-beam, 140 mm
7 Girder steel I-beam, 300 mm conically tapered

8 Roof structure:
   Double lock roof, copper-titanium-zinc sheet, 7 mm structural matting, sound-insulating trapezoidal sheet, 41 mm
9 Steel I-beam, 100 mm
10 Skylight glazing: laminated safety glass 2× float, 8 mm
11 Steel I-beam, 450 mm
12 Sealing sheet as emergency cover
   Ceiling element:
   Plywood board, 27 mm thermal insulation cellulose, 220 mm oriented-strand board, 12 mm
13 Steel channel section, 200 mm
14 Timber post and beam element:

Particle board cement-bound, 18 mm, thermal insulation cellulose, 160 mm, vapour barrier, oriented-strand board, 15 mm
15 Floor construction:
   Oriented-strand board, sanded, oiled, 18 mm, soft fibre board, 12 mm thermal insulation rigid foam, 140 mm, moisture barrier reinforced concrete floor slab, 250 mm granular sub-base lean concrete, 100 mm
16 Material store

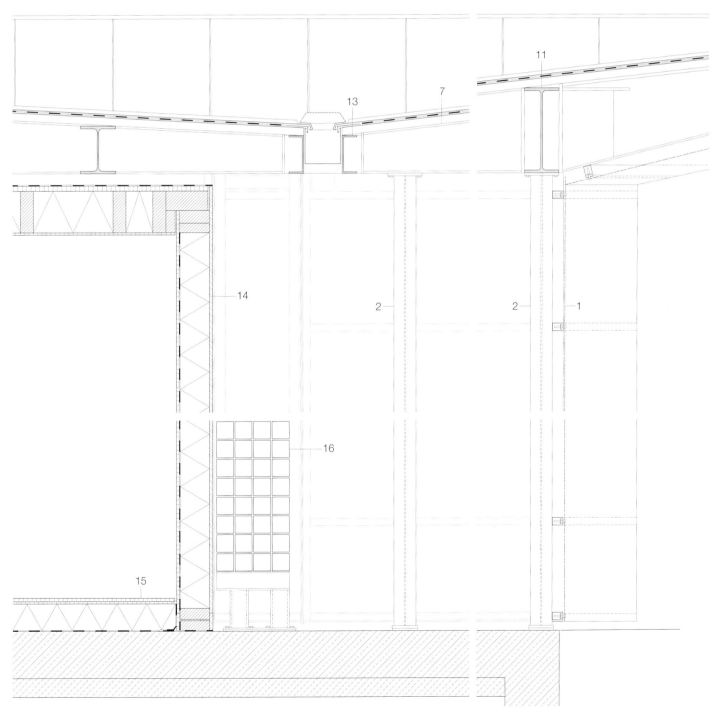

Newspaper kiosks in London

Designer: Heatherwick Studio, London

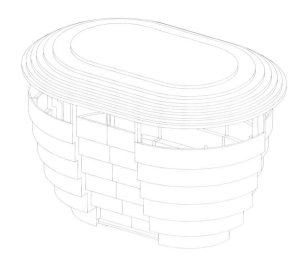

These oval kiosks with stepped outer shell combine an attractive design with protection from vandalism and integrated newspaper display shelving.

The London districts of Kensington and Chelsea decided to replace their boring rectangular booths with new kiosks featuring a fresher design. The declared aim was to provide better protection from vandalism and simpler working conditions for the sales personnel.

The girth of the oval structure increases from bottom to top as a result of a stepped outer shell. The geometry performs various functions: Even when closed, the kiosks attract the interest of passers-by on account of their sculptural form; the cladding consisting of bands of patinated brass has a stylish look and denies graffiti artists the necessary space for their work; inside, the steps serve as wooden shelves for displaying newspapers and magazines.

A window strip running all the way around the kiosk directly under the stepped roof lends the latter a certain weightlessness and provides for adequate natural lighting. At night, the kiosk shines from within.

Instead of the cumbersome roll-up door of old, the kiosk is opened simply by sliding the curved front over the adjoining sections of the facade. The oval opens up halfway to reveal the generously sized counter. The sales personnel behind the counter stand on a raised floor offering a good inside and outside view while also enjoying good protection from the weather. The shelves are already filled, with no need to spend time setting up shop in the morning and clearing the shelves at the end of the day.

The kiosks can stand in the open or against a wall, as part of the rear side is straight. The prefabricated constructions are transported by lorry to the installation site in one piece. Due to their high weight of around 2 t, which results from additional weighting in the area of the base plate, they do not require any additional fixation. The structure consists of vertical CNC-milled flat steel bars of 130 mm in width which support the roof cantilever and girder. They are fixed to curved asymmetric double-T girders which serve as a guide rail for the nylon rollers of the doors. Additional double-T girders reinforce the base plate. Six adjusting screws compensate any unevenness in the street paving. The profile of the flat steel bars corresponds to the steps of the shelving and the outer shell. 2 mm thick steel sheeting is welded between the flat steel bars and then lined with plywood on the inside and brass as the outer cladding.

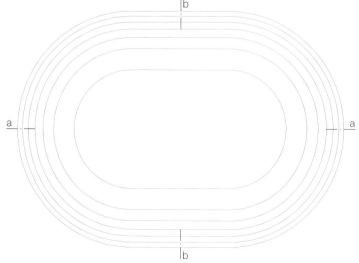

94

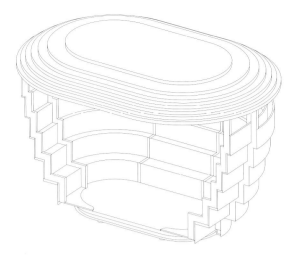

Axonometric projection – Outer shell of the structure
in closed and open state

Top view · Sections
Scale 1:50

Project data:

Usage:	Sales
	Fixed
Structure:	Steel
Headroom:	approx. 2.35 m
Gross volume:	11.25 m³
Gross floor area:	2.60 m²
Dimensions:	4.43 × 3.03 × 2.83 m
Construction costs:	€34,700 (£30,000)
Year of construction:	2009
Construction period:	12 weeks

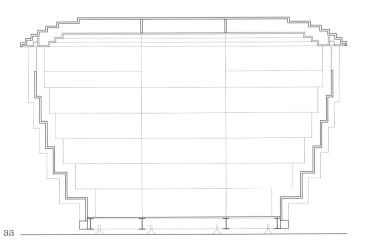

aa

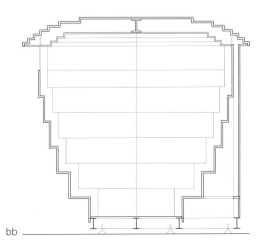

bb

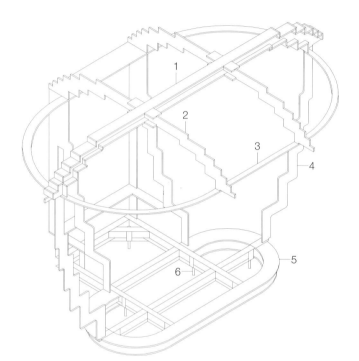

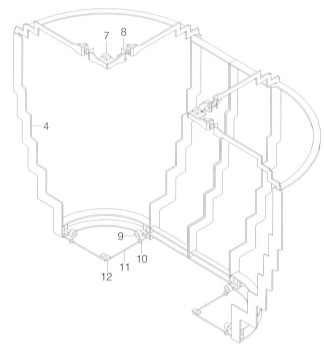

Axonometric projection
Steel frame and door element

1 Main roof girder I-section, 130 mm
2 Roof cantilever flat steel bar
3 Roof edge support, curved flat steel bar,
   64/8 mm
4 Building/door ribs, shaped sheet steel,
   130/15 mm
5 Curved edge beam, in asymmetric design as
   running rail for the doors, 142/108 mm
6 Adjustable feet
7 Top pivot
8 Rod as top retainer for door and tolerance
   compensator
9 Shaft and upper wheel
10 Rod as bottom door lock
11 Bottom wheel
12 Bottom pivot

Kiosk at lake "Staufensee" near Dornbirn

Architects: Wellmann Ladinger, Bregenz

Project data:

Usage:	Sales
	Fixed structure
Structure:	Fair-faced concrete
Clear room height:	2.30–3.70 m (main room)
	2.10 m (sanitary facilities / storeroom)
	1.55 m (sleeping berth)
Gross volume:	96 m³
Gross floor area:	25.56 m²
Floor space (total):	18.60 m²
Dimensions:	3.60 × 7.10 m
Construction costs:	€67,500
Year of construction:	2005
Construction period:	5 months

The monolithic, reinforced concrete kiosk with an archaic shape not only offers sustenance for hikers – it also provides its owner with a place to spend the night.

The kiosk, a solid structure that has been "cast" in raw reinforced concrete, is located on a flat piece of land by the river above Dornbirn, in the gorge which holds the Dornbirner Ach River, between Rappenloch and Alploch. The hut, which is only 7.10 × 3.60 m in size, offers hikers a place to rest and buy food. Its elementary, primitive shape sets it clearly apart from the natural surroundings.

Clear exterior form

This sharply delineated monolithic structure offers no visible architectural details. The walls and roof are joined seamlessly, without any gutters. The entrance door and large top-hung window are fitted flush with the facade. They have been made entirely from rough-sawn white fir, forming a counterpart to the rough, sandblasted structure of the concrete, which bears signs of the wooden formwork. An additional narrow window strip on the southwest side, in front of which a white fir grate is set flush with the wall, ensures that the building receives natural light even when the top-hung window is closed.

As the building ages, the white fir facade elements will gradually turn grey, growing ever more similar to the colour of the concrete. The raised window shutter and open entrance door, the inside of which has been painted black to serve as a price board, signal that the kiosk is open for business.

Contrasting interior

The interior of this concrete structure has been modelled on that of a traditional farmhouse. The archaic coarseness of the concrete exterior is in stark contrast to the materials and warm colours used for the interior, which boasts boarding made of formwork panels painted reddish brown and a concrete floor coated with a black sealant.

In addition to the central sales room, which is equipped with a counter and an integrated shelf system, a separate auxiliary area houses a storeroom and a bathroom with basic amenities. An additional level was added beneath the gable above the auxiliary area. It is reached via a simple stepladder and serves as a relaxation area or a place to spend the night if the owner does not feel like making the trek into the valley in the evening.

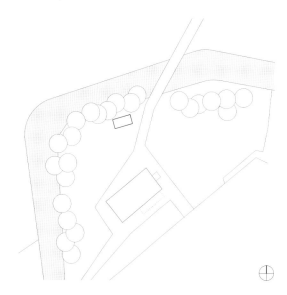

Site plan
Scale 1:500

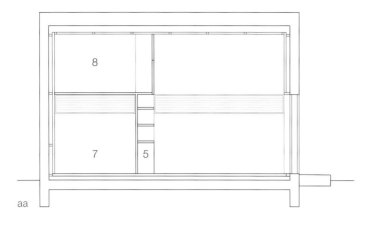

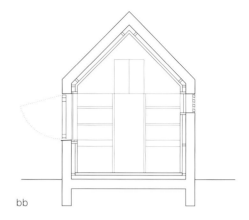

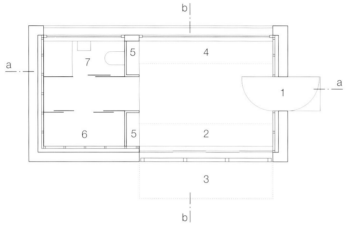

aa

bb

Sections · Ground floor plan
Scale 1:100

1 Entrance
2 Sales area
3 Top-hung window
4 Kitchen area
5 Service installations /
   shelves
6 Storeroom
7 Shower / WC
8 Sleeping berth

Vertical section · Horizontal section
Scale 1:20

9 Reinforced concrete, impermeable to water,
  sandblasted, rough-sawn wooden
  formwork, 250 mm
  lathing, 100/50 mm
  in between
  mineral wool insulation, 100 mm
  vapour barrier, 2 mm
  counterlathing, 37 mm
  veneer plywood formwork panels,
  painted reddish brown, 21 mm
10 White fir boarding, 25 mm
  tubular steel frame, 80/80 mm
  with insulation in between, 80 mm

lift arm operated by gas pressure cylinder
veneer plywood boarding, 10 mm
coated black
11 Galvanised sheet-steel window sill, 6 mm
12 Sliding window element in aluminium
  profile, stainless steel cover, 3 mm
13 Veneer plywood formwork panels, 37 mm
14 White fir grate, 4× 63/63 mm
15 Window strip with double glazing in
  white fir frame
  aluminium cover profile, 2 mm
16 Cement screed, sealed, 60 mm
  vapour barrier, 2 mm
  thermal insulation XPS, 100 mm
  cardboard separating layer, 2 mm
  reinforced concrete floor slab, 250 mm

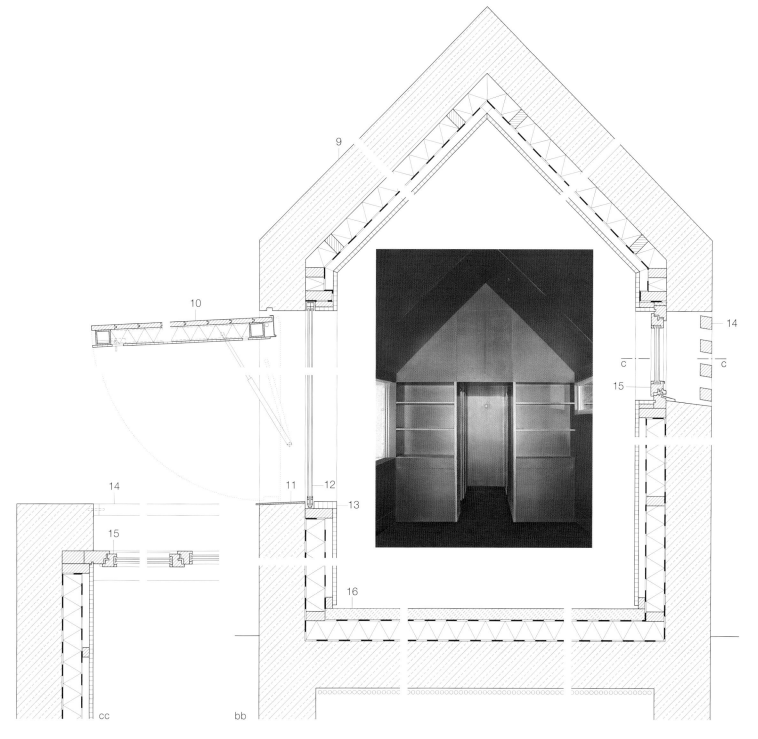

Temporary bar in Porto

Architects: Diogo Aguiar and Teresa Otto, Porto

Axonometric projections of the structure
Section · Ground floor plan   Scale 1:50
Detailed section   Scale 1:10

At night, the temporary bar is transformed from an abstract white cube into an illuminated attraction for night owls.

Every year, the University of Porto's faculty of architecture holds a competition to design a temporary bar. The objectis for students to create an extraordinary item of architecture within a short time and on a limited budget that is representative of the university. Within a month of the winner for 2008 being declared, the temporary bar had already been completed with the help of numerous students. Its modular design made it possible to use a large number of prefabricated parts. The facade is comprised of 420 white plastic (polypropylene) storage boxes of varying heights. In spite of a grid which is uniform throughout (30 × 42 cm), the variation in the projection of the boxes brings the facade to life. The individual models were prefabricated in a hall, where the plastic boxes were bolted onto a timber frame substructure. A total of 46 modules in four different sizes were used, ranging from a row of three boxes to a set of 4 × 3 boxes. Once the modules were on site, they needed simply to be attached to the load-bearing structure fashioned from rectangular steel tubing.
Part of the facade can be folded out, creating an opening for the bar. As a result of the depth of the boxes and the desire to keep the interior free, special, extra-long hinges had to be developed. The flap is attached at the side using stainless steel rods in the reveal. A network of LEDs inside the structure illuminates the white cubes at night, the colours changing in time to the music.

Project data:

Usage:	Restaurant Temporary
Structure:	Steel frame, timber frame
Clear room height:	4.55 m
Gross volume:	43 m³
Gross floor area:	9 m²
Dimensions:	3.00 × 3.00 × 4.80 m
Year of construction:	2008
Construction period:	1 week

1 Polycarbonate boards 20 mm
2 Tubular stainless steel frame 80 mm
3 Timber frame substructure 40/20 mm
4 Plastic box PE 300/420 mm
5 Stainless steel bracket 20/20/2 mm
6 Stainless steel bracket 100/30/4 mm
7 Stainless steel hinge, diam. 10 mm
8 Stainless steel rod, diam. 12 mm
9 Flat stainless steel profile 4 mm
10 Flat stainless steel profile, curved 40/40/4 mm

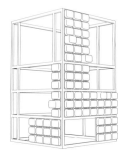

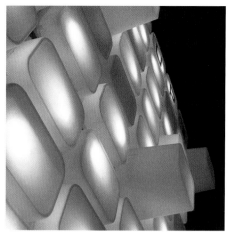

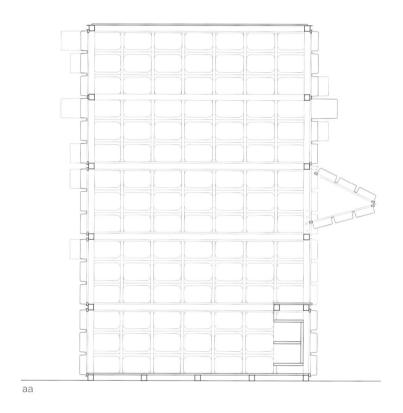

aa

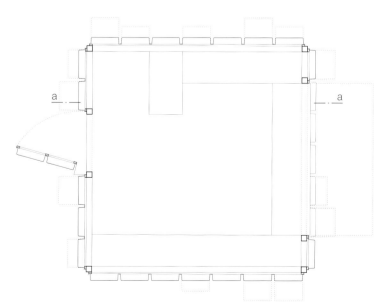

a — — — — — a

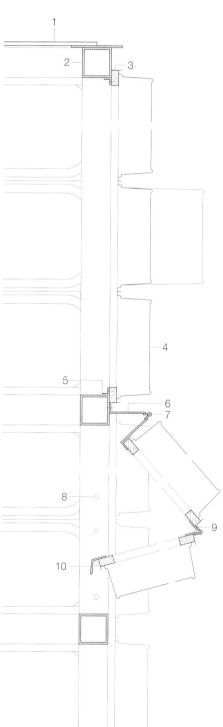

1

2   3

4

5

6
7

8

9

10

Tree house Restaurant near Auckland

Architects: Pacific Environments Architects, Auckland

The Tree house Restaurant, venue for an advertising campaign, encircles the redwood tree like a butterfly's cocoon.

The objective was to take a childhood dream, combine it with an adventure restaurant and transform the result into a powerful televised advertising campaign. The project was commissioned by Yellow, New Zealand's Yellow Pages business directory – to demonstrate the versatility of Yellow Pages – the architect and all other suppliers were listed there.

The architects, who were put in charge of selecting the location, a suitable tree, the form and the structure of this tree house restaurant, ended up choosing a location north of Auckland where they found a 40 m high redwood tree at the edge of the forest which offered a view overlooking a meadow and a river.

Form as a reflection of nature

The tree house encloses the 1.70 m diameter tree trunk like a butterfly's cocoon, and is sensitive to its natural surroundings. A 60 m long walkway leads guests naturally through the forest and up a gentle slope to the restaurant 10 m above the ground. The experience begins on the way up to the restaurant: discreet night-time illumination creates a special atmosphere and a lantern effect guiding guests to the tree house.

Inspiration for its structure was also found in nature, with two offset semicircles reminiscent of a shell. A small balcony opposite the entrance affords a panoramic view of the surrounding landscape. The restaurant seats 24, with service staff. Catering and other facilities are located at ground level.

Materials and structure

The materials used are in keeping with the surroundings, constructed almost entirely of wood. Two dead redwood trees nearby provided wood for the walkway. The tree house itself is suspended from the tree trunk by four steel sleeves, to which triangular wooden frames have been attached to support the platform and the building's envelope. The facade is fashioned from curved fins made from glued-laminated pine which emphasises the verticality while ensuring natural light and attractive views. Spaces between the fins have been weatherproofed with acrylic glass panes. With the campaign complete, it is possible for the tree house to be removed or re-located.

Project data:

Usage:	Restaurant
	Temporary
Structure:	Wood
Clear room height:	3 m
Gross floor area:	44 m²
Dimensions:	10 × 8 m
Year of construction:	2008
Construction period:	3–4 months

Site plan
Scale 1:800

1 Tree house Restaurant
2 Access walkway
3 Film crew vehicle
4 Catering
5 Access road
6 Cul-de-sac where vehicles can turn around

Floor plan · Section
Scale 1:100

1 Redwood tree trunk, diam. 1,700 mm
2 Glued-laminated pine fins: 450/42 mm, with
  280/42 mm in between
  poplar lathing
3 Floor construction:
  Wooden plank flooring treated pine
  100/40 mm
  lathing treated pine 150/50 mm
  wooden beams treated pine 2× 300/50
4 Two-piece steel sleeve for mounting onto the
  tree trunk; attached to the tree trunk using
  dowels
5 Wooden struts treated pine 100/100 mm with
  acrylic glass panes in between

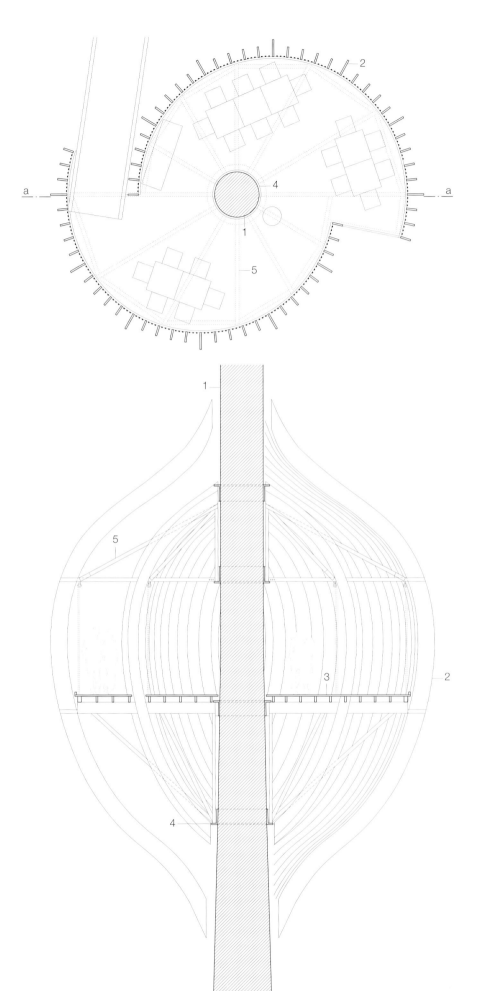

aa

St. Benedikt Chapel in Kolbermoor

Architects: kunze seeholzer architektur & stadtplanung,
Munich

**The simple yet powerful form of the small chapel
is distinguished by the contrast of light and
shadow, solidity and lightness.**

Solid and with a clarity of form, St. Benedikt Chapel is located
in a clearing in the Spinnereipark in Kolbermoor. The small,
fair-faced concrete structure, with a base that is barely
10 m² in size, is oriented along an east-west axis. The roofed
entrance area, whose high concrete arch and bell are evoca-
tive of a church tower, are approached across a large forecourt. The natural stone flooring found in the interior begins
here in the entranceway, linking the interior with the exterior.
Visitors enter the chapel through the room-high red cedar
portal, where they find an interior distinguished by the contrast between fair-faced concrete and wooden pews. The
smooth concrete shell has been brightened with titanium
dioxide. The materials' impact is derived from their original
texture and feel. The light entering perpendicularly from
above directs the view of those entering the chapel from the
crucifix on the rear wall upwards towards the sky. As the
walls have no windows, all of the illumination comes from a
skylight running round three sides of the ceiling. The concrete roof appears to hover above the centre of the room.
The ceiling and walls are joined solely by three stainless steel
tubes embedded into the concrete on both long sides. The
tubes at either end of each wall function as structural supports, while the middle tube serves as a drainpipe, directing
rainwater from the flat roof through the exterior wall to the
open wooden gutters. The ageing of the wood and movement of the water in this visible drainage system are meant to
symbolise the course of life.

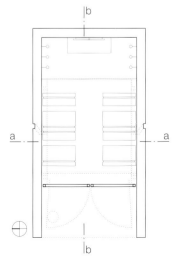

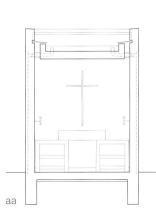

aa

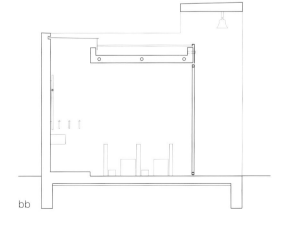

bb

Floor plan
Sections
Scale 1:100

Project data:

Usage:	Religious building
	Fixed
Structure:	Fair-faced concrete
Clear room height:	3 m
Gross volume:	67.50 m³ (including covered entrance area)
Gross floor area:	17.10 m² (including covered entrance area)
Main floor area:	10 m²
Dimensions:	3.08 × 5.54 m
Year of construction:	2007
Construction period:	5 months

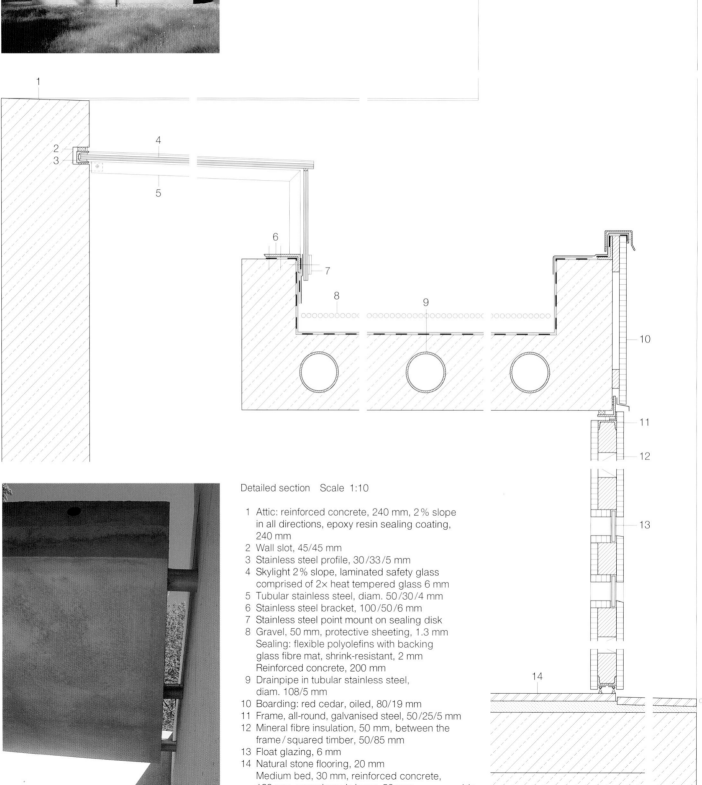

Detailed section   Scale 1:10

1 Attic: reinforced concrete, 240 mm, 2 % slope
   in all directions, epoxy resin sealing coating,
   240 mm
2 Wall slot, 45/45 mm
3 Stainless steel profile, 30/33/5 mm
4 Skylight 2 % slope, laminated safety glass
   comprised of 2× heat tempered glass 6 mm
5 Tubular stainless steel, diam. 50/30/4 mm
6 Stainless steel bracket, 100/50/6 mm
7 Stainless steel point mount on sealing disk
8 Gravel, 50 mm, protective sheeting, 1.3 mm
   Sealing: flexible polyolefins with backing
   glass fibre mat, shrink-resistant, 2 mm
   Reinforced concrete, 200 mm
9 Drainpipe in tubular stainless steel,
   diam. 108/5 mm
10 Boarding: red cedar, oiled, 80/19 mm
11 Frame, all-round, galvanised steel, 50/25/5 mm
12 Mineral fibre insulation, 50 mm, between the
   frame / squared timber, 50/85 mm
13 Float glazing, 6 mm
14 Natural stone flooring, 20 mm
   Medium bed, 30 mm, reinforced concrete,
   160 mm, granular sub-base, 50 mm   bb

Chapel in Lustenau

Architect: Hugo Dworzak, Lustenau

A fascinating, versatile little sanctuary on wheels.

Lustenau football club is famous for the unique atmosphere that prevails after home games. The special post-match backdrop is provided by the so-called Austriadorf, a market-like collection of sales stands for souvenirs, food and drink that serves as a meeting place for those attending the matches every other week.

A recent new addition to the "Austriadorf" is a mobile chapel which can also be used for other occasions, such as weddings or baptisms. The chapel on four wheels fits into a standard parking space measuring 5.00 by 2.50 m, making it suitable for temporary stays at other locations also. Its gable roof in the form of an equilateral triangle symbolises the Holy Trinity.

The chapel is designed as a timber frame construction. Inside it is lined with wood laths positioned at regular intervals. Three benches and the four hub cap covers serve as seating. Fluorescent lamps fitted between the timber frame construction and the outer fabric illuminate the interior at night, setting the chapel aglow through its transparent outer skin. A small door is provided at the front of the structure for daily use. For larger gatherings the side wings and the front can be opened by means of pneumatic springs to form a cross pattern, resulting in a covered outside area. The chapel then becomes the altar, while the stadium acts as the main body of the corresponding "church".

Section · Floor plan
Scale 1:50

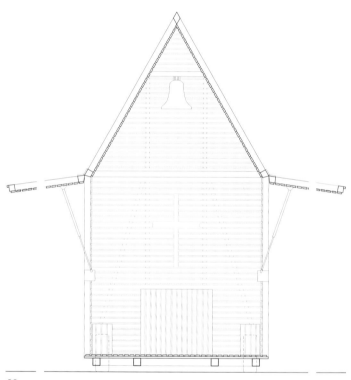

aa

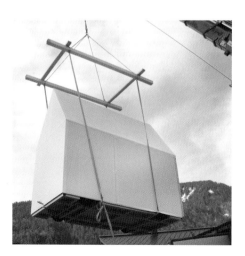

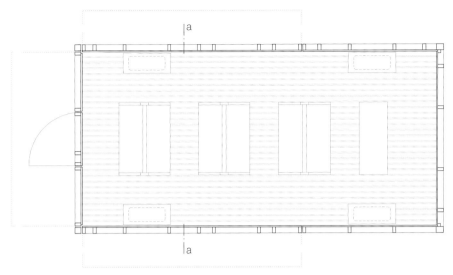

Project data:

Usage:	Religious building
	Mobile
Structure:	Timber post and beam
Clear room height:	4.85 m
Gross volume:	50 m³
Gross floor area:	12 m²
Dimensions:	5.00 × 2.50 m
Construction costs:	€40,000 (gross)
Year of construction:	2007
Construction period:	2 months

"Sehstation" in North Rhine-Westphalia

Architect: Andy Brauneis, Augsburg

Project data:

Usage:	Town "look-out"
	Mobile, temporary
Structure:	Timber frame
Gross volume:	approx. 315 m³
Gross floor area:	approx. 54 m²
Dimensions:	12.00 × 6.80 m
	Height: max. 6.90 m
Construction costs:	€42,000 (gross)
Year of construction:	2008
Assembling period:	1,5 days

The mobile, walk-in "Sehstation", or "Big Window" aims to prompt people to see their towns from a fresh new perspective.

The mobile pavilion is the starting point for the "Sehen lernen" ("Learning to see") campaign organised by the Europäisches Haus der Stadtkultur, which travelled to nine towns in North Rhine-Westphalia in 2008/09 with the aim of giving people a heightened awareness of the towns in which they live. The "Sehstation", or "Big Window", aims to bring people into closer contact with the architecture around them by means of an interactive approach. At Friedensplatz Square in central Oberhausen it focuses on the Parkstadt Oberhausen. Ten other larger-than-life "Sichtfenster" (windows) were installed at selected locations throughout the town. Audio collages relate historical and present-day information on the respective locations. The mobile installation consisting of wooden slats is designed as a walk-in eyepiece. The cuboid is tapered in steps, emphasized as frames in fresh colours. From outside, the object appears as a wooden construction with fine nuances of colour; inside it is perceived as a colourful sculpture. The structure consists of individual veneered laminated wood panels of consecutively increasing length which are bolted immovably together with threaded rods, with alternating horizontal and vertical overlaps at the corners. The entire construction consists of twelve individual sections, each of approx. 1 m in width and each with frame edges of identical length. The "Sehstation" stands on a prefabricated plywood frame construction stiffened with oriented strand boards on the outside. Mobile concrete foundations bear the attendant loads.

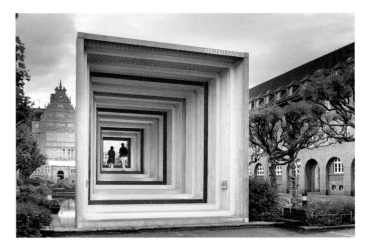

Floor plan • Section
Scale 1:200

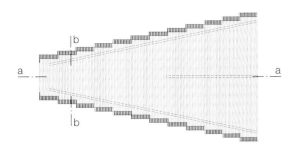

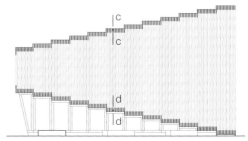

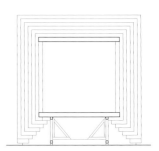

aa   bb

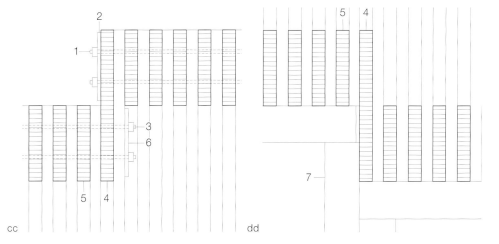

Vertical section, ceiling and base
Scale 1:20

1 Threaded rods, diam. 12 mm
2 Steel plate, 180/180/10 mm
3 Countersunk nuts, diam. 12 mm
4 Veneered laminated wood, 400/33 mm
5 Veneered laminated wood, 200/33 mm
6 Steel plate, 180/180/20 mm
7 Wooden post and beam structure
  solid wood, 100/100 mm
  with multilayered wood boarding on one side

Mobile log house

Architects: olgga architectes, Paris

The mobile log house looks like a temporary art installation – until it is taken by lorry to a new location.

Like a cargo of timber, the log house moves towards its destination on the bed of a lorry. In summer 2009 it was displayed at a French art festival in Nantes where it was on show alongside other examples of microarchitecture and shelters in Frossay, near the Loire. The design for this conjunction of architecture and art was created back in 2006, as part of the "Petites machines à habiter" competition.

The log house evokes associations of a broken branch. The two parts of the building, 3 and 6 metres long respectively, contain a functional area and a living area. They are arranged at an angle, acting as a funnel which entices the visitor to enter the space between them. The building's envelope is comprised of untreated maritime pine logs. The walls merge seamlessly into the monopitch roof, creating a uniform facade. The gable sides facing each other are covered almost entirely with wooden discs that are 16 cm in diameter and protrude to different degrees from the wall, practically concealing the doors. The structures give the appearance of logs that have been stacked for storage. The far end of each structure is fully glazed, providing views into and out of the structures. In addition to this contrast of open and closed, the wood also takes on very different forms in the facade and interior. On the outside, it is raw, with its shape and surface remaining in their natural state, while the interior is smooth, in the form of a solid plywood wall. At 2.50 metres in width, the log house has been designed to perfectly match the dimensions of a lorry. When the structures have reached their destination, a mobile crane places each on wooden planks positioned at different angles to the buildings. No other foundation is necessary. This makes it easier to set up, dismantle and transport the buildings. The journey continues, as the mobile cottage was auctioned off on the internet after the festival.

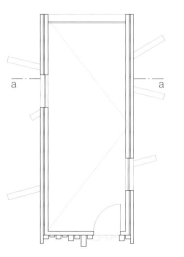

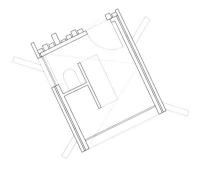

Project data:

Usage:	Accommodation
	Mobile
Structure:	Wood
Clear room height:	1.60–2.70 m
Gross volume:	48.40 m³
Gross floor area:	22.50 m²
Dimensions:	2.50 × 6.00 m and 2.50 × 3.00 m
Construction costs:	€22,000
Year of construction:	2009
Construction period:	1 month

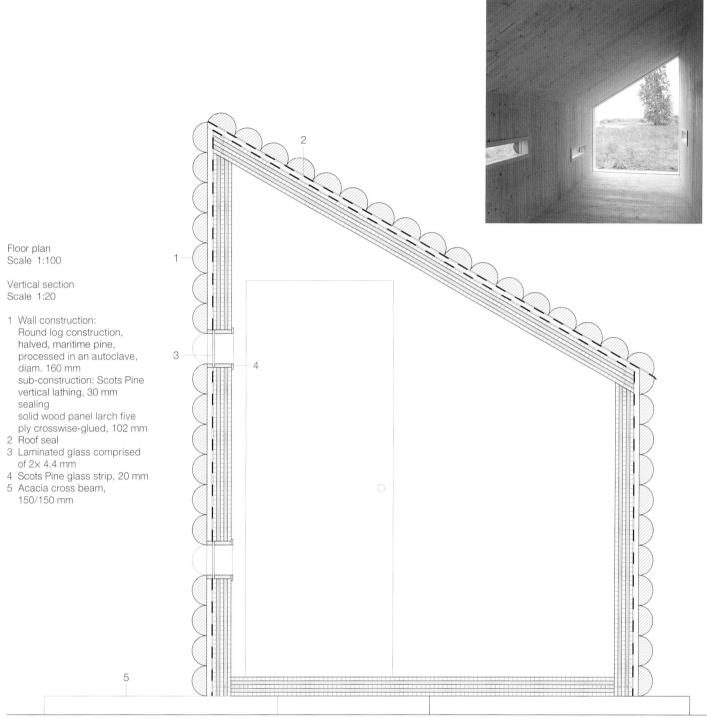

Floor plan
Scale 1:100

Vertical section
Scale 1:20

1 Wall construction:
   Round log construction,
   halved, maritime pine,
   processed in an autoclave,
   diam. 160 mm
   sub-construction: Scots Pine
   vertical lathing, 30 mm
   sealing
   solid wood panel larch five
   ply crosswise-glued, 102 mm
2 Roof seal
3 Laminated glass comprised
   of 2× 4.4 mm
4 Scots Pine glass strip, 20 mm
5 Acacia cross beam,
   150/150 mm

aa

Transformbox

Architect: Bernhard Geiger with Armin Kathan, Innsbruck

Floor plan · Sections
"RescueHomeBox"
Scale 1:50

Detailed sections
Scale 1:10

1 Room module 1
2 Room module 2
3 Room module 3
4 Room module 4
5 Castors for transport
6 Foldable bench/bed combination

plywood, 10 mm
7 Pull-out table top
   plywood, 10 mm
8 Pull-out loft bed
9 Ship's oven, 455/350/345 mm
   retractable chimney
10 Wall structure:
   Aluminium sheet, 0.9 mm
   lightweight building board,
   45 mm
   marine plywood, 4 mm
11 Acrylic glass window, 4 mm
   mounting using strap hinges

Foldable "boxes" in a variety of sizes create spaces that can be used as an emergency shelter, a miniature housing unit or an event box.

The Holz Box Tirol architectural firm has been working intensively on the development of prefabricated wooden structures that offer maximum functionality in a minimum of space for a number of years now. Following their "Minibox" and "Maxibox", Bernhard Geiger has spent the past few years developing the concept for the "Transformbox". These 'residential cubes' are part of a spatial concept in which practical units are housed in foldable volumes. The "Rucksackhaus", or backpack house, is the first to have been created to date, and has been conceived as an emergency shelter for one person. Additional "Transformboxes" are to be created in future in accordance with the same principle, e.g. the "RescueHomeBox", which will house two to four people, and the multi-storey "InterHomeBox" for six to eight people. The sizes of these versatile boxes vary in accordance with the desired interior volume and transport possibilities. Thanks to their modular structure, multiple "homes" can be combined to create larger units. When folded up, the smallest housing unit measures 60 × 50 × 100 cm. Once it has been unfolded, however, it offers a total volume of 1.27 m³. Equipped with a carrying and stand system, the "Rucksackhaus" is ideal as a portable one-person shelter. Thanks to its low transport volume and weight, the box can be set up quickly at various locations using its stand system. Integrated storage space within all "Transformboxes" makes it possible to leave furnishings, supplies and baggage inside the boxes even when they have been folded up. The "RescueHomeBox" offers a total volume of 10.19 m³, and its simple strap hinges allow it to be easily unfolded. The two seats have been integrated into the first, lowermost module, which holds all of the foldable volumes. Here, the foldable benches can be used for desk work, as well as for a bed to sleep on. The second box contains shelves and the oven. WC, shower, kitchenette with refrigerator and additional shelving are found in the third room module. The final module, which is home to the loft bed, also serves as the lid for the box. The boxes have been designed to be self-sufficient energy-wise, with photovoltaic cells on the shell generating electricity for operating the electronic devices. If produced in volume, the "RescueHomeBox" and "InterHomeBox" would fit on a lorry trailer or flat bed lorry, from which they can be placed in the desired location using a crane or helicopter.

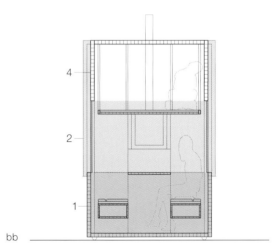

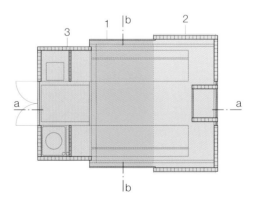

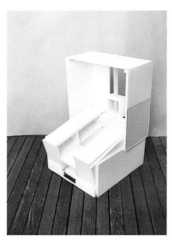
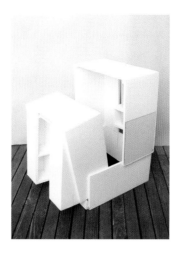
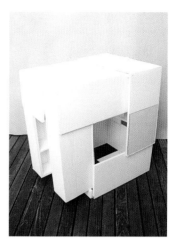

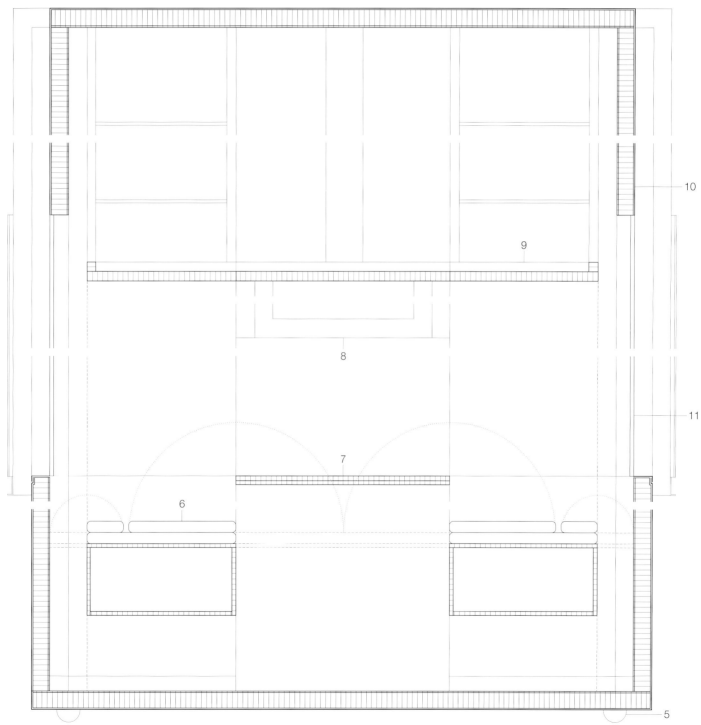

Sections "Rucksackhouse"
Scale 1:20

1 Room module 1
2 Room module 2
3 Room module 3
4 Room module 4
5 Castors for transport
6 Height-adjustable stands
   aluminium, diam. 15 mm
7 Pivoted folding table
   plywood, 4 mm
8 Foldable bench/bed combination
   plywood, 8 mm
9 Storage space
10 Sandwich-lightweight
   building board, 10 mm
11 Acrylic glass window, 3 mm
   Mounting using strap hinges

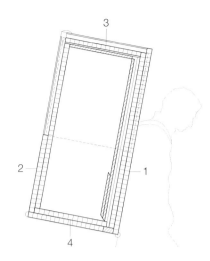

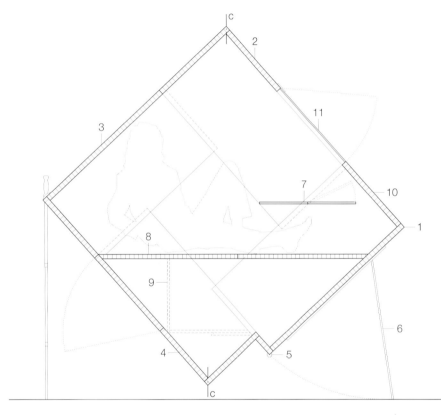
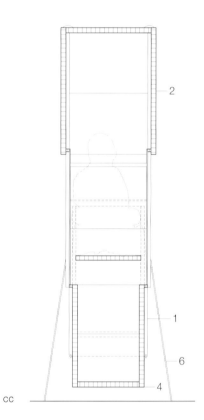

Project data – "Rucksackhouse":

Usage:	Emergency shelter
	Temporary
Structure:	Wood
Clear room height:	approx. 172 cm
Gross volume:	1.27 m³ (unfolded)
	0,30 m³ (folded up)
Gross floor area:	0.6 m² (folded up)
Dimensions:	60 × 50 × 100 cm
Year of construction:	2010
Construction period:	1 month

Convertible pavilion

Architects: Kalhöfer-Korschildgen, Cologne

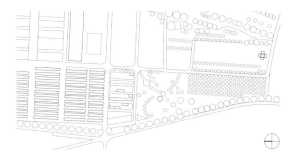

This pavilion can be transformed at will in several stages from an archetypal closed hut into an open shelter, according to the vagaries of the weather and the prevailing atmosphere.

"Let's build three huts!" was the battle cry of the Elisabeth Montag Foundation, which is dedicated to establishing a dialogue between art and architecture.
One of the "huts" which was subsequently installed at the site of a former municipal nursery in Bonn takes the form of an archaically simple yet versatile pavilion. Under the banner "A fleeting sanctuary" ("Raum auf Zeit – Zeit im Raum), the temporary structure offers visitors a weatherproof shelter in which to experience fascinating interactions between inside and outside, structure and artefact.

The pavilion has been sited at a point where overgrown tree plantations, dilapidated greenhouses and open landscape converge. Its compact design contrasts with its surroundings. When the variable side panels are closed, the structure serves as an archetypal hut offering shelter, refuge, comfort and privacy.
Reduced to its essential cubic shape, the structure reaches out into the surrounding terrain on all sides by way of cable-stayed steel beams. These beams serve as rails which allow the side panels to be raised, opening up the interior in steps. In fully open state, the structure consists solely of a roof hovering on a metal frame to afford protection from the sun and rain. The architects have addressed the topic of flexibility by way of a deliberately simple approach employing modern, industrially manufactured materials.

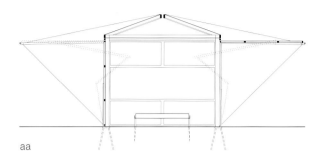

aa

The pavilion's supporting structure consists of L-shaped steel columns on base plates which bear a rigid tent roof construction made of rectangular steel tubing. The four side panels are simple garage doors in tip-up door frames which open outwards, in contrast to their original function. The outer skin consists of white, waterproof polyethylene film, with red scaffold screening mesh serving as an inner lining. The two membranes are fixed to the steel profiles by means of heavy-duty adhesive tape.

Fitted out with a centrally positioned item of furniture which lends itself to a variety of uses, the pavilion serves as a public and private place in one, offering a unique space in which to contemplate the surroundings and absorb a wealth of different atmospheres.

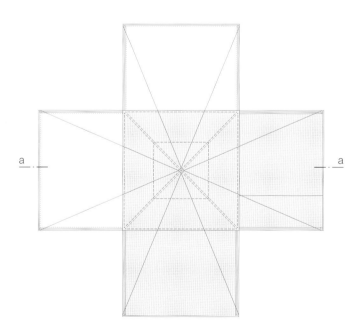

a

a

Site plan
Scale 1:3500

Section · Top view
Scale 1:100

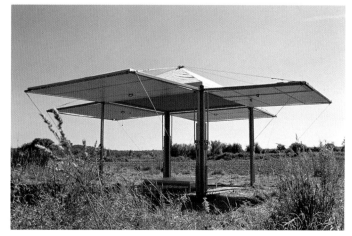

119

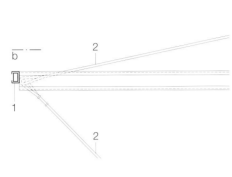

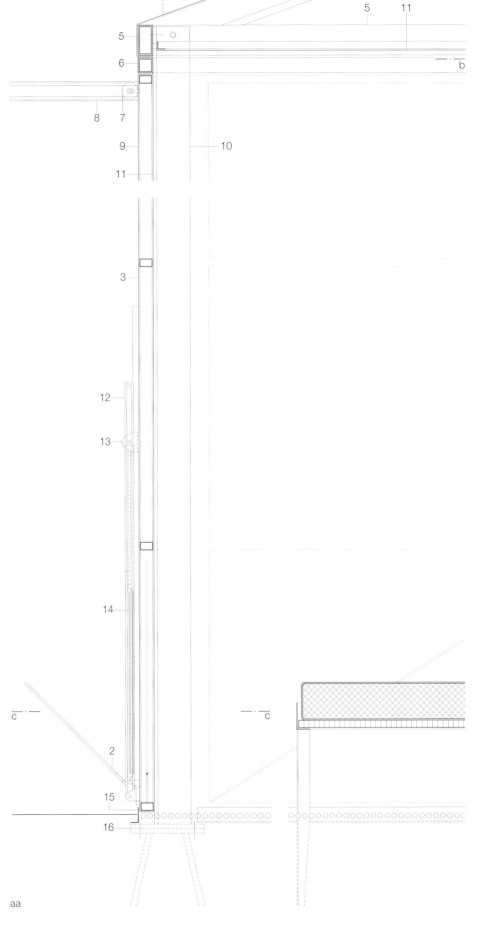

Detailed sections
Scale 1:10

1 Steel spacer profile, 20/30/1 mm
2 Steel staying cable, diam. 6 mm
3 Polyethylene film outer covering,
  mesh-reinforced, waterproof, white
4 Tubular steel hip rafters, 40/80/2 mm
5 Tubular steel eaves frame, 40/80/2 mm
6 Outer frame of door element:
  Tubular steel (vertical), 40/70/1 mm
  Tubular steel (horizontal), 40/40/1 mm
7 Polyamide roller
8 Galvanised steel channel section running rail
  25/50/1 mm
  with tubular steel bracing, 30/40/2 mm
9 Tubular steel door frame, 20/40/2 mm
10 Steel angle column, 100/100/10 mm
11 Inner lining of red scaffold screening mesh
12 Galvanised steel awning profile
13 Galvanised steel lever arm bearing
14 Steel spring
15 Steel profile stop angle, 25/40/2 mm
16 Base plate:
  2 steel profiles, 200/200/12 mm
  with ground anchor – 4 steel bars,
  diam. 40 mm

Project data:

Usage:	Pavilion
	Mobile
Structure:	Steel
Clear room hight:	2.50 m
Gross volume:	30 m³
Gross floor area:	10.50 m²
Dimensions:	3.20 × 3.20 × 3.30 m
Construction costs:	€19,000
Year of construction:	2005
Construction period:	2 weeks

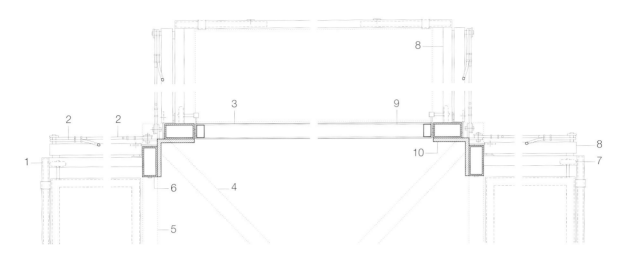

bb

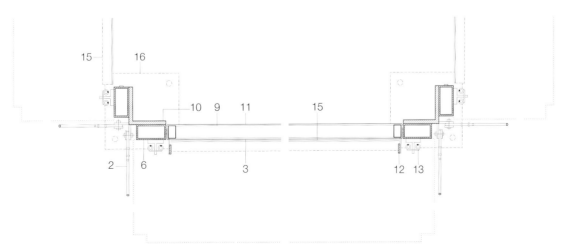

cc

121

Tea house in Frankfurt am Main

Architect: Kengo Kuma & Associates, Tokyo,
with formTL, Radolfzell

This small tea house is a haven of calm and relaxation with its translucent, inflatable shell which glows from within at night-time.

The new tea house stands in the garden of the Museum of Applied Art in Frankfurt am Main. The inflatable textile shell evokes numerous associations, from half a peanut to two golf balls welded together. Inside, a rectangular area measuring 20 m² contains nine tatami mats, with a folding partition separating the preparation room. The room in which the tea ceremony takes place features a charcoal pit in the floor for heating the water.

The sculptural room is available for use on special occasions. The membrane is then delivered on a rolling truck and zipped onto the metal frame running around the concrete base plate; this foundation is not required inside. The high-tech PTFE fabric exudes a textile character, is translucent and particularly robust. Despite its resistance to any external influences, it remains flexible. Welded air-tight, the space between the two layers of the textile skin is inflated like an air bed by means of a ventilation system. The two shell layers are joined by a total of 306 plastic cords installed at a spacing of 60 cm. The "soft shell" stands upright at an internal pressure of 1000 Pa; at a pressure of 1500 Pa it is adequately stable and will even withstand a storm. To enable Japanese tea ceremonies during hours of darkness, the air chamber is illuminated from inside by LED light strips which are integrated into the base frame.

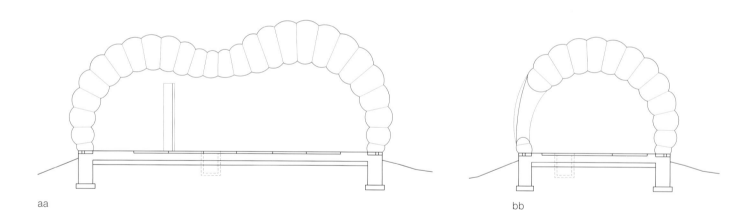

aa   bb

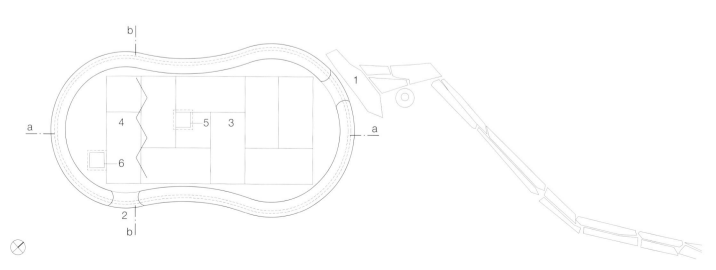

Project data:

Usage:	Events
	Mobile, temporary
Structure:	Self-supporting
	pneumatic membrane
	construction
Clear room height:	2.40 m (tea room),
	2.20 m (preparation
	room)
Gross volume:	56.46 m³
Gross floor area:	31.30 m²
Dimensions:	9.00 × 4.60 × 3.40 m
Construction costs:	€300,000
Year of construction:	2007
Construction period:	2 months

Sections
Floor plan
Scale 1:100

1 Entrance to tea room
2 Entrance to preparation room
3 Tea room
4 Preparation room
5 Fireplace
6 Storage

Axonometric projection – set up sequence
A Concrete base plate with access path
B Installation of tatami mats
C Installation and inflation of the membrane
   construction

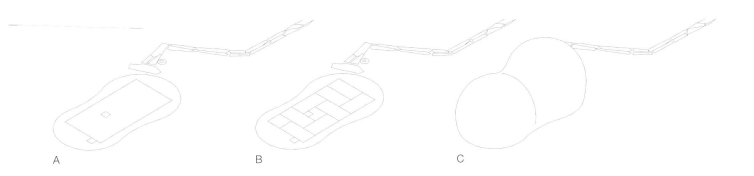

A   B   C

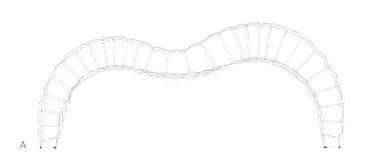

A

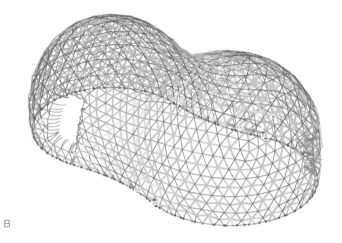

B

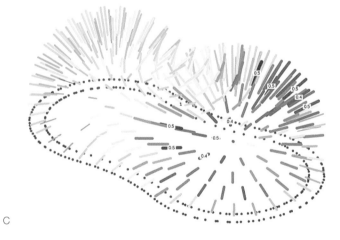

C

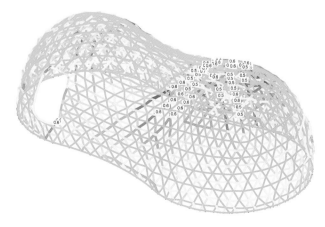

D

Statics – load case side wind
A Deformation
B Stress on outer membrane
C Stress on connecting cords
D Stress on inner membrane

In the load case "initial stress" inner membrane, connecting cords and outer membrane bear the load evenly. In the load case "side wind" deformations occur and a new equilibrium of forces arises between the loads acting from outside and the counteracting forces from inside. The colours show the stress in the membranes and the cords (tension increasing from green to red). A notable aspect is the local strong increases in forces in the connecting cords and in the membranes when wind or heavy rain presses in the pavilion in the middle by up to 40 cm. The connecting cords prevent the two shell layers from separating; the air package in between the two layers is additionally compressed. This results in local increases in membrane stress and in the tensile forces in the connecting cords, the sum effect of which is to further stabilise the shell. The stability and load-bearing capacity of this construction method are attributable to this "constant volume" principle.

Detail – base connection of membrane cushion
Scale 1:5

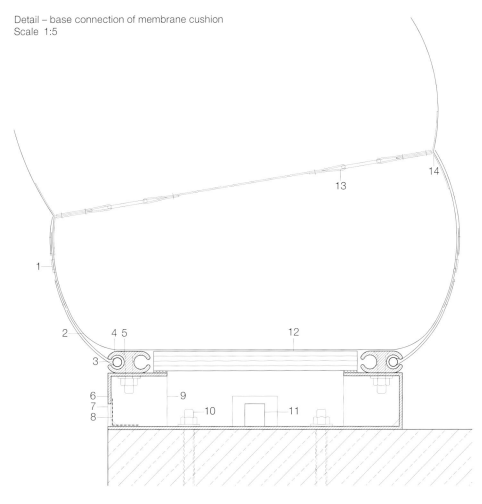

1 Zipper, segment length, 2000 mm
2 PTFE fabric, 630 g/m², with laminated-on fluorofilm, 38 % translucence
3 Cotter, diam. 12 mm
4 Aluminium profile
5 Countersunk bolt, diam. 12 mm
6 Metal frame, 75/400 mm
7 Drainage hole
8 Insect screen
9 Steel plate bracing, 76/67/4 mm
10 Connection anchor, diam. 12 mm
11 LED lighting, illuminates inner and outer membrane
12 Acrylic glass cover, 275/26 mm
13 Plastic connecting cord
14 Round membrane reinforcement, PTFE fabric with full-surface bonding on inside, with tab for connecting cords, diam. 100 mm

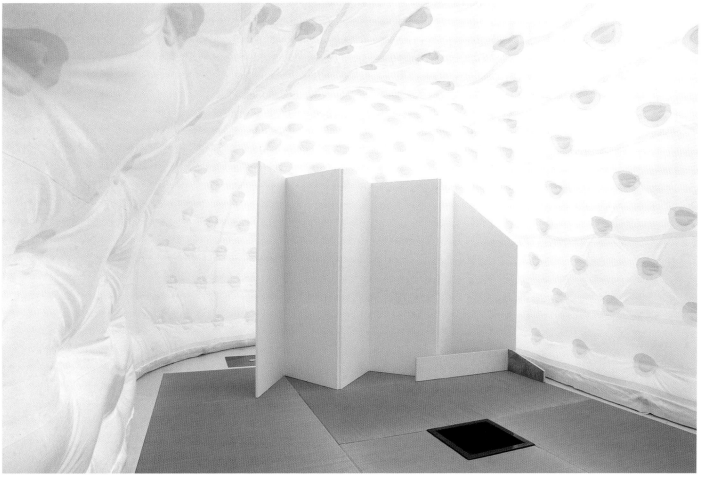

Aero House

Architects: Richard Horden, Wieland Schmidt,
Technical University of Munich,
Helmut Richter, Technical University of Vienna,
with students

A digital process was used to create this futuristic capsule made from high-quality materials – from the design through to its execution.

The Aero House is a light, transportable miniature housing unit that can be adapted to a wide range of locations and quickly set up as a temporary space. The capsule offers a comfortable refuge from the weather for one or two people. It can be transported on the roof of a car, and quickly transformed into a hovering sleeping pod on legs. Its tripod base allows the house to maintain its balance on widely varying surfaces. The capsule, which is 1.30 metres above ground level, is accessed through a folding door on the bottom at the rear. Openable elements in the front windows provide the necessary ventilation. With a length of approx. 2.7 metres, this double-bent hollow body weighs only 26 kg. In contrast to its rigid exterior shell, which has been fashioned from 10 mm thick carbon sandwich elements, the interior has been furnished in a soft nylon fabric. The idea for this structure was developed in a seminar at the Technical University of Munich, with the support of the Technical University of Vienna. In 1996, students had already developed a portable housing unit which they

christened the "Fish House", and which was intended primarily as a temporary shelter for fishers on the Danube. Twelve years later, students in the architecture and product development faculties at the Technical University of Munich worked with various faculties and companies to create a prototype, which was presented for the first time in 2009.

The planning and production process

By tailoring the planning to the production processes, it was possible to reduce to a minimum the number of conventional plans and drawings required. Planning data were obtained using digital 3D models and fed directly into production. The objective was to create a structure which was as light as possible, and the students quickly settled on the material for the shell, as only carbon fibre-reinforced plastic provided the desired reduction in weight while also meeting the demands for the stability of the outer shell. To start with, a 3D model of the existing 1:6 model of the "Fish House" was created using a 3D laser scanner, so that individual points on its surface could be calculated. The results of this effort were not very precise, however, so an extremely high-precision scanner from the automotive industry was used to scan the model again, in order to obtain exact 3D data. This flexible optical measurement device is based on the principle of triangulation. Fringe patterns are projected and measured by two cameras in order to calculate 3D coordinates for each of the observed camera pixels. The result is a polygon mesh of a million points stretching across the entire surface of the object. In order to derive a homogenous surface from this polygonal mesh, a series of sections are generated in three directions. By using software that guarantees mechanical precision and seamless integration into the design process, it was possible to use the digital models to create a perfectly smooth surface that could be controlled via a few points. In the next step, a computer-controlled 5-axis-CNC-milling machine was used to construct two reusable moulds for the floor and roof of the carbon shell. These were ground, painted and coated with release agent to prepare them for the laminating process. Students performed the laminating process under expert supervision, using a vacuum process to create the sturdy composite of carbon fibre, resin and an insulation layer. After both parts of the capsule had been put together, a metallic paint was applied in a multistep process.

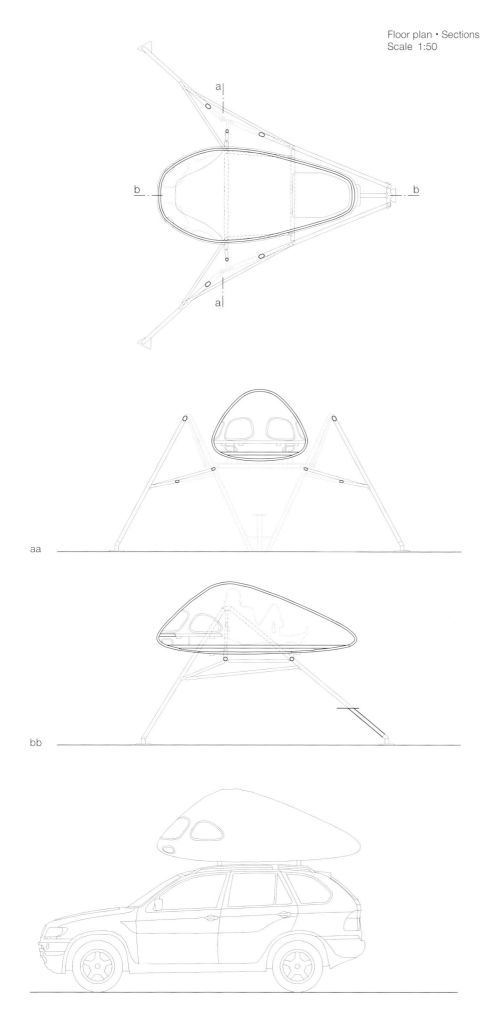

a

b ·   · b

a

aa

bb

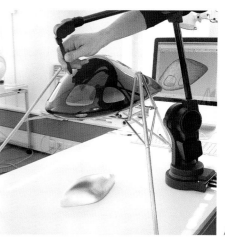

A

B

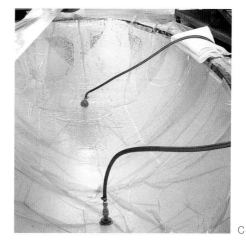

C

D

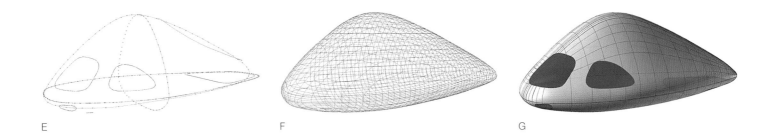

E

F

G

A "Fish House" scanned using a 3D laser scanner.
B Students as they wet-laminate the lower shell with carbon fibre-reinforced plastic.
C Vacuum process for the shell. A vacuum pump is used to exert 900 kg/m² of pressure on the shells as they harden.
D Painting the assembled capsule.
E 3D model after the points have been calculated using the 3D laser scanner.
F Sectional views of the high-precision 3D model in accordance with the principle of triangulation.
G 3D model with homogenous and controllable surface before the production process.

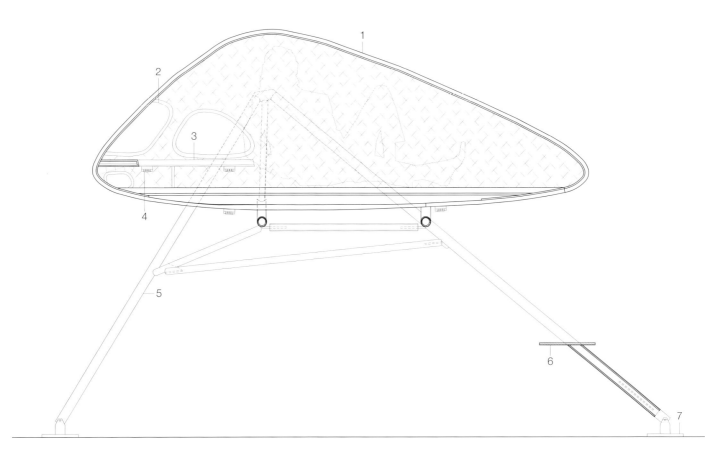

Section
Scale 1:20

1 Wall structure:
  Composite material comprising carbon
  fibre-reinforced plastic with acrylic glass
  foam core, 10 mm
  nylon fabric interior lining
2 Acrylic glass, 4 mm
3 Particle board shelf, 15 mm
4 LED lighting
5 Tube, diam. 55 mm, made of
  carbon fibre-reinforced plastic
6 Aluminium step, 5 mm
7 Aluminium foot joint and
  foot plate, 5 mm

Project data:

Usage:	Accommodation
	Mobile
Structure:	Stand: Carbon fibre-reinforced plastic
	Capsule: Sandwich construction made from
	carbon fibre-reinforced plastic
Clear room height:	0.80 m
Gross volume:	1.40 m³
Gross floor area:	2.60 m²
Dimensions:	2.70 × 1.30 m
Weight:	Stand: 18 kg
	Capsule: 26 kg
Construction costs:	€18,000 (gross)
Year of construction:	2009
Construction period:	4 weeks

"Desert Seal" tent

Architects: Architecture and Vision, Munich / Bomarzo

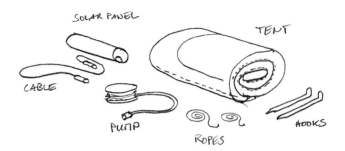

This tent can be set up in just 15 minutes to provide sleeping quarters that are well equipped for desert conditions, with a fan, solar panel and reflective outer skin.

The design of this inflatable tent for hot, arid regions is based on the microclimate which prevails in the desert. During the day the temperatures drop substantially the further one is from the ground – an effect which is also exploited by camel riders on the high backs of their animals.

A fan powered by a flexible solar panel continually blows in cooler air from above. Batteries store the solar energy to supply warmer air to the lower part of the tent during the night, when the temperatures directly over the ground drop sharply. The slight pressure inside helps to stabilise the bivouac in addition to the structure of inflatable tubes. Aluminium panels hold the fan on top and the air outlet at the bottom in position at the narrow ends. The aluminium-lined outer skin reflects the daytime heat.

The construction weighting 5 kg is completely rolled up for transportation and is inflated by means of a pump. Hooks are then inserted, the air mattress is placed inside and the solar panel is strapped in place. The concept originated from an European Space Agency technology transfer programme. A low transport volume and low weight resulting from pneumatic structures, the use of locally available resources and a tolerable interior climate in a hostile environment are crucial factors in space, too. The high-tech tent has yet to make it into space, but it has found a place in the MoMA collection in New York.

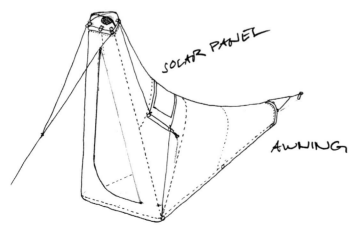

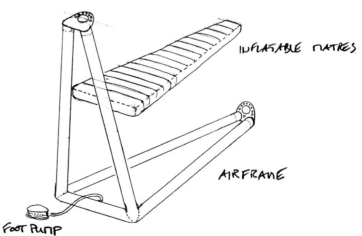

Sketches of individual components · complete bivouac · pneumatic structure

Construction sequence

Elevations   Scale 1:50
Temperature above ground during daytime

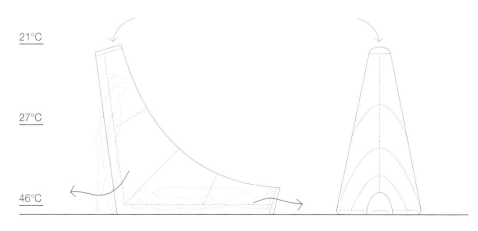

21°C

27°C

46°C

Project data:

Usage:	Survival, accomodation
	Mobile
Structure:	Membrane, inflatable
	A-frame construction
Clear room hight:	0.35 – 2.10 m
Gross volume:	0.90 m³
Gross floor area:	1.60 m²
Dimensions:	2.35 × 1.25 × 2.26 m
Construction costs:	€4700 (first prototype)
Year of construction:	2005
Construction period:	2 weeks
Set-up:	By one person in 15 min.

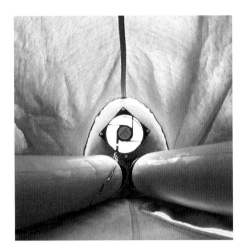

Detailed section of top end
Scale 1:2.5

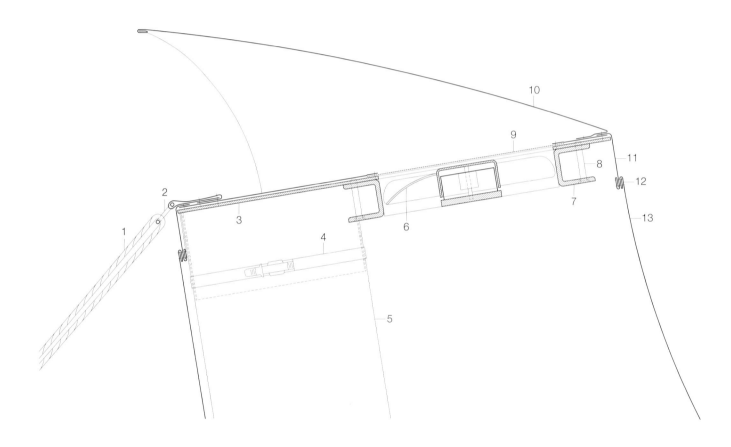

1 Polyamide rope, 3 mm
2 Stainless steel D-ring
3 Shaping end element in aluminium, 2 mm:
   Perforated head plate with welded-on tubes
   (aluminium tubes bonded to pneumatic tubes)
4 Safety lock, tensioning strap
5 Supporting structure: polyethylene pneumatic
   tubes, polyurethane-coated, yellow, diam.
   120 mm
6 12 volt fan, diam. 120 mm
7 Fan frame
8 Stainless steel screw, diam. 4 mm
9 Synthetic fleece dust and sand filter
10 Cover for protection from dust and sand,
   polyurethane-coated polyethylene, yellow
11 Polyurethane-coated polyethylene, yellow
12 Reinforced seam, double-stitched
13 Polyester outer skin with aluminium lining,
   heat-reflecting

Rucksack House

Artist: Stefan Eberstadt, Munich

The Rucksack House – sculpture, parasite and private "out-house" in one – wanders from one house facade to the next.

Housebuilding commonly focuses on straight facades and standardised ground plans. The Rucksack House is an attempt to improve the quality of housing on an individualised basis, thereby exploring the dividing line between architecture and art. Formwork panels as cladding, the unusual arrangement of the windows and the archaic nature of the suspension cables pointedly define this add-on unit as a foreign body. The wood-panelled steel cage consisting of rectangular tubes hangs like a rucksack from steel cables which pass over the roof of the building behind, making two diversions before they are anchored in the rear facade. A lorry crane lifts the cube into position in front of the facade and four bolts are inserted into corresponding holes drilled into the building beforehand. The suspension cables are then attached while the cube is still suspended from the crane. Inside, the cube houses a "hovering light room" outside of the apartment to which it is docked. The room protrudes into public space, maintaining its privacy inside despite being exposed by windows on five sides. The interior does not define any specific use. Wall panels can be folded down to form a platform for lying on, a table and a stool. Produced as a temporary installation at a former cotton spinning mill in Leipzig, the structure was designed without thermal insulation. Additional static measures were undertaken in view of the substance of the old building structure to which the cube is attached. The Rucksack House has been shown at plan05 in Cologne (see p. 55) and several architecture festivals.

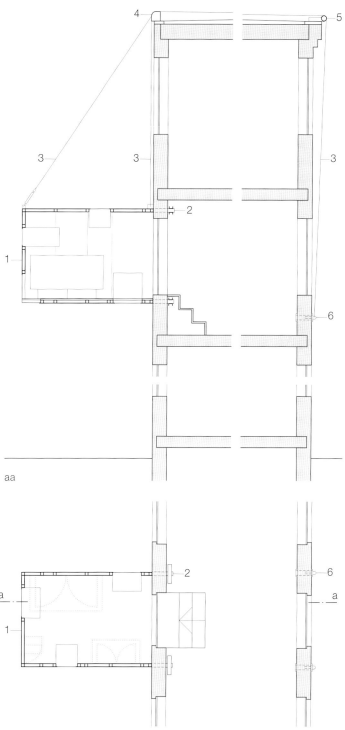

aa

Project data:

Usage:	Accommodation
	Temporary
Structure:	Steel
Clear room height:	2.30 m
Gross volume:	22.50 m³
Gross floor area:	9 m²
Dimensions:	2.50 × 3.60 × 2.50 m
Construction costs:	€25,000 (prototype without installation)
Year of construction:	2004
Construction period:	2 months
Duration of suspension process:	4–5 hours

Section · Floor plan   Scale 1:100

1 Rucksack House
2 Anchor bolts
3 Steel cable, diam. 16 mm
4 Squared timber deflector
5 Tubular steel deflector
6 Rear anchorage in masonry

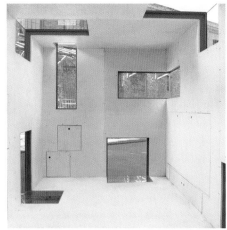

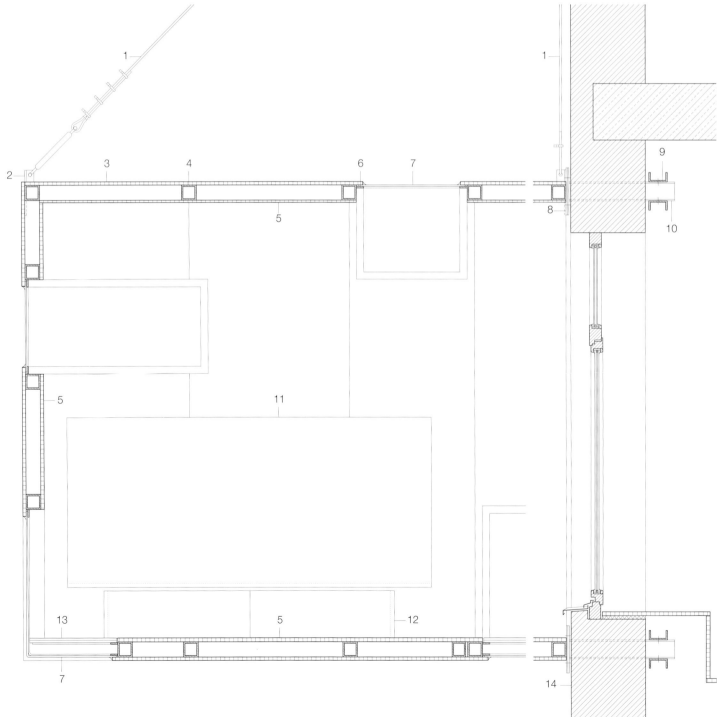

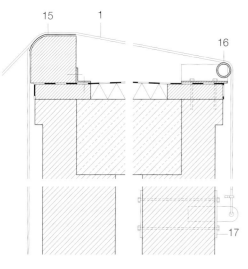

Section through street facade
Section through rear anchoring with steel cable
Scale 1:20

1 Stainless-steel cable with turnbuckle,
   diam. 16 mm
2 Steel angle with eye, welded to steel frame
3 Resin-coated lam. construction board, 18 mm
4 Steel SHS cage, 80/80/3.2 mm
5 Lam. birch construction board, ceiling 12 mm,
   wall 18 mm, floor 21 mm
6 Support for glazing flat steel bar, 4 mm
7 Extruded perspex fixed glazing, bent to 90°
   angle at edge of structure, sealed with
   silicone, 8 mm
8 Steel plate, welded to steel cage,
   250/250/20 mm

9 Steel restraining channel, 100 mm
   500 mm long
10 Steel I-beam, 100 mm, with
   flange plate, 250/250/20 mm
11 Wall panel, 2,000/900/18 mm magnetically
   fixed, pivoting down as divan
12 Plywood flap, folding out
   as support for divan
13 Cast perspex sheet floor reinforcement,
   25 mm
14 Existing brick wall, 400 mm
15 Steel sheet, 4 mm, on timber bearer,
   250/250 mm
16 Steel tube, diam. 120 mm, welded to steel
   channel
17 Steel anchor plate, 250/250/15 mm,
   with bolts, 4× diam. 16 m

Mobile roof terrace in Cologne

Architects: Kalhöfer-Korschildgen, Cologne

Raising the roof to new pastoral heights. This mobile roof terrace conjures up a picnic setting and provides storage space for garden furniture.

A picnic on a sunny day with the requisite table and folding chairs, with a grandstand view from one's own rooftop: A mobile panel fitted with garden furniture, crockery and lighting and a built-in flight of stairs is all it takes. Following the renovation of their residence, the occupants of a semi-detached house dating from the 1970s are now able to make full use of their roof, too. The panel is raised by means of a simple hand crank. A motor-powered variant was also tested and offered as an alternative, but the building's owner found the manual solution more in keeping with the overall character of the project. In a retracted state the panel serves to partition off the stairs and provides compact storage space for the garden furniture. When opened up on the terrace, it becomes a backdrop providing a decorative border for the "picnic area". The residents are able to remove and set up the integrated furniture in next to no time. The surface of the panel is embellished with floral patterns which harmonise well with the hand-laid artificial turf floor.
The construction is based on a standard self-supporting sliding door which has been turned by 90 degrees and faced with timber boarding and painted sheet steel. The door runs in vertical rails installed on either side and is raised manually by means of cables which are fixed to the bottom edges and diverted by guide pulleys on the frame of the roof hatch. A counterweight facilitates raising and lowering of the panel and a wing bolt at the top edge fixes the door in position on the roof.

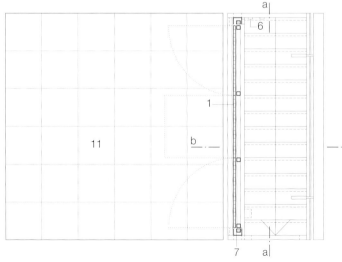

Project data:

Usage:	Accomodation
	Fixed
Structure:	Steel, plywood facing with
	sheet steel lining
Gross floor area:	13.2 m²
Dimensions:	4.40 × 3.00 m (mobile roof terrace)
	9.05 × 7.24 m (total roof surface area)
Construction costs:	€29,000 (gross, for roof terrace with entrance)
Year of construction:	2008
Construction period:	1 month

Floor plan · Sections
Scale 1:50

1 Sliding door
2 Legs for fold-out tabletop
3 Console for garden chairs
4 Cable winch with rollback lock
5 Guide pulley for cabling
6 Power socket
7 Rail
8 Counterweight
9 Lock
   Flat steel bar with
   wing bolt
10 Ventilating flap
   motor-operated
11 Artificial turfing

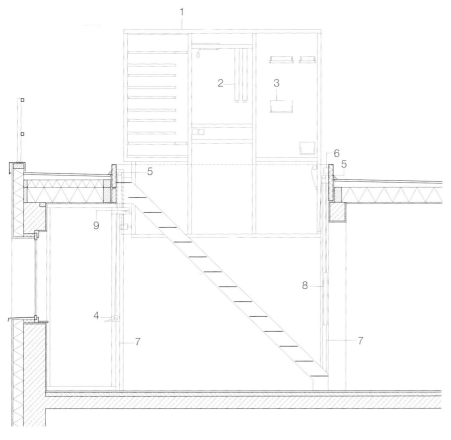

aa

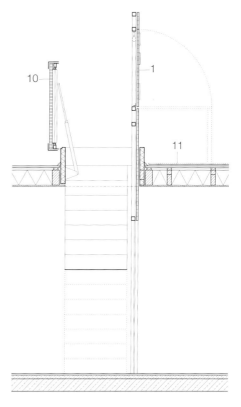

bb

Detailed section
Scale 1:10

1 Acrylic glass three-web
  panel, 32 mm
  acrylic glass, transparent,
  8 mm
  PVC frame
2 Aluminium sheet frame,
  2× 2 mm
  thermal insulation
  mineral wool, 60 mm
3 Safety matting, 30 mm
  with artificial turf covering
  two-ply bitumen sheeting
  boarding, 24 mm

sloping wood, 30–60 mm
beams, 60/60 mm
vapour barrier
beams, 60/140 mm, with
thermal insulation in between
gypsum plaster board, 10 m
4 Timber frame, 100/60 mm
5 Painted sheet steel, 1 mm
  laminated wood panel,
  24 mm
  tubular steel 60/60 mm
6 Magnetic film with
  rose motif
7 Sheet steel console, 1 mm
8 Guide wheel for cabling
9 Step in welded flat steel, 8 mm

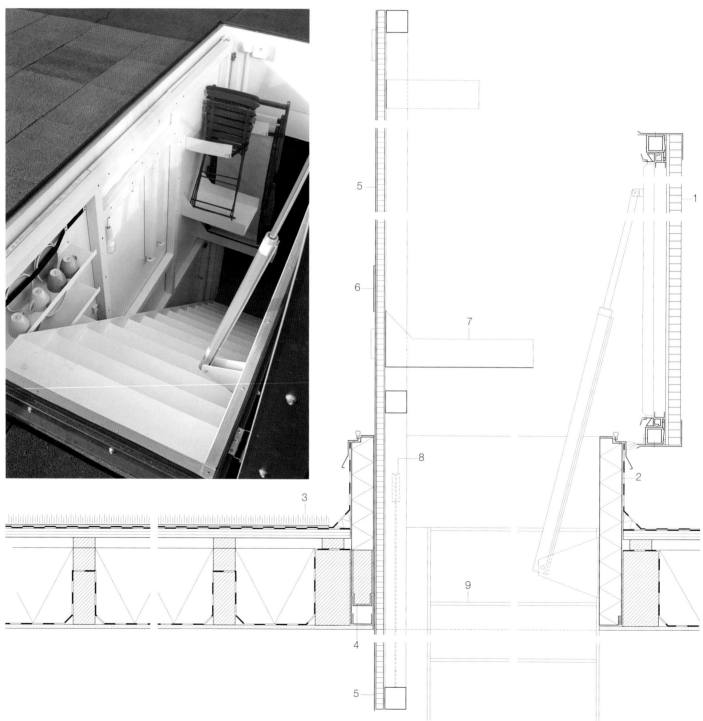

Bedroom and playroom furniture

Architects: h2o architectes, Paris

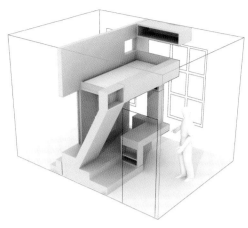

Whether it be as a room divider for a separate children's room or as a shared play area, loft bed furniture is able to perform multiple functions simultaneously.

Following the birth of another child, a children's room in an apartment in Paris' 10th arrondissement is to be divided into two areas so that each child can have their own zone. Instead of a partition wall, the architects decide to place an element in the centre of the room which functions as a room divider, loft bed and play facility at the same time. This room high, 2.96 × 1.28 m element features a complex design. The back offers a nearly smooth wall surface, while the front is practically an invitation to play, with a table, shelves, niches, stairs and stepped platforms for climbing, drawing and hiding. When the integrated sliding doors are closed, the rear portion serves as a sleeping area for the younger child, while the older daughter can play to her heart's content on the other side. Shelves and compartments are ideal for storing books and toys, and even the base itself can be used for storage, as this space conceals chests with lids. The furniture element was built using 20 mm thick MDF boards attached to a squared timber sub-construction which was assembled and bolted together on location. The structure is self-supporting and self-reinforcing. The bed area rests on the stairs and the shelves, which are designed as supports. Attached to both the ceiling and floor, this furniture element can be easily removed to allow the room to be used in other ways. The silk matt, light grey-blue coating lends this elegant element an air of lightness, providing an unobtrusive backdrop for the children's colourful world.

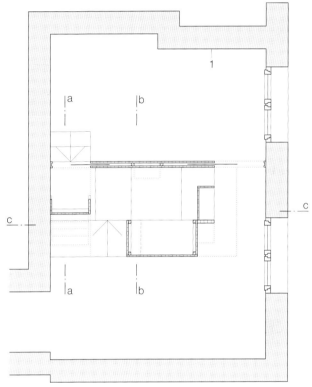

Plan · Section   Scale 1:50

1 Existing wall
2 Games table
3 Loft bed
4 Storage space

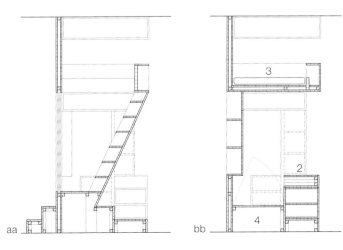

139

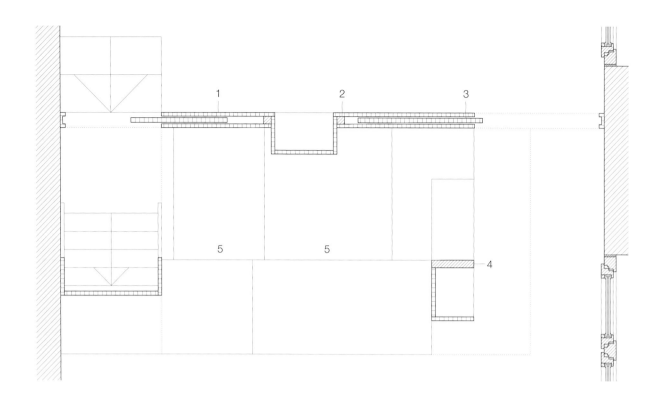

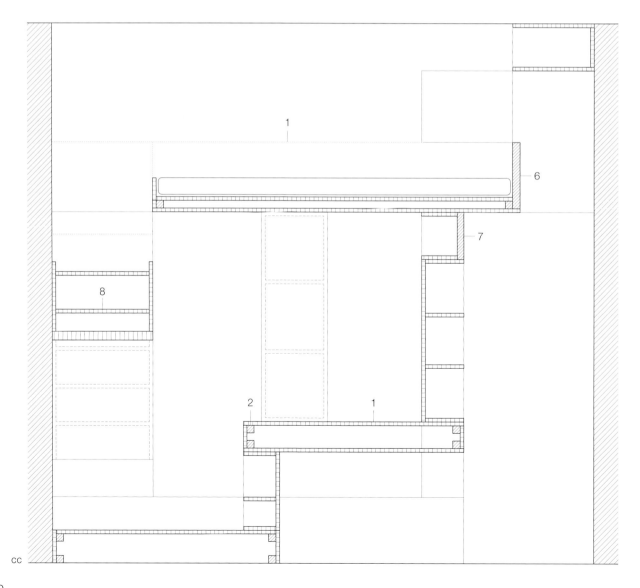

Horizontal section · Vertical section
Scale 1:20

1 MDF boards with a grey-blue coating,
  20 mm thick
2 Squared timber 50/50 mm
3 Sliding door MDF 20 mm
4 Squared timber support 40/230 mm
5 Storage space lid MDF 20 mm
6 Squared timber beam 40/370 mm, front MDF
7 Squared timber beam 40/230 mm, front MDF
8 Step MDF 20 mm

Project data:

Usage:	Accommodation
	Fixed
Structure:	Wood
Clear room height:	1.90 m
Gross floor area:	3.50 m²
Dimensions:	2.96 × 1.28 × 2.86 m
Construction costs:	€5,000 (net)
Year of construction:	2009
Construction period:	2 weeks

Summer houses in Berlin

Architects: Hütten & Paläste, Berlin

"MiLa" project data:

Usage:	Leisure facility
	Fixed
Structure:	Wooden post and beam
Clear room height:	3.25 m
Gross volume:	51.50 m³
Gross floor area:	16 m²
Dimensions:	5.00 × 3.17 m
	Eaves height: 2.25 m, roof ridge height: 3.50 m
Construction costs:	€10,500 (gross, cost of materials)
Year of construction:	2006
Assembling period:	3–4 days

The special appeal of the MiLa, DuLa and CaLa summer houses stems from their unconventional layouts and individual designs.

For many people, allotments are the epitome of staid suburban tastelessness, while others value them as a sanctuary away from the hustle and bustle of town and city life and a place to grow one's own produce. In recognition of these merits, the gardeners' association Landesverband Berlin der Gartenfreunde e. V. commissioned architects Hütten & Paläste to develop types of summer houses which would appeal to young families in particular. This resulted in "MiLa", "DuLa" and "CaLa". Special features common to all the house types are their layouts offering plenty of space inside, despite their highly compact design, and large fully openable glass doors. The ground plans all meet the strict requirements of German law on allotments, which stipulate a maximum size of 24 m². Another common feature of all the house types is the gable roof, the advantage here being that the aforesaid law permits a height of 3.50 m for gable roofs, while flat and monopitch roofs are restricted to 2.60 m. This would rule out use of the attic, which figured as an integral part of the architects' design in each instance.

Different types of summer house for different needs

The mini-house MiLa incorporates all the key functions assignable to a summer house in a ground plan of 16 m². The spacious, light and airy recreation room which can be opened up towards the garden forms the centre of the house. The practical functions are accommodated in the adjoining room to the left – a compost toilet, a worktop for handling the harvest and a spacious tool cabinet. Above these rooms is an attic bedroom which can be used for a variety of purposes, with a large skylight offering night-time views of the sky. The wide terrace in front of the house offers 5 m² of space for sun-lovers. The wooden post and beam structure is provided with light insulation to prevent overheating in the sunshine. The facade consists of robust yellow wooden panels – a mass-produced article from the concrete casting industry. MiLa is available in yellow, red, fir green, dark brown and natural finish.

DuLa features large sliding elements which open up to provide a seamless connection between the roof-ridge-high recreation room and the garden. This lends the 6 × 4 m family-style summer house a special open and spacious character. The windows next to the entrance door can also be opened fully, creating a counter which can be used simultaneously on the inside and outside.

In addition to its open, practical layout, the 6.30 × 3.80 m CaLa house also offers users a choice of facade variants. It comes with spruce bevel siding in various colours, for example, with wooden tiles, with a plaster facade or with wooden shingles.

The complete house is available for delivery around eight weeks after receipt of order. The prefabricated units are assembled in three to four days. Those wishing to can also assemble the summer house themselves.

A

B

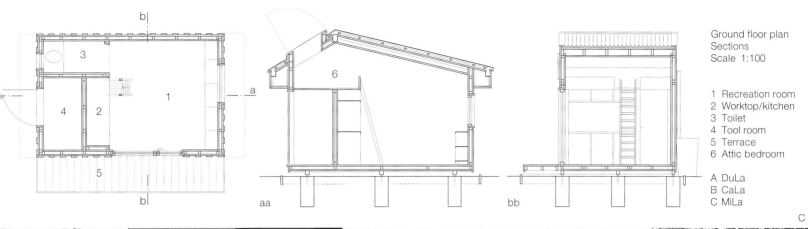

Ground floor plan
Sections
Scale 1:100

1 Recreation room
2 Worktop/kitchen
3 Toilet
4 Tool room
5 Terrace
6 Attic bedroom

A DuLa
B CaLa
C MiLa

C

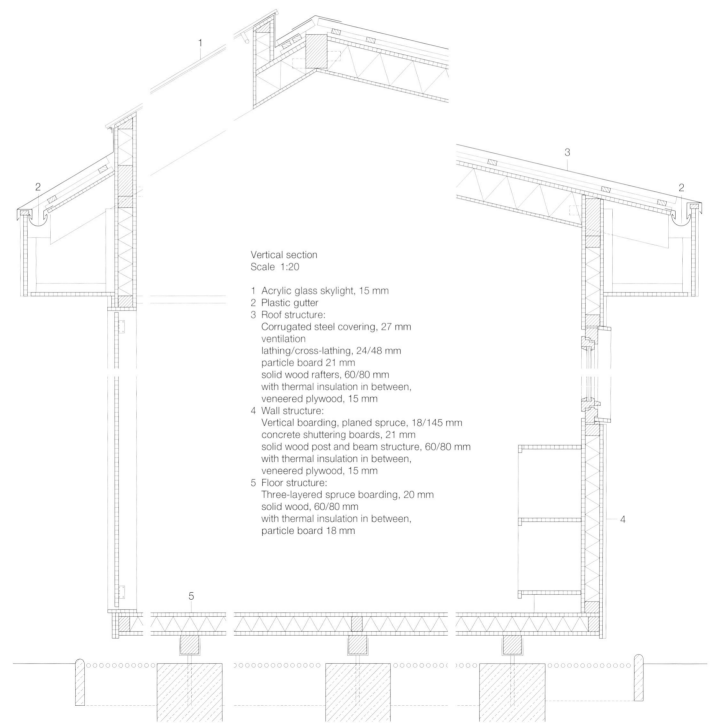

Vertical section
Scale 1:20

1 Acrylic glass skylight, 15 mm
2 Plastic gutter
3 Roof structure:
  Corrugated steel covering, 27 mm
  ventilation
  lathing/cross-lathing, 24/48 mm
  particle board 21 mm
  solid wood rafters, 60/80 mm
  with thermal insulation in between,
  veneered plywood, 15 mm
4 Wall structure:
  Vertical boarding, planed spruce, 18/145 mm
  concrete shuttering boards, 21 mm
  solid wood post and beam structure, 60/80 mm
  with thermal insulation in between,
  veneered plywood, 15 mm
5 Floor structure:
  Three-layered spruce boarding, 20 mm
  solid wood, 60/80 mm
  with thermal insulation in between,
  particle board 18 mm

Beach houses in Domburg

Architects: WTS Architecten, Vlissingen

Compact in design to facilitate transportation by lorry, these small houses nevertheless offer all the necessary amenities for holidays at the beach.

Holidaymakers in the North Sea town of Domburg can live their dream of inhabiting their own beach house – at least for the duration of their holiday. Here in the south-west of the Netherlands, ten beach houses with their own terraces are available for rent from April to the end of October. At the end of the season the small houses with gable roof are removed and placed in safe storage for the winter. Their dimensions have been limited to 3.52 × 7.52 m, so as to enable them to be loaded onto lorries in one piece. The houses are built around steel frames consisting of U-profiles which fit precisely onto the transport lorries.
A timber-framed construction which rises over the steel frame is lined with oriented-strand boards. As the houses are situated very closely together, fire-retardant gypsum fibre boards are installed as inner linings on the ceilings and walls to prevent fire from spreading from one building to the next. The outer shell of HPL panelling shimmers in silver grey, blending harmoniously into the dune landscape.
The fully glazed gable end offers a view of the beach and sea with the entrance door situated on the opposite side facing the dunes.
A small kitchenette and a sanitary area are provided, while a steep single-flight wooden staircase leads up to the low attic which serves as a sleeping area. This layout ensures that the 26 m² of floor space is adequate for a family with three children. A generously sized terrace leads down to the beach.

Section
Ground floor plan
Scale 1:100

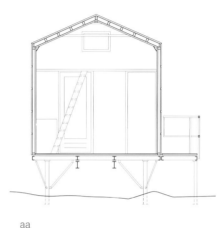

aa

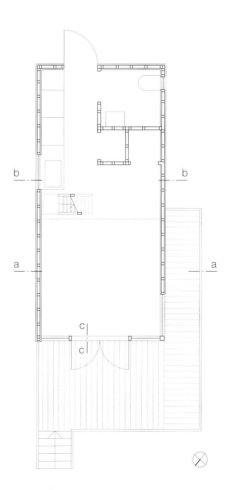

Project data:

Usage:	Accommodation
	Temporary
Structure:	Steel frame, timber frame
Clear room height:	2.10 m (main room)
	0.53–1.06 m (attic)
Gross volume:	87 m³
Gross floor area:	26 m²
Attic floor space:	10 m²
Terrace:	12 m²
Dimensions:	3.52 × 7.52 m
Construction costs:	approx. €40,000
Year of construction:	2008
Construction period:	5 months for 5 beach houses
Installation:	1 day per house

145

Detailed sections
Scale 1:10

1

2

3

4

5

6

7

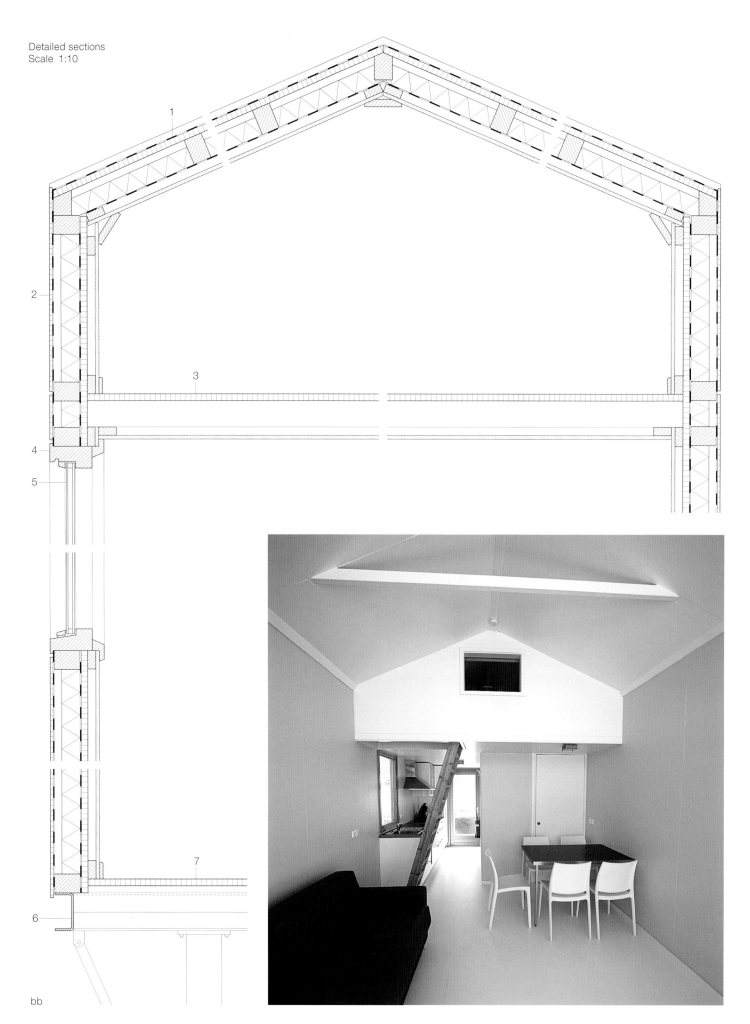

bb

146

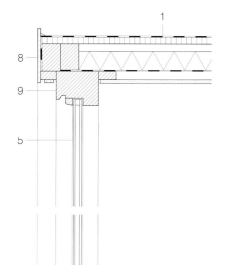

1 Roof structure:
  Plastic roof covering layer
  oriented-strand board, 18 mm
  Rafters and purlins, 70/50 mm, with
  50 mm mineral wool insulation in between
  vapour barrier, lathing, 22 mm
  fibrous plaster sheeting, 10 mm
2 Wall structure:
  HPL panelling with visible screws,
  silver-grey, 8 mm, black sealing
  timber frame, 70/50 mm, with
  50 mm mineral wool insulation in between
  vapour barrier
  oriented-strand board, 18 mm
  lathing, 22 mm
  fibrous plaster sheeting, 10 mm
3 Floor construction:
  oriented-strand board, 18 mm
  timber beams, 70/50 mm

  lathing, 22 mm
  fibrous plaster sheeting, 10 mm
4 Meranti timber frame, 67/114 mm
5 Thermopane glazing, 4 mm float glass +
  12 mm cavity + 6 mm float glass
6 Edge girder, cold rolled steel profile,
  100/50/5 mm
7 oriented-strand board, 18 mm
  steel I-section, 100 mm, with
  70/50 mm timber beams in between
8 HPL panel, silver-grey, 8 mm
9 Timber frame, 90/114 mm
10 Timber frame terrace door,
  Meranti, two-leaf
11 Thermopane glazing, 4 mm float glass +
  8 mm cavity + 6 mm float glass
12 Terrace floor hardwood planking, 22 mm
13 Slide rails for transportation,
  steel I-section, 180 mm

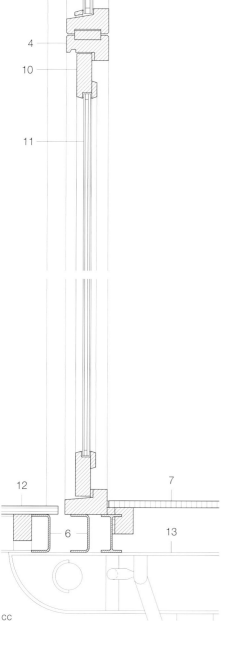

cc

Residential building in Tokyo

Architects: Claus en Kaan Architecten,
Amsterdam/Rotterdam with
Souhei Imamura/Atelier IMAMU, Tokyo

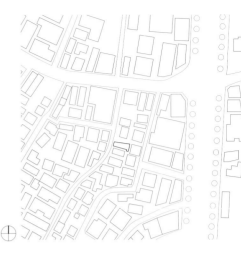

Site plan
Scale 1:2000

This sculptured structure, comprised of a series of cuboids, employs simple means to make the most of the limited space on offer.

Tokyo has the paradoxical quality of being both a city and village at the same time. Tokyo shows its urban face at its metro hubs, yet when one ventures into its alleys, the city's dense fabric proves an invitation to discover places more reminiscent of a village. The residential building is located on a nondescript pathway in the middle of an established housing development in the geographic centre of the transfer stations Shibuya, Shinjukua and Akasakamitsuke. The building's strange form is in keeping with legal planning restrictions: only 80 % of the 45 m² property could be built on, to a maximum height of 12 metres and set back by 60° from the street. The architects made a virtue of necessity, stacking a variety of volumes on top of one another.

Minimally furnished rooms
The room programme has been divided into three areas: the two-storey building that serves as the base fills almost the entire property, leaving only a thin garden strip. This structure houses the kitchen, living room, bedroom and bathroom. Another two-storey volume has been built on top of this base building and set back from it. This houses the "salon" and gallery, 4 m high with an area of 9.72 m², which fronts on the roof terrace. Following the stairs up from here takes one to the roof level, which is home to a circular pavilion. The relationship between inside and outside is given a different treatment on each level. While the lower rooms open out onto a small garden, the upper cube provides views of the city. The roof pavilion located on the top floor reveals only a view of the sky. In spite of the limited ground space available, the minimalist, entirely white interior and open plan design lend it an appearance of spaciousness.

Stairway
The design element linking all of the storeys is the folded steel staircase. Its 70 % slope and stair tread size of only 15.9 cm would be inconceivable in Europe. It is mounted on a steel stair string which disappears into the wall level, where it is invisibly bolted onto the building's supporting steel structure. The steel skeleton has been covered with sandwich panels and the exterior has been uniformly covered with corrugated aluminium.

Floor plans · Sections
Scale 1:200

1 Terrace
2 Study room
3 Living room
4 Bathroom
5 Bedroom
6 Dining room

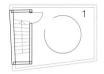

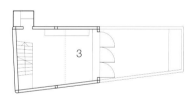

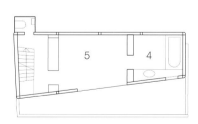

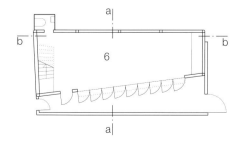

Vertical section
Scale 1:20

1 Galvanised sheet-steel, 0.8 mm
   timber board, 9 mm
   thermal insulation with a gradient, 120 mm
   timber board, 9 mm, vapour barrier
   gypsum plasterboard, 12.5 mm
2 Two layer water proofing sheet
   thermal insulation, 30 mm
   vapour barrier
   sloping concrete, 150–200 mm
3 Aluminium sheet, 0.8 mm

4 Edge beam steel profile, 148 mm
5 Wall construction:
   Corrugated aluminium, 0.8 mm
   galvanised sheet-steel, 0.2 mm
   plywood board, 9 mm
   gypsum plaster board, 12.5 mm
   thermal insulation, 100 mm
   gypsum plasterboard, 12.5 mm
6 Light steel profile support, 140/56/1.5 mm
7 Flooring urethane paint finish
   Heating-screed, 60 mm, sealing sheet
   insulating board, 15 mm
   reinforced concrete, 150 mm

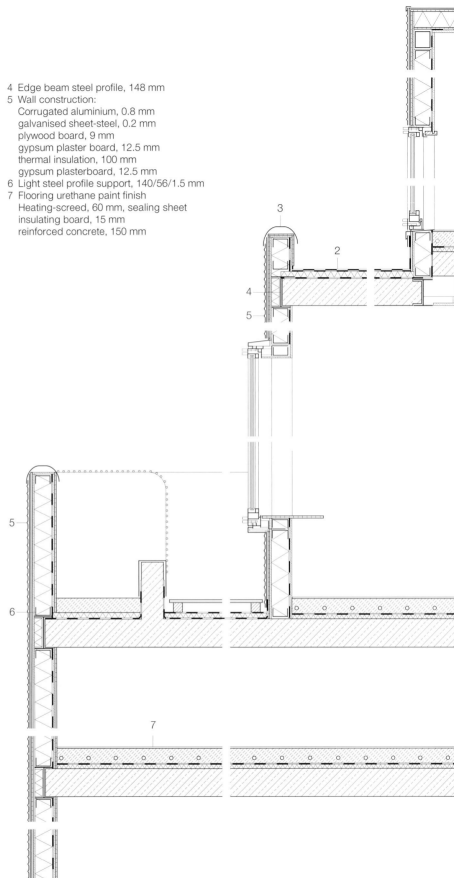

Project data:

Usage:	Accommodation
	Fixed
Structure:	Steel frame
Clear room height:	2.275 – 4.40 m
Gross volume:	169 m³
Gross floor area:	68 m²
Property size:	49 m²
Dimensions:	11.00 m × 4.50 m
Construction costs:	36 million yen
Year of construction:	2008
Construction period:	10 months

Residential building in Munich

Architects: meck architekten, Munich

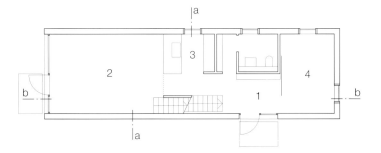

With its dark facade, this narrow house with a width of only 4.80 metres presents a skilful contrast to the surrounding buildings.

The owner wanted to use the small remaining property in the middle of a heterogonous residential area in southeast Munich for the construction of an affordable detached house that made optimum use of the space available. As a result of its small size and strict conditions – the building's location only permits a building size of 4.80 × 16.00 m – planning and developing this detached house presented quite a challenge for the architects.

Effective utilisation thanks to fluid spaces

This narrow house has been tailored to the life of a family of five. The architect and owners worked together to create a concept for the interior that provided privacy for each member of the family, while also allowing for communal areas that would be large enough for all of them. The resulting plan has created rooms that are compactly arranged, practically doing away with the need for halls. The entrance area, with bathroom and cloakroom, merges seamlessly with the kitchen. The kitchen in turn forms a single unit with the dining room and living room, which boast a spacious opening onto the garden. The study, which faces the street, has been fitted with a sliding door that allows it to be turned into a separate space when necessary. When this door is open, the entire ground floor can be experienced as a single room. The various zones of the house are distinguished their varying room heights. While the room height is 2.26 m in the entrance area, it opens up to a height of 2.83 m towards the living area.

The upper storey can be reached from the living room via a narrow stairway. The first floor has been divided into three children's rooms of equal size, all of which open up onto the central play hall, which also serves as a music room and library. The architects incorporated the shelves necessary for housing the extensive book collection as key stylistic elements. Each of the children is able to reach their own private bedroom and private area beneath the roof by using a ladder. Seamless connections between the rooms not only allow the living space to be put to effective use, but also underscore the interconnectedness of the various areas of life.

Space-saving construction and details

From the outside, this narrow house is set apart from its surroundings by its vertical facade embellishment. This is comprised of boards in three different widths, the unfinished surfaces of which have been lasered in ebony colours. A structure made up of prefabricated timber panel elements is found beneath this shell. This offered an ideal solution not only on account of the reduction in construction costs resulting from prefabrication, but also because of the thin walls it made possible, allowing for the utilisation of every last centimetre. The well-insulated wall elements are 29.50 cm thick and entirely prefabricated, including the exterior cladding, all installations, recesses and the interior panel. Even the windows have already been installed in the walls. They have been designed to go with the furnishings, and can be opened towards the outside. As a result, the full width of the window sills can be utilised.

The minimalist design of both the interior and exterior serve to highlight the house's unique aesthetic appeal.

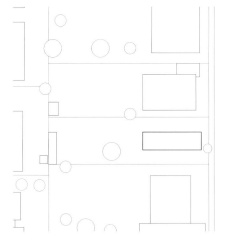

Site plan
Scale 1:1000

Floor plans
Scale 1:200

1 Entrance
2 Living room
3 Kitchen
4 Study
5 Children's room
6 Bedroom
7 Play hall / library

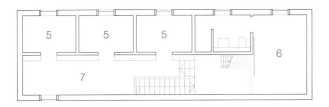

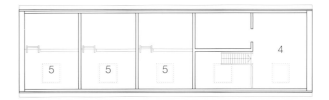

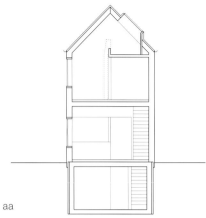

aa

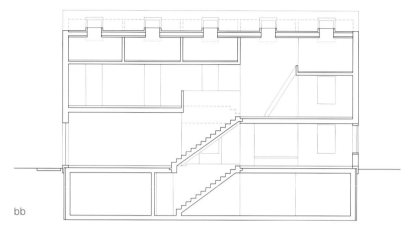

bb

Sections
Scale 1:200

Vertical section
Scale 1:20

1 Roof structure:
   Double lock standing seam covering
   titanium zinc sheeting, 0.8 mm
   undersheeting
   spruce cladding, 27 mm
   solid wood rafters, 280 mm
   with thermal insulation in between, squared
   timber, 24 mm
   gypsum plasterboard, 12.5 mm
2 Wall structure:
   Rough-sawn spruce in
   three board widths, 24 mm
   ventilation, lathing, 30 mm
   black weather proofing membrane
   gypsum fibreboard, 12,5 mm
   timber post and beam, 200 mm
   with thermal insulation in between
   vapour barrier
   2-layer gypsum fibreboard, 12.5 mm
3 Spruce window element
   painted white
4 Floor construction, 1st floor:
   Heating screed as wearing screed, 65 mm
   insulation, 40 mm
   footfall sound insulation, 120 mm
   polythene sheeting
   rough-sawn wooden ceiling construction,
   180 mm
   lathing, 24 mm
   gypsum plasterboard, 12.5 mm
5 Floor construction, ground floor:
   Heating screed as wearing screed, 65 mm
   insulation, 120 mm, polythene sheeting
   reinforced concrete roof, 180 mm
6 Base element reinforced concrete, 50/400 mm

Project data:

Usage:	Accommodation Fixed
Structure:	Basement: Reinforced concrete Ground and upper floors: Timber frame construction
Clear room height:	2.26–2.83 m
Gross volume:	775 m³
Gross floor area:	272 m²
Dimensions:	4.80 × 16.00 m Eaves height: 6 m Ridge height: 8.40 m
Year of construction:	2009
Construction period:	8 months

154

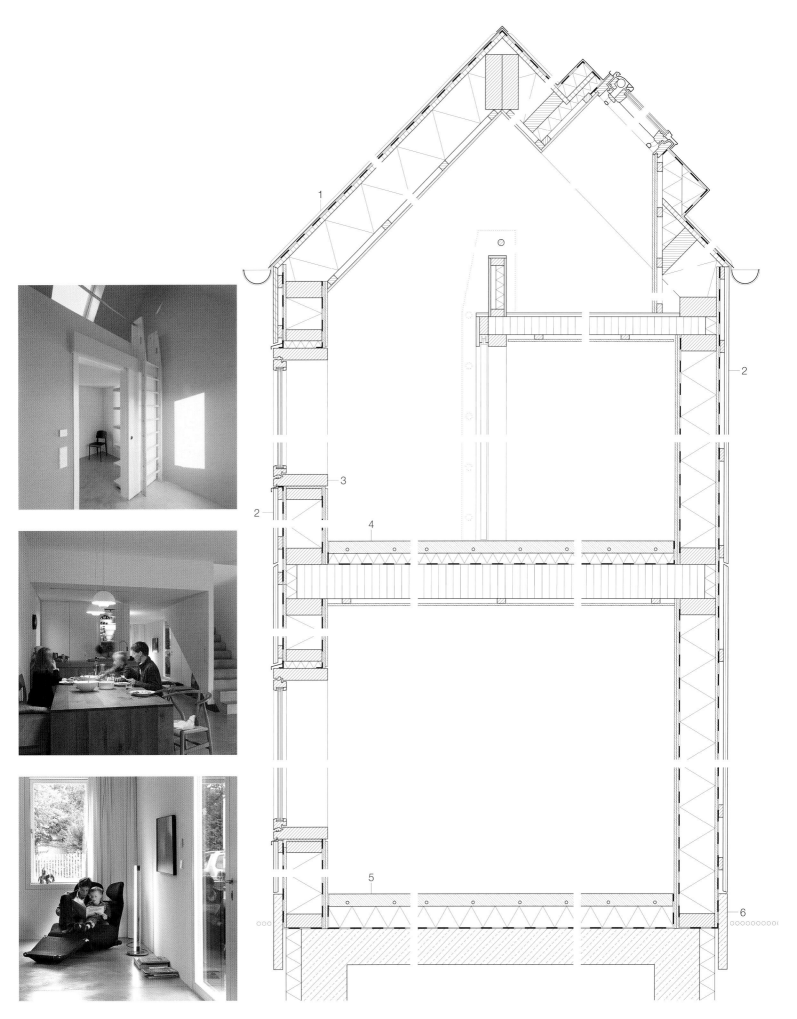

Renovation of students' apartments at the Olympic Village, Munich

Architects: arge werner wirsing bogevischs buero, Munich

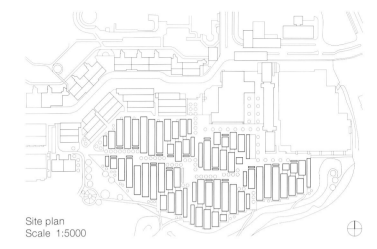

Site plan
Scale 1:5000

Mini-houses demonstrate in impressive style how space can be used effectively and architectural quality can come to the fore even in the most constricted conditions.

Student hostels from the 1970s generally take the form of serial structures with long corridors and standardised interior fittings – characteristics which do not necessarily make a positive impression in most examples of architecture from this era. The mini-row houses of the former Olympic women's village are an exception to this rule. Designed by Munich architect Werner Wirsing, their narrow aisles and squares are interwoven in the manner of a tight-knit carpet. Stringing together 800 identical precast concrete housing units did not produce an anonymous community, however. With 24 m² of living space, a gallery level with roof terrace and their own cooking and sanitary area, the mini-houses offered adequate privacy combined with an outward-looking character which naturally gave rise to a lively communal atmosphere.

Renovation and optimisation

After almost 40 years of use, the maisonette apartments were due for thorough refurbishment, and in 2006 the students' welfare association responsible commissioned Werner Wirsing together with bogevischs buero to renovate the houses by way of a critical approach befitting their status as a historical monument. This essentially entailed demolishing and rebuilding virtually the entire site, while at the same time offering an opportunity to reinterpret and develop the idea of individualised student accommodation.

In terms of the broader urban development context, the residential complex is identical to the original. At first glance, the row houses featuring interior-insulated fair-faced concrete without metal facia strips are the spitting image of their predecessors. In accordance with the specifications of the students' welfare association and the guidelines on public subsidies, the architects have, however, increased the number of residential units to 1052 by reducing their axial width from 4.20 m to 3.15 m and the living space to 18 m².

Numerous ingenious details have been evolved to broaden the scope available to the students and to ensure that every square centimetre is utilised to the full. These include tailor-made built-in furniture and storage space in the first steps of the staircase leading to the upper floor.

The two ground-floor windows facing onto the access aisles are another key feature. As in the former women athletes' village, these cannot be opened for reasons of fire safety – ventilation takes place either via the front door or an ingenious ventilation opening over the door. These windows are nevertheless instrumental to integrating the ground floor into the outside environment. Those wishing to keep out prying eyes can close off the window niches with easy-to-fit opaque plexiglass panels. This creates a form of showcase window which the first residents have already used to show off arrangements of beer mugs, flowers or photos to passers-by. These individual displays are somewhat reminiscent of the motley array of colourful facades which the students bestowed on the old row houses. As artwork on the facades is still expressly permitted, it should not be too long before the old spirit of the students' quarter returns – the architectural conditions for such a revival are certainly in place.

Floor plans
Scale 1:100

Sections · Floor plans
Scale 1:200

A Ground floor 2009
B Upper floor 2009
C Ground floor 1972
D Upper floor 1972
E Overview upper floors
F Overview ground floors

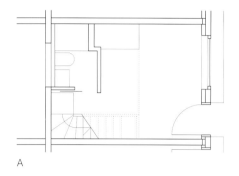

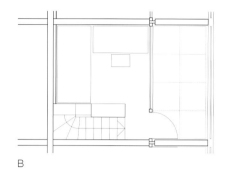

A   B

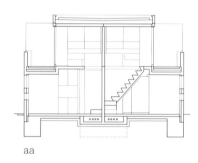

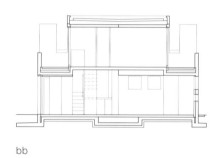

aa   bb

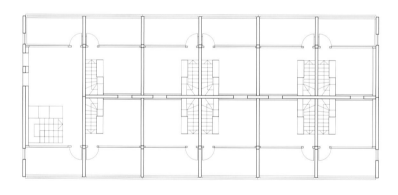

E

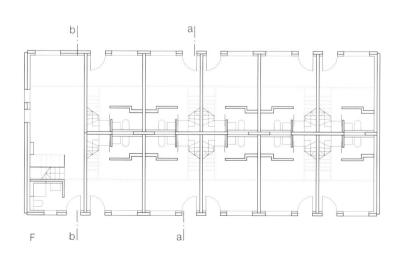

F   b   a

Project data:

Usage: Accomodation
Fixed
Structure: Precast reinforce concrete
Clear room height: 2.10–2.38 m
Gross volume: 72.85 m³
Gross floor area: 32.16 m²
Dimensions: 4.20 × 3.15 m
complete 1052 units
Year of construction: 2010
Construction period: 2008–2010

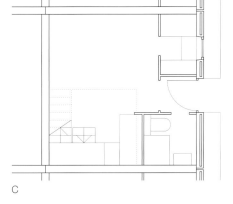

C

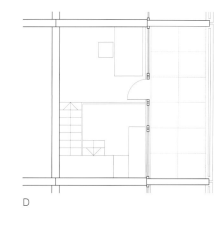

D

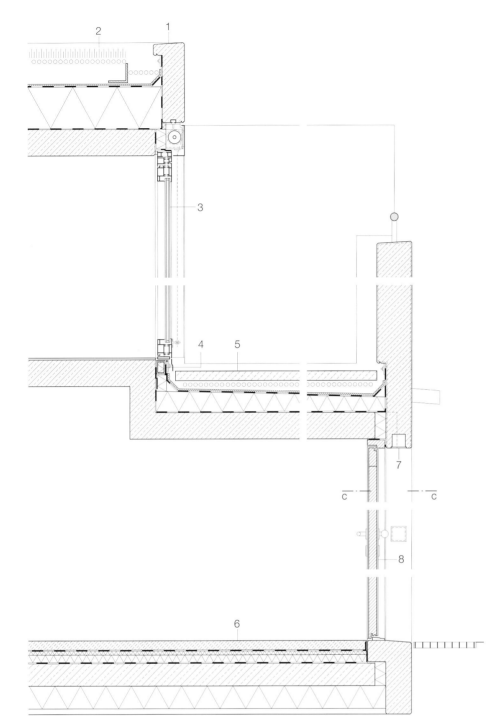

Vertical section · Horizontal section
Scale 1:20

1 Precast reinforced concrete unit, 120 mm
  element length 3.12 m, fixation
  with 2 stainless steel angles, 20/250/170 mm
2 Roof structure:
  Extensive greenery, root protection
  2-layer sealing course
  sloping installation, 180 mm, vapour barrier
  precast reinforced concrete roof, 140 mm
3 Fixed windows, toughened glass 2× 6 mm
4 Tubular steel, 70/50/6 mm
5 Terrace structure:
  Concrete blocks, 50 mm
  2-layer sealing course
  sloping insulation, 100 mm, vapour barrier
  reinforced concrete roof, 140 mm
6 Floor structure:
  Epoxy resin coating, 2 mm
  cement screed, 55 mm
  separation layer, footfall sound insulation
  mineral fibre boards, 20 mm
  thermal insulation, 40 mm, sealant, 5 mm
  in-situ concrete floor slab, 120 mm
  thermal insulation, 120 mm, base course
7 Light positioned centrally in door lintel
8 Solid wooden door, HPL surface, 0.8 mm
9 Fair-faced concrete, 140 mm
  thermal insulation
  foamed glass panels, 80 mm
  bonded gypsum plasterboard, 12.5 mm
10 Insulating strip

bb

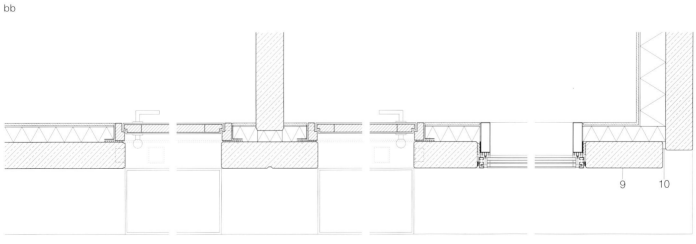

cc

Capsule hotel in Kyoto

Creative director & Product design: Fumie Shibata, Tokyo
Sign & Graphic design: Masaaki Hiromura, Tokyo
Interior design: Takaaki Nakamura, Tokyo
Architect: Sigma Architectural Design, Kyoto

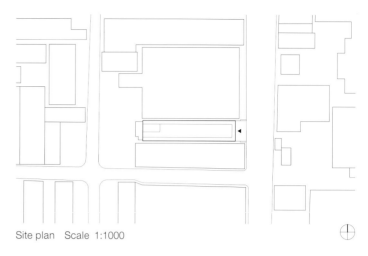

Site plan   Scale 1:1000

The 9hours hotel offers its guests an innovative service concept from tooth brush and slippers to individual sleeping capsules.

A capsule hotel which sets new standards for this typically Japanese type of accommodation opened in December 2009 on a plot measuring just 6 m in width. Evolved in the 1970s, to date capsule hotels have served primarily as low-price abodes for commuters in major cities.
The innovative design of the 9hours hotel is now aimed at new target groups. While the capsules measuring 1.20 × 2.34 m are no larger than the standard cells for this type of hotel, the design here is both functional and aesthetic, with the aim of offering guests a high standard of comfort and a pleasant atmosphere despite the minimal space available. The colour scheme helps to differentiate the respective areas of the hotel, from gleaming white in the entrance and lounge through shades of grey in the wash rooms to the black-floored corridors in the sleeping areas. The latter are divided up into separate storeys for male and female guests respectively, with corresponding showers, wash rooms and lockers. The sleeping capsules consist of glass fibre-reinforced plastic. The individual cells rest on a steel sub-construction, presenting a honeycomb-like appearance in the corridor. The hotel's name alludes to the recommended duration of stay – seven hours sleep and one hour each for showering and dressing. In keeping with its function

as sleeping quarters, the building is introverted in character, with no windows apart from the glass entrance doors.

The hotel and design concept

The 9hours hotel was developed by a general creative director in collaboration with a graphic designer and an interior designer. Clear and simple pictograms lead the way through the building, also serving as a guide on how to use the hotel: The guest checks in, places his shoes and luggage in the lockers at reception and takes the lift to the floors on which the wash rooms are situated. Here he deposits his clothing in a locker and is provided with pyjamas, slippers, a bottle of water and a tooth brush. Towels and soap dispensers also bear the hotel logo and the inside of the sleeping capsules have been designed especially for the hotel, featuring a gelcoat finish with a silky shimmer. An elegant minimalist black control panel for the lighting and an alarm clock are flush-fitted at the rear of the capsule. A dimmable LED light is integrated into the ceiling, while small personal items can be placed in two niches at the sides. The capsules have no doors. A polyester fabric roller blind offers privacy but no protection from noise. The mattress and pillow are thus all the more crucial to relaxation, and feature a special ergonomic design employing various materials. The guest lies in the capsule as if in a cocoon, enjoying a degree of privacy in this quintessentially Japanese style of dormitory.

Project data:

Usage:	Accommodation
	Fixed structure
Structure capsule:	glass-fibre-reinforced plastic
Height capsule:	1.08 m
Gross volume capsule:	2.48 m³
Gross floor area capsule:	2.30 m²
Dimensions capsule:	2.15 × 1.07 m
Year of construction:	2009
Construction period:	11 months

1 + 7 + 1 = 9ʰ

 Shower   Sleep   Rest   9 hours

1. Registration & Reservation
First register as a member at the 9h website and then make a reservation.

2. Check-In
After checking in, get your locker key and capsule number.

3. Floors
At 9h Ladies and Gentlemen Floors are different and have separate elevators. To reach the Locker Room, take the elevator accordingly.

4. Lockers
Put your luggage in the locker and change into "9h loungewear".

5. Lounge Area
To eat, drink or to use computers, please use the lounge area.
*A "Ladies Only" lounge area is available for the comfort of our female guests.

6. Shower Rooms
Bath towels, shampoo and conditioner are provided, feel free to use them.

7. Amenities
Toothbrush sets and hairdryers are also available for use.

8. Capsules
Rest well with the Sleep Ambient Control System in your capsule unit.

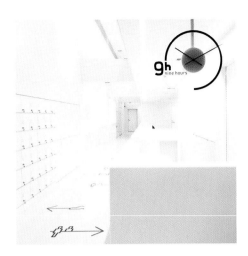

Floor plans • Section
Scale 1:250

1 Entrance
2 Reception
3 Lockers
  for footwear
4 Lounge
5 Lift
6 Store
7 Air space
8 Showers
9 Wash room
10 Lockers
11 Sleeping quarters

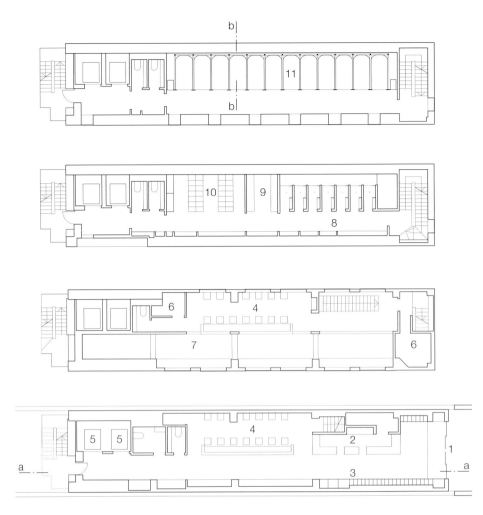

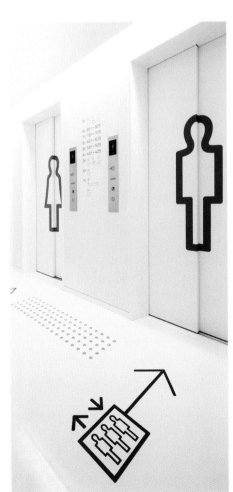

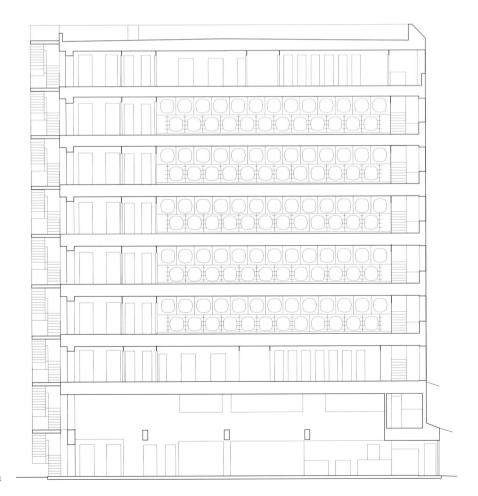

aa

164

Sleepwear and sanitary articles in hotel design;
presentation of the prototypes in an exhibition

Room Slippers
Slipper bag

館内スリッパ

*日帰りの使用と生まるまま一サービス……
スリッパとなりました

素材：下底品
サイズ：男性用、女性用
サントレ：ツキ式会社

スリッパ袋

袋には館内での基本的な過ごし方が書いてあります 館内用の小物入れとしての
使用をおすすめします

素材：紙
サイズ：男性用、女性用
望月印刷株式会社

for men   for women

gh   gh

Lounge wear with
high desorption

高放湿性館内着

長時間着ることになる館内着はスポーツ
ウェアに近く、伸縮性や通気性の良い
素材を使用しております 見た目はもち
ろんのこと、寝ても、くつろいでも快適な
状態を保ちます。

素材：ポリエステル
サイズ：S M L XL XXL
サントミック株式会社

Shampoo / Conditioner /
Body Wash

シャンプー・コンディショナー
ボディーソープ

髪や肌にやさしい天然素材を使用し、
すべてシリコンフリー、性別を問わず多く
の方々に使っていただくことを意識した
自然な香り。9hだけの特別な処方と香り
のオリジナルアメニティー。

香り：linden blossom
玉の肌石鹸株式会社

歯ブラシ・歯磨きチューブ

清潔感のあるクリアなハンドルは、グリップ
がしっかりとしている事によりつかみや
すくブラッシングしやすい。

Toothbrush / Toothpaste

歯磨きチューブ（キシリトール配合）
医薬部外品指定
株式会社JT日経事

ミネラルウォーター

富士の麓にて採取された、バナジウム
を多く含むナチュラルミネラルウォー
ターです。水と緑奥深い山々に囲まれた
「西桂町」の工場で採取され、そのまま
パックしました。

株式会社富士クリスタルビバレッジ

Mineral Water

タオル

エジプト綿使いのシルクのような柔らかな
肌触り。高い吸水性でシャワー後のお体
を包みます。

バスタオル 78cm×155cm
フェイスタオル 40cm×85cm
素材：綿100%
東洋紡リビングサービス株式会社

Towel

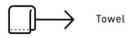

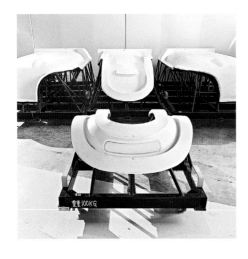

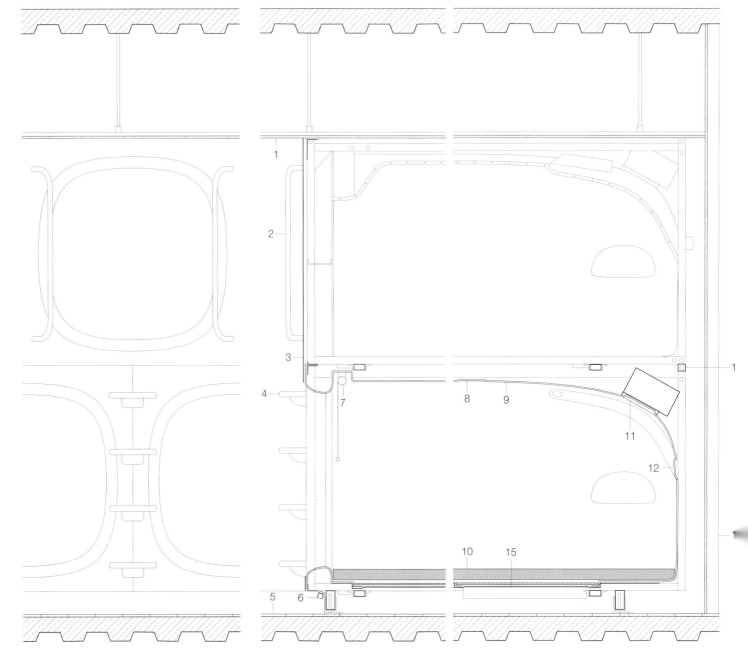

1
2
3
4
5
6
7
8
9
10
11
12
15

bb

View • Vertical section of capsules
Scale 1:20

1 Suspended ceiling of laminated white gypsum
   plasterboard, 12.5 mm
2 Tubular steel grab bar, melamine resin-coated,
   black, diam. 25.4 mm
3 Melamine resin-coated sheet steel front panel,
   black, 3.2 mm
4 Cast aluminium step
   melamine resin-coated, black
5 Rubber tiling, 500/500/2,5 mm
   concrete on trapezoidal sheet steel
6 LED base lighting
7 Polyester fabric screen
8 Smoke detector
9 Glass fibre-reinforced plastic
   gelcoat finish, polished, 4 mm
10 Polyester mattress
11 LED lighting with acrylic glass cover
12 Electronic control panel, glass fibre-
   reinforced plastic with self-coloured black
   gelcoat finish, 2.4 mm
13 Tubular steel bearing structure, 40/40 mm
14 Lightweight steel construction, 12.5 mm
   gypsum plasterboard
15 Lighting control

Architects – Project Data

Observation tower on the Mur River

Owner: Gemeinde Gosdorf Orts- und Infrastrukturentwicklungs KG
Architects: terrain: loenhart&mayr architekten und landschaftsarchitekten, München/Graz; Klaus K. Loenhart, Christoph Mayr
Structural planning: osd - office for structural design, Frankfurt a. M.; Klaus Fäth, Harald Kloft, project leader: Jürgen Scholte-Wassink
Constructed: 2010

www.terrain.de; info@terrain.de
www.o-s-d.com; office@o-s-d.com

Klaus K. Loenhart
1994 Diploma at the Munich University of Applied Sciences; 1999 Master in Design, 2000 Master in Landscape Architecture at Harvard University GSD in Cambridge; Prof./Institute Manager at the Technical University of Graz since 2006.

Christoph Mayr
1993 Diploma at the Munich University of Applied Sciences; 1998–2000 Partner in LBGM Architekten, 2000–2002 with MSP & Partner Architekten in Munich.

2003 terrain: loenhart&mayr founded.

Klaus Fäth
1981 Diploma at the Technical College Darmstadt; 1991–1998 Stöffler-Abraham-Fäth; 1998–2002 Fäth + Fäth; Professor at the University of Applied Sciences in Frankfurt a.M. since 1998.

Harald Kloft
1990 Diploma and 1998 Doctorate at the Technical University of Darmstadt; 1998–2001 Bollinger + Grohmann; Professor at the Technical University of Kaiserslautern since 2002, 2007–2009 in Graz.

2002 osd founded.

"Top of Tyrol" summit platform

Owner: Wintersport Tirol AG & Co, Stubaier Bergbahnen KG
Architects: LAAC Architects, Innsbruck; Kathrin Aste, Frank Ludin
Employee: Thomas Feuerstein
Structural planning: aste Konstruktion, Innsbruck
Soil mechanics: Ingenieurbüro Wietek – IBW, Innsbruck
Constructed: 2008

www.laac.eu
info@laac.eu

• Steel construction: Bitschnau GmbH, Nenzing
• Metalwork: Raggl Metallbau, Völs
• Construction: Felbermayr Bau GmbH & Co KG, Imst
• Carpentry: Zimmerei Haas, Neder im Stubaital
• Helicopter: Heli Tirol, St. Johann im Pongau

Frank Ludin
2004 Diploma at the University of Innsbruck; Partner in astearchitecture since 2005.

Kathrin Aste
2000 Diploma at the University of Innsbruck; 2004 Foundation of astearchitecture, Innsbruck.

with LAAC Architects since 2010.

Temporary bamboo pavilions

Owner: Ministry of Foreign Affairs via the Goethe Institute in China
Architect: Markus Heinsdorff, Munich; Installation artist and designer
Structural planning consultant: W. G. Schachl, Munich
Statics: Tongji University, architectural and engineering firm, Shanghai
Construction: Oriental Expo Services, Shanghai
Navett, Diamond Pavilion
Planning: Werkhart International, Beijing
Constructed: 2007–2008
Dome, Conference, Central, Lotus Pavilion
Planning: MUDI Architects, Shanghai in cooperation with Tong Lingfeng, Architect, Shanghai
Structural planning consultant: schlaich bergermann and partner, Stuttgart
Constructed: 2008–2009

www.heinsdorff.de
markus@heinsdorff.de

Markus Heinsdorff
1976–1981 Studied at the Academy of Fine Arts in Munich;
2007–2010 Visiting Professor at the Southeast University in Nanjing and Chongqing University; Visiting Professor at the School of Architecture and Urban Planning in Huazhong and the University of Science and Technology in Wuhan since 2009.

Transport shelters in Darmstadt

Owner: City of Science Darmstadt/Building Construction and Machine Office Darmstadt
Architects: netzwerkarchitekten, Darmstadt
Employees: Uta Varrentrapp, Andrea Weber, Sebastian Meuschke, Thorsten Mergel, Irena Penic, Jan Schipull, Tim Sperling
Supporting structure: ProfessorPfeiferundPartner, Darmstadt
Constructed: 2005

www.netzwerkarchitekten.de
kontakt@netzwerkarchitekten.de

Thilo Höhne
1995 Diploma at the Technical University of Darmstadt; 1999–2000 Lectureship at the Technical University of Darmstadt.

Karim Scharabi
1997 Diploma, 2002 Assistant Professor and lectureship at the Technical University of Darmstadt.

Philipp Schiffer
1996 Diploma, 1998–2000 Lectureship at the Technical University of Darmstadt.

Jochen Schuh
1995 Diploma at the Technical University of Darmstadt.

Markus Schwieger
1995 Diploma, 2001 Lectureship at the Technical University of Darmstadt; 2007–2008 Substitute Professor at the University of Kassel.

Oliver Witan
1995 Diploma at the Technical University of Darmstadt; 1999–2002 Asst. Professor Technical University of Darmstadt and HfG Offenbach.

1998 netzwerkarchitekten founded.

Market stalls in Augsburg	Theatre podium in Rotterdam	Pavilion at Lake Geneva	Pavilion in Zurich

Owner: Office for Consumer Protection and Market Trading, Augsburg
Architects: Tilman Schalk Architekten, Stuttgart
Outdoor installations: Helleckes Landschaftsarchitektur, Karlsruhe
Structural planning: Ingenieurbüro Bytow, Königsbrunn
Building installations planning: Wimmer Ingenieure, Neusäss
Electrical planning: Municipal Department of Works, Augsburg
Constructed: 2009

www.schalkarchitekten.de
schalk@schalkarchitekten.de

Tilman Schalk
1995 Diploma at the University of Stuttgart; 1990–2001 Freelance in Germany; 1997 Tilman Schalk Architekten founded; 2000–2008 Research Assistant at the University of Karlsruhe.

Owner: Rotary Club Rotterdam North, OBR Rotterdam
Architects: Atelier Kempe Thill architects and planners, Rotterdam; André Kempe, Oliver Thill
Employees: David van Eck, Teun van der Meulen, Kingman Brewster,Takashi Nakamura, Frank Verzijden
Structural planning: ABT, Velp
Constructed: 2009

www.atelierkempethill.com
office@atelierkempethill.com

· General contractor: J.P. van Eesteren B.V., Barendrecht
· Concrete structures: Keijzer Betonwerken B.V., Zutphen
· Prestressed concrete: Heijmans Beton en Waterbouw B.V., Rosmalen
· Steel facade: Konstruktiebedrijf Visser B.V., Veenwouden
· Aluminium facade: Gebr. Van den Burg, Rotterdam
· Electrical installations: Endenburg Elektrotechniek, Rotterdam

André Kempe
1990–1996 Technical University of Dresden; Visiting Professorships at the Technical University of Delft, Academie van Bouwkunst Arnhem and Rotterdam since 1999.

Oliver Thill
1990–1996 Technical University of Dresden; Visiting Professorships at the Technical University of Delft, Academie van Bouwkunst Arnhem and Rotterdam and the Berlage Institute Rotterdam since 1999.

2000 Atelier Kempe Thill founded.

Owner: City of Geneva
Architects: Bakker & Blanc Architectes, Lausanne; Marco Bakker, Alexandre Blanc
Employees: Nuala Collins, Yves Dreier, Thierry Sermet
Structural planning: Alho Systembau, Wikon
Constructed: 2008

www.bakkerblanc.ch
info@bakkerblanc.ch

· Steel system construction: Alho Systembau, Wikon

Marco Bakker
1979–1983 Hogere Technische School Leeuwarden; 1985–1986 EPF Lausanne; 1983–1988 Technical University of Delft; Professor at Bern University of Applied Sciences since 2008; Visiting Professor at EPF Lausanne since 2009.

Alexandre Blanc
1982–1986 Collège Calvin Genève; 1986–1990 Studied at EPF Lausanne; Visiting Professor at EPF Lausanne since 2009.

1992 Bakker & Blanc Architectes founded in Fribourg and Biel; Bakker & Blanc Architectes in Lausanne since 2003; Office in Zurich since 2007.

Owner: City of Zurich
Architects: phalt architekten, Zurich
Project management: Cornelia Mattiello-Schwaller
Structural planning: Schnetzer Puskas Ingenieure AG, Zurich
Building installations: HLS Engineering GmbH, Zurich
Electrical planning: Walter Salm, Meier & Partner AG, Zurich
Constructed: 2008

www.phalt.ch
info@phalt.ch

· Profiled hot-dip galvanised steel sheet: IBS GmbH, Bad Vöslau
· Facade lining, roof and steel construction: Kaufmann Spenglerei + Sanitär AG, Egg near Zurich
· Element construction in wood, windows: Arbos AG, Dinhard

Frank Schneider
2003 Diploma at EPF Lausanne; 1999– 2007 Gigon Guyer Architekten, Herzog & de Meuron and EM2N Architekten.

Mike Mattiello
1996 Diploma, 1996–1997 Assistant Professor at the University of Applied Sciences in Burgdorf; 1997–2006 Steinmann + Schmid, Stücheli Architekten, Interbrand Zintzmeyer + Lux and W3 Architekten.

Cornelia Mattiello-Schwaller
2002 Diploma at EPF Lausanne; 2002–2006 EM2N Architekten, Zurich.

2006 phalt architekten founded.

Newspaper kiosks in London	**Kiosk at lake "Staufensee" near Dornbirn**	**Temporary bar in Porto**	**Tree house restaurant near Auckland**

Newspaper kiosks in London

Owner: The Royal Borough of Kensington & Chelsea; Daniel Moylan
Designer: Heatherwick Studio, London
Design development: Heatherwick Studio in cooperation with Nader Mokhtari
Structural planning: TALL engineers, London
Constructed: 2008

www.heatherwick.com
studio@heatherwick.com

· Manufacturer: Manage Ltd & sub-contractors
· Fit out sub-contractor: 2D:3D, London
· Frame sub-contractor: Guttridge, Spalding

Thomas Heatherwick
1989–1992 Studied three-dimensional design at Manchester Polytechnic and 1992–1994 at the Royal College of Art in London; 1994 Heatherwick Studio founded; Honorary Doctorate of the Sheffield Hallam University, the University of Brighton, the University of Dundee and Manchester Metropolitan University; lectures at Bartlett School of Architecture, Victoria and Albert Museum in London and Yale University.

Kiosk at lake "Staufensee" near Dornbirn

Owner: Roswitha Konstatzky, Dornbirn
Architects: Wellmann Ladinger, Bregenz; Judith Wellmann, Martin Ladinger
Constructed: 2005

office@wellmann-ladinger.com

· General contractor: Oberhauser & Schedler, Andelsbuch
· Interior work and furnishing: Tischlerei Metzler, Andelsbuch
· Electrical installations: Elektro Willi GesmbH, Andelsbuch
· Plumber: Dorfinstallationstechnik, Andelsbuch

Judith Wellmann
1992–1998 Technical studies at the Technical University of Innsbruck; 1996 École d'Architecture, Paris-Belleville; 1999–2002 Baumschlager & Eberle Architekten, Lochau; 2003–2005 Business studies at the University of Applied Sciences in Dornbirn; with Dietrich I Untertrifaller Architekten, Bregenz since 2003; freelance projects with Martin Ladinger since 2003.

Martin Ladinger
1994–2000 Technical studies at the Technical University of Graz; 1998–1999 Studied at Danube University Krems; 2004 Licensing Examination; 2000–2003 Baumschlager & Eberle Architekten, Lochau; Cukrowicz Nachbaur since 2003; freelance projects with Judith Wellmann since 2003.

Temporary bar in Porto

Owner: Associação de Estudantes da Faculdade de Arquitectura (AEFAUP)
Architects: Diogo Aguiar and Teresa Otto
Graphic design: Diogo Aguiar and Teresa Otto
Structural planning and technology: Acústica F.E.S., Lda – Estruturas, Iluminação e Som, in collaboration with students of AEFAUP
Constructed: 2008

www.diogoaguiar.com
info@diogoaguiar.com
www.teresaotto.com
info@teresaotto.com

Diogo Aguiar
2006 Year abroad at the Federal University of Rio de Janeiro; 2007 UNStudio in Amsterdam; 2008 Diploma at the Oporto University School of Architecture; 2009 ADPJMA in Lisbon; 2010 LIKEarchitects founded.

Teresa Otto
2005 Year abroad at the Facoltà di Architettura Valle Giulia, Università La Sapienza in Rome; 2006–2007 Collaborated with Architects RCR Aranda Pigem Vilalta in Olot; 2008 Diploma at the Oporto University School of Architecture; 2009 Zinterl Zt Architects in Lisbon; 2010 LIKEarchitects founded.

Tree house restaurant near Auckland

Owner: Yellow Treehouse Restaurant
Architects: Pacific Environments Architects, Auckland; Peter Eising, Lucy Gauntlett
Project Managers: The Building Intelligence Group, Auckland
Structural planning: Holmes Consulting, Auckland
Constructed: 2008

www.pacificenvironments.co.nz
info@pacificenvironments.co.nz

· Construction company: NZ Strong; Citywide Construction Ltd
· Wooden slats: McIntosh Timber Laminates
· Lighting: ECC Lighting & Furniture
· Crane: NZ Access
· Earthwork: C&L Sorenson
· Wood: Timberworld

Peter Eising
1984 Bachelor of Architecture Degree at the Auckland University; 1988–2006 Director at Architects Patterson, later Patterson Co Partners Architects; Director at Pacific Environments Architects since 2006.

Lucy Gauntlett
2002 Bachelor of Architecture Degree at the Auckland University; 2002–2005 Architects Patterson; 2006 Founder of Lucy G Photography; Working for Pacific Environments Architects since 2006.

St. Benedikt Chapel in Kolbermoor

Owner: Franz Stettner, Kolbermoor
Architects: kunze seeholzer architektur & stadtplanung, Munich
Employee: Marta Binaghi
Structural planning: Stefan Baur Ingenieurbüro für Bauwesen, Berlin
Constructed: 2007

www.kunze-seeholzer.de
info@kunze-seeholzer.de

- Master builder: Gröbmeier + Spielvogel GmbH, Bad Feilnbach
- Joiner: Schreinerei Krug, Kolbermoor
- Natural stone: Mario Riedesser, Kempten
- Roof waterproofing: Hans Brummer GmbH, Vogtareuth
- Glazier: Glaserei Moser, Kolbermoor

Stefanie Seeholzer
2003 Diploma at the Technical University of Munich; freelancer since 2003.

Peter Kunze
1992 Diploma at the Munich University of Applied Sciences; freelancer since 1993.

2003 kunze seeholzer architektur & stadtplanung founded.

Chapel in Lustenau

Owner: SC Austria Lustenau
Architect: Hugo Dworzak, Lustenau
Art on building: Udo Rabensteiner
Constructed: 2007

www.hugodworzak.at
office@hugodworzak.at

- Wood construction: Stephan Muxel, Au
- Solar protection: M. Berthold GmbH, Rankweil

Hugo Dworzak
1987 Diploma at the University of Innsbruck; 1989 Master of Architecture at the Pratt Institute in New York; 1990 Architekturwerkstatt Dworzak founded; Teaching at the University of Innsbruck since 1994; Lecturer at the University of Liechtenstein since 1999.

"Sehstation" in North Rhine-Westphalia

Owner: Europäisches Haus der Stadtkultur e.V. Gelsenkirchen
Architect: Andy Brauneis, Augsburg
Structural planning: Ingenieurbüro Christian Schüller, Gersthofen
Sound collage: Nicolette Baumeister, Munich
Constructed: 2008

- Wood construction: Bernd Schmid, Augsburg

Andy Brauneis
1984–1986 Trained as a carpenter; 1994 Diploma in Architecture and Urban Planning at the University of Stuttgart; 1995 Lederer Ragnarsdóttir Oei; 1996–1997 Kehrbaum Architekten; own studio in Augsburg since 1998; Lectureship at the University of Applied Sciences in Augsburg since 2000; 2003–2009 Baukunstbeirat of the city of Augsburg.

Mobile log house

Owner: Le Lieu Unique, Nantes
Architects: olgga architectes, Paris
Project leader: Guillaume Grenu
Constructed: 2009

www.olgga.fr
contact@olgga.fr

- Timberwork: Home Bois Distribution, Langon

Alice Vaillant
1995–2002 Studied at the École d'Architecture de Paris-La Villette and Paris-Belleville; 2002 Diploma at the École d'Architecture de Paris-Belleville.

Guillaume Grenu
1995–2001 Studied at École d'Architecture de Normandie and Paris-La Villette; Year abroad at the University of Portsmouth; 2001 Diploma at École d'Architecture de Normandie.

Nicolas Le Meur
1997–2006 Studied at École Supérieure d'art et de Design de Reims; 1998–2006 Course of studies at École d'Architecture de Normandie; 2006 Diploma at École d'Architecture de Normandie; with olgga architectes since 2008.

2006 olgga architectes founded.

Transformbox	Convertible pavilion	Tea house in Frankfurt am Main	Aero House

Transformbox

Architects: Bernhard Geiger with Armin Kathan
Constructed: 2010

bernhard.geiger@holzbox.at
www.transformbox.at

Bernhard Geiger
Architectural studies in Innsbruck; Worked for the architectural firm Manzl, Ritsch, Sandtner; 1997 Founding member of Holz Box Tirol where he has since served as a freelance project leader; independent development of various "transformboxes" since 2008.

Armin Kathan
Studied at the University of Innsbruck and the Academy of Applied Art in Vienna; Worked for architectural firms in Austria and the USA; Collaboration with Erich Strolz in a joint undertaking since 1993; 1997 Founding member of Holz Box Tirol, later Managing Director of Holz Box ZT GmbH.

Convertible pavilion

Owner: Elisabeth Montag Foundation, Bonn
Architects: Kalhöfer - Korschildgen, Cologne
Project leader: Stefan Korschildgen
Employees: Felix Franke, Marcel Franken, Lei Lei, Miriam Lück
Structural planning: Vreden, Henneker & Partner, Bonn
Constructed: 2005

www.kalhoefer-korschildgen.de
mail@kalhoefer-korschildgen.de

· Metal construction: Trimborn Metallbau GmbH, Bad Honnef
· Upholstery: Eiting-Räume, Cologne

Gerhard Kalhöfer
Studied at RWTH Aachen and the Düsseldorf Art Academy; Creation of numerous mobile constructions; Professor in architectural theory and design at the University of Applied Sciences in Mainz since 1998.

Stefan Korschildgen
1992 Diploma at RWTH Aachen; Visiting student at the University of Washington Seattle and the Düsseldorf Art Academy; Professor at Peter Behrens School of Architecture Düsseldorf since 2001; 2006 Visiting Professor at RMIT University Melbourne.

1995 architectural firm Kalhöfer - Korschildgen founded, Paris/ Aachen; since 2000, Kalhöfer - Korschildgen, Cologne.

Tea house in Frankfurt am Main

Owner: Museum for Applied Art Frankfurt, Frankfurt am Main
Architects: Kengo Kuma & Associates, Tokyo and formTL, Radolfzell
Employees at Kengo Kuma: Katinka Temme, Takumi Saikawa
Employees at formTL: Gerhard Fessler, Bernd Stimpfle, Udo Ribbe, Manuel Neidhart
Structural planning: formTL, Radolfzell
Constructed: 2007

www.kkaa.co.jp
kuma@kkaa.co.jp
www.form-TL.de
info@form-TL.de

· General contractor foundation: Takenaka Europe GmbH
· Membrane shell: Canobbio S.p.A.
· Supporting air: Gustav Nolting GmbH, Detmold

Kengo Kuma
1979 Master at the University of Tokyo; 1985–1986 Visiting student at Columbia University; 1990 Kengo Kuma & Associates founded; 2001–2008 Teaching appointment at Keio University; Professor at the University of Tokyo since 2009.

Gerd-Michael Schmid
1988 Diploma in Architecture at the University of Stuttgart; 1989–1991 Federal Ministry for Research and Technology – Photovoltaic research; 1994–1999 Project Leader, Managing Director of IPL Radolfzell up to 2004; Managing Partner at formTL in Radolfzell since 2004; Teaching appointment at the University of Applied Sciences in Frankfurt since 2009.

Aero House

In collaboration with:
Technical University of Vienna
1996: Gerhard Abel, Willi Frötscher, Ursula Hammerschick, Silvia Hörndl, Martin Janecek, Birgitta Kunsch, Paul Linsbauer, Christian Lottersberger, Michael Quixtner, Margit Rammer, Helmut Richter, Hannes Schillinger, Andreas Vogler, Anne Wagner, Sakura Watanabe

Technical University of Munich, winter semester 2004/05: Proof of Concept Prototype: Richard Horden, Lydia Haack
Students: Florian Dressler, Georg Herdt, Matthias Plassmann

Technical University of Munich, summer semester 2008: Final planning and production: Richard Horden, Wieland Schmidt
Students: Steffen Knopp, Inga Mannewitz

Technical University of Munich, summer semester 2009: Interior design: Richard Horden, Moritz Mungenast
Students: Frederike Krinn, Catharina Reutersberg

Design: 1996
Constructed: 2009

www.light.ar.tum.de
sekr.horden@lrz.tu-muenchen.de

Material sponsoring:
Sika Deutschland GmbH, Bad Urach
Lange & Ritter GmbH, Gerlingen

· Carbon construction: Carbon-Werke Weißgerber GmbH & Co KG, Wallerstein
· Aluminium sections: Alu Meier GmbH, Munich

"Desert Seal" tent

Architects: Architecture and Vision, Munich/Bomarzo; Arturo Vittori, Andreas Vogler
Structural planning: Aero Sekur, Aprilia
Constructed: 2005

www.architectureandvision.com

· Production: Aero Sekur, Aprilia
· Model: Self Group Rivignano
· Flexible photovoltaic film: Flexcell, Yverdon-les-Bains

Andreas Vogler
1994 Diploma in Architecture at ETH Zurich; 1996–2002 Research Assistant at the Technical University of Munich, Prof. Richard Horden; 1995–1999 Richard Horden Associates in London; 1998–2005 Own architectural firm in Munich; 2003–2005 Visiting Professor at the Royal Academy of Fine Arts in Copenhagen.

Arturo Vittori
1998 Diploma in Architecture at Università degli Studi di Firenze; 1997–2006 Santiago Calatrava, Jean Nouvel, Francis Design, Future Systems and Anish Kapoor.

2003 Architecture and Vision founded.

Rucksack House

Artist: Stefan Eberstadt, Munich
Structural planning: a.k.a. Ingenieure, Munich; Thomas Beck
Constructed: 2004

stefan.eberstadt@stefaneberstadt.de

· Steel construction: Dobetsberger Anlagenbau, Michaelnbach
· Cables, suspension: Teufelsberger Seil, Wels
· Acrylic glass: Wolfgang Derschmidt, Alxing bei Grafing
· Plywood panels: WISA, UPM Wood Products, Helsinki

Stefan Eberstadt
1982–1988 Studied sculpture at the Academy of Fine Arts in Munich and in London; Studio in Jetzendorf near Munich since 2009; 1993 Bavarian State Prize and Art Prize of the Bavarian Academy of Fine Arts; 2007 E.ON Culture Prize Bavaria; his works can be found in numerous private and public collections.

Mobile roof terrace in Cologne

Owner: Ruth Langenkamp, Gerald Schroeder
Architects: Kalhöfer-Korschildgen, Cologne
Project leader: Gerhard Kalhöfer
Employee: Philip Braselmann
Structural planning: Jürgen Bernhardt, Cologne
Graphic design: Kalhöfer & Rogmans, Cologne; Marc Rogmans
Constructed: 2008

www.kalhoefer-korschildgen.de
mail@kalhoefer-korschildgen.de

· Steel construction, stairs, mobile wall: Fröbel Metallbau GmbH, Brühl
· Roof construction, roof covering: Christian Franzen, Kall
· Safety mats with artificial turf: Ph Gummitechnik GmbH & Co. KG, Bad Berleburg
· Light dome: Astroplast Schärdel GmbH, Weiherhammer

Gerhard Kalhöfer
see p. 172

Stefan Korschildgen
see p. 172

Bedroom and playroom furniture

Owner: private owner
Architects: h2o architectes, Paris; Charlotte Hubert, Jean-Jaques Hubert, Antoine Santiard
Constructed: 2009

www.h2oarchitectes.com
contact@h2oarchitectes.com

Jean-Jaques Hubert
1999 Diploma in Architecture at École d'Architecture de Nantes; 2001–2002 Jakob + MacFarlane; 2002–2007 Bernard Tschumi Architects in Paris; Teaching appointment at École Supérieure des Arts et Techniques in Paris since 2006.

Charlotte Hubert
1999 Diploma in Architecture at École d'Architecture de Paris-Belleville; 1999–2005 Bruno Decaris; 2003 Completion of monument preservation at Centre des Hautes Études de Chaillot.

Antoine Santiard
2001 Diploma at EPF Lausanne; 2001–2002 Jakob + MacFarlane; 2002–2008 Bernard Tschumi Architects in Paris; Teaching appointment at École d'Architecture de Paris-Malaquais since 2007; Partner in h2o architectes since 2008.

2005 h2o architectes founded.

Summer houses in Berlin

Beach houses in Domburg

Residential building in Tokyo

Residential building in Munich

Owner: Maren Mielke
Architects: Hütten & Paläste, Berlin;
Nanni Grau, Frank Schönert
Structural planning: Hütten &
Paläste, Berlin
Constructed: 2006

www.huettenundpalaeste.de
info@huettenundpalaeste.de

Nanni Grau
1991–2001 Studied architecture
and design in Berlin, Sydney and
Coburg; Worked at Studio Daniel
Liebeskind, Eisenmann Architects,
East and MacGabhann Architects;
Research Assistant in the Chair of
Design and Building Construction
at Berlin University of the Arts since
2009.

Frank Schönert
1990–2004 Studied architecture
and molecular biology in Berlin,
Dessau, Münster and Karlsruhe;
Worked for Foster + Partners,
Scholl Architekten and Hamann
Pott Architekten; Research Assist-
ant in the Chair of Design and
Building Construction at Berlin Uni-
versity of the Arts since 2007.

2005 Hütten & Paläste founded.

Owner: Kooper Passenier V.O.F.,
Mirjam Passenier & Koos Kooper,
Westkapelle
Architects: WTS Architecten, Vliss-
ingen; Glenn de Groot, Don Monfils
Employee: Jana Vlasova
Constructed: 2008

www.wtsarchitecten.nl
wts@wtsarchitecten.nl

Glenn Douglas de Groot
1979–1981 Bachelor of Design
Studies at the University of Queensland; 1973–1984 Bachelor of Architecture at the University of
Queensland; 1984–1991 Worked
for various architectural firms in
Australia; 1991–1997 Worked for
various architectural firms in Rotterdam; 1997–2006 WTS Architecten,
Vlissingen; Partner in WTS Architecten since 2006.

Don Frédéric Monfils
1977–1978 Studied physics,
1979–1983 Studied architecture at
the Institute of Technology in Vlissingen; 1985–1995 Studies at the
Academie van Bouwkunst in Rotterdam; 1997 Diploma; 1990–2006
Director of the Laboratorium voor
Architektuur in Middelburg; Partner
in WTS Architecten since 2006.

Owner: private owner
Architects: Claus en Kaan Archi-
tecten, Amsterdam/Rotterdam
in cooperation with Souhei Ima-
mura/Atelier IMAMU, Tokyo
Structural planning: Shinitsu
Hiraoka, Tokyo
Constructed: 2007

www.clausenkaan.com
cka@cka.nl

• General contractor: Maekawa
  Construction Co., Yokohama

Felix Claus
1987 Diploma at the Delft University
of Technology; Professor at ETH
Zurich; Teaching appointment at
ETSA Madrid; Visiting Lecturer at
the Berlage Institute of the Delft
University of Technology and the
Amsterdam Academy of Architecture.

Kees Kaan
1987 Diploma at the Delft University
of Technology; Visiting Lecturer at
various universities since 1993;
Professor at the Delft University of
Technology and Visiting Professor
at RWTH Aachen since 2006; 2007
Visiting Professor at the Syracuse
University in Florence.

1987 Claus en Kaan Architecten
founded.

Owner: Gerhard and Katharina
Matzig
Architects: meck architekten,
Munich; Andreas Meck
Project leader: Francesca Fornasier
Constructed: 2009

www.meck-architekten.de
office@meck-architekten.de

• General contractor: KOBUS –
  Hausmanufaktur, Unterreit
• Joinery, windows, bookshelf,
  kitchen: Schreinerei Reichen-
  berger, Göggenhofen

Andreas Meck
1985 Diploma at the Technical University of Munich; 1989 Foundation
of architectural firm in Munich;
1994–1998 Teaching appointment
at the Munich University of Applied
Sciences; Professor for design and
building construction at the Munich
University of Applied Sciences
since 1998; 1998–2000 Partnership
with Stephan Köppel.

2001 meck architekten founded.

Renovation of students' apartments at the Olympic Village, Munich

Owner: Student Union Munich
Architects: arge werner wirsing
bogevischs buero, Munich
Structural planning: Sailer Stepan
und Partner, Munich
Landscape architects: Keller &
Damm Landschaftsarchitekten
Stadtplaner Partnerschaft, Munich
HLS planning: Ingenieurbüro
Konrad Huber, Munich
Electrical planning: Rücker und
Schindele, Munich
Sealing and building physics:
Müller BBM, Munich
Constructed: 2009/10

www.bogevisch.de
buero@bogevisch.de

Werner Wirsing
1949 Diploma at the Technical College Munich; Own architectural firm in Munich since 1948; Teaching appointments in Ulm and Munich since 1967; Honorary Member of the Bavarian Academy of Fine Arts since 2009.

Ritz Ritzer
1993 Diploma at the Technical University of Munich; 1993–1997 Hebensperger-Hüther-Röttig Architekten; 1997–2001 Teaching appointment at the Technical University of Munich; 2000–2003 Project team with Matthias Reichenbach-Klinke.

Rainer Hofmann
1993 Diploma at the Technical University of Munich; 1995 Master at Iowa State University; 1995–2002 Teaching appointments in London; 1996–2000 Worked for various architectural firms in Germany and Great Britain.

1996 bogevischs buero founded.

Capsule hotel in Kyoto

Owner: Cubic Corporation, Tokyo
Creative director & Product design:
Fumie Shibata, Tokyo
Sign & Graphic design: Masaaki
Hiromura, Tokyo
Interior design: Takaaki Nakamura,
Tokyo
Architects, structural planning:
Sigma Architectural Design,
Kyoto
Light planning: Panasonic Denko,
Tokyo
Constructed: 2009

www.design-ss.com
info@design-ss.com

• Sleeping capsule:
  www.kotobuki.co.jp

Authors

Christian Schittich (Ed.)
Born 1956
Architectural studies at the Technical University of Munich;
followed by seven years of practical experience, journalistic work;
since 1991, editorial staff of DETAIL, Review of Architecture + Construction
Details;
editor responsible since 1992, editor-in-chief since 1998;
author and editor of numerous specialist publications and articles.

Lydia Haack
Born 1965
Architectural studies at the Architectural Association London and
Munich University of Applied Sciences;
1996–2004 Research Assistant at the Technical University Munich,
Prof. Richard Horden; Teaching appointment at Augsburg University of
Applied Sciences since 2009;
Worked at Doris und Ralph Thut, Munich and Michael Hopkins & Partners,
London; since 1996 Haack + Höpfner . Architekten BDA.

John Höpfner
Born 1963
Architectural studies at the Architectural Association London and
Munich University of Applied Sciences;
1994–1999 Research Assistant at the Technical University Munich,
Prof. Thomas Herzog;
2005–1998 Teaching appointment at Queens University Belfast;
Worked at Michael Hopkins & Partners, London and Richard Rogers
Partnership, London; since 1996 Haack + Höpfner . Architekten BDA.

Peter Cachola Schmal
Born 1960
1981–1989 Architectural studies at the Technical University of Darmstadt;
Worked in various architectural firms in Germany;
1992–1997 Research Assistant at the Technical University of Darmstadt,
Prof. Jo Eisele;
1997–2000 Teaching appointment for Designs II at the University of Applied
Sciences in Frankfurt am Main;
Curator of the Deutsches Architektur Museum (DAM) since 2000,
Director since 2006.

Philipp Sturm
Born 1976
1997–2004 Studied political science, sociology and modern history in
Frankfurt am Main;
2004–2006 Traineeship in the Cultural Office of the City of Frankfurt am
Main;
Freelance culture manager since 2007;
Coordination of numerous exhibitions featuring photography, design and
architecture as well as projects in public space.

Andreas Wenning
Born 1965
Trained carpenter, architectural studies in Bremen;
Worked in architectural firms in Germany and Australia;
2003 Foundation of the architectural firm baumraum, realisation of projects
in Europe, Brazil and the USA;
Lectures and teaching appointments, numerous publications in Germany
and abroad.

Gerhard Kalhöfer
Born 1962
Architectural studies at RWTH Aachen and the Art Academy Düsseldorf;
1995 Kalhöfer-Korschildgen Paris/Aachen, from 2000 Cologne;
Creation of numerous mobile constructions;
Professor in architectural theory and design at the University of Applied
Sciences in Mainz since 1998;
Teaching and research activities relating to mobile real estate.

Oliver Herwig
Born 1967
German, American studies, history and art history in Regensburg,
Williamstown, Champaign-Urbana and Kiel;
1994–1997 Editor in Tübingen;
Freelance journalist in Munich since 1998;
Lecturer in design theory in Basel, Karlsruhe and Linz since 2005;
Writes regularly for Süddeutsche Zeitung, Neue Zürcher Zeitung and
Baumeister.

Illustration credits

The authors and editor wish to extend their sincere thanks to all those who helped to realize this book by making illustrations available. All drawings contained in this volume have been specially prepared in-house. Photos without credits are form the architects' own archives or the archives of "DETAIL, Review of Architecture". Despite intense efforts, it was not possible to identify the copyright owners of certain photos and illustrations. Their rights remain unaffected, however, and we request them to contact us.

from photographers, photo archives and image agencies:
- p. 8:
  Pyot, Laurent, Paris
- pp. 10, 16, 23:
  Kletzsch, Sascha, Munich
- p. 12 top:
  Wirths, Karsten/wikipedia.de
- p. 13 bottom:
  Aerolux Ltd., UK-Blackpool
- p. 14 bottom:
  Hirai, Hiroyuki, Tokyo
- p. 15 top:
  Moormann, Nils Holger, Aschau
- p. 15 middle:
  Bredt, Marcus, Berlin
- p. 15 bottom:
  EDGE Design Institute Ltd., Hongkong
- p. 17:
  Ishimoto, Yasuhiro, Tokyo
- p. 18 top:
  Demange, Francis/gamma, Paris
- p. 18 middle, bottom:
  Novaki, Zoran, Munich
- pp. 20 bottom, 149:
  Ano, Daici, Tokyo
- pp. 21, 29 bottom:
  Sumner, Edmund/view/arturimages
- p. 24:
  Berg, Anders Sune/
  The Danish & Nordic Pavilions, 2009/La Biennale di Venezia
- p. 25:
  Eirich, Juliane, Munich/New York
- p. 26 top left:
  akg-images, Berlin
- p. 26 bottom left:
  Giedion-Archiv, Zurich
- p. 27 left:
  Malagamba, Duccio, Barcelona
- p. 27 right:
  Heinsdorff, Markus, Munich
- pp. 28 bottom, 134:
  Kaltenbach, Frank, Munich
- p. 29 top:
  Guttridge, Nick/view/arturimages

- p. 30 bottom:
  Hill, Christopher, London
- p. 32:
  Garve, Roland, Lüneburg
- pp. 34 bottom right, 35 top, bottom left, 36:
  Jardine, Alasdair, Bremen
- p. 35 bottom right:
  Döring, Michael
- p. 38:
  Dürr, Michael, Vienna
- p. 40 bottom:
  Dechau, Wilfried, Stuttgart
- p. 42 middle, bottom:
  Bereuter, Adolf, Dornbirn, Austria
- p. 43 top:
  Holzenleuchter, Jürgen, Berlin
- p. 43 bottom:
  Leppert, Quirin, Munich
- p. 44 top:
  Lenzo, Massimo, Pisa
- pp. 45 top right, 118–121:
  Gliese, Carsten, Cologne
- p. 46 bottom:
  lbertram/flickr.com
- p. 47 bottom left:
  Lange, Jörg, Wuppertal
- p. 48:
  Ishida, Richard/flickr.com
- p. 49:
  Franz, Christoph/raumlaborberlin, Berlin
- p. 50:
  Heinrich, Michael, Munich
- p. 52:
  Alessi S.P.A., Crusinallo, Italy
- p. 53:
  Knoll, Walter, Herrenberg
- p. 54 middle, bottom:
  Hoberman, Chuck, New York
- p. 55 top left:
  Schäfer, Hans Günter, Cologne
- p. 55 top right:
  Schäfer, Hana, Cologne
- pp. 55 bottom, 152–154, 155 top, 156, 174 bottom right:
  Holzherr, Florian, Munich
- p. 56 top:
  Leistner, Dieter/arturimages
- p. 56 bottom:
  Speller, Steve/
  spellermilnerdesign.co.uk
- p. 57 top:
  Sönnecken, Eibe, Darmstadt
- p. 58 top:
  Otto, Frei, Warmbronn
- p. 58 middle:
  Habermann, Karl J., Munich
- p. 58 bottom:
  Koch Membranen, Rimsting
- pp. 62, 65 bottom:
  Lins, Marc, New York
- p. 63:
  Hamm, Hubertus, Munich
- p. 64 middle, bottom:
  archive_terrain.de, Munich

- pp. 74–77:
  Hempel, Jörg, Aachen
- pp. 78–81:
  Engel, Christoph, Karlsruhe
- pp. 82–84:
  Schwarz, Ulrich, Berlin
- pp. 90–93:
  Wehrli, Dominique Marc, Regensdorf, Switzerland
- pp. 94, 95, 96 top right, bottom:
  Palma, Cristobal/Providencia, Santiago, Chile
- p. 96 top left:
  Schittich, Christian, Munich
- pp. 97, 98:
  Baisch, Nina, Lindau
- pp. 100, 101:
  Neto, Sandra, und Aguiar, Diogo
- pp. 105, 106 top, 107:
  Averwerser, Jann, Munich
- p. 109:
  Geiger, Harald, Lustenau, Austria
- pp. 110, 111 left:
  Hoernig, Robert, Dortmund
- pp. 112, 113:
  Delafraye, Fabienne, Paris
- p. 122:
  Martin-Peláez, Maria
- pp. 123, 125 bottom:
  Dettmar, Uwe
- p. 124 top:
  MAK Frankfurt
- pp. 124 middle, bottom, 125 top:
  Schmid, Gerd
- pp. 126, 128, 129:
  Krier, Yves, Munich
- pp. 130, 132 top right:
  Mattioli, Mauro, Viterbo, Italy
- pp. 131, 132 bottom:
  Laurière, Céline, Toulouse
- p. 133:
  Koch, Silke, Leipzig
- p. 135:
  Bach, Claus, Weimar
- pp. 136–138:
  Hempel, Jörg, Aachen
- pp. 139, 141:
  Chalmeau, Stéphane, Nantes
- p. 143:
  Angelmaier, Claudia, Leipzig
- pp. 148, 151:
  Richters, Christian, Münster
- p. 150 top:
  Ohashi, Tomio, Tokyo
- p. 150 middle:
  Zwarts, Kim, Maastricht
- p. 155 middle, bottom:
  Müller-Naumann, Stefan, Munich
- pp. 158–161:
  Masmann, Jens, Munich
- pp. 162-164, 167:
  Nacása & Partners Inc., Tokyo
- pp. 165, 166:
  Yoshida, Akihiro/9h, Kyoto
- p. 170 bottom left:
  Franco, David

- p. 171 3rd from left:
  Gibbs, James, New York

from books and journals:
- p. 13 top:
  Aicher, Otl, Die Küche zum Kochen, Berlin 1994, p. 13
- p. 26 bottom right:
  Chan-Magomedow, Selim O., Pioniere der sowjetischen Architektur, Dresden 1983, p. 213

Articles and introductory b/w photos:
- p. 8:
  Ikos Flexible Research Station; Gilles Ebersolt, Paris
- p. 10:
  "micro compact home"; Horden Cherry Lee Architects, London / Haack und Höpfner . Architekten, München
- p. 24:
  Installation shot from "The Collectors"/The Danish & Nordic Pavilions, 2009/53rd International Art Exhibition, La Biennale di Venezia
- p. 32:
  Korowai tree house in New Guinea
- p. 38:
  "turnOn" in motion; AllesWirdGut, Vienna
- p. 50:
  "Iris Dome", Hannover, Expo 2000; Hoberman Associates, New York
- p. 60:
  Temporary bamboo pavilions Markus Heinsdorff, Munich

Dust-jacket:
Newspaper kiosks in London
Designer: Heatherwick Studio, London
Photo: Cristobal Palma, Providencia, Santiago, Chile

Project data are provided as is by the responsible architectural offices. The publisher is not responsible for correctness of provided data.